Theology Beyond Metaphysics

Theology Beyond Metaphysics

Transformative Semiotics of René Girard

Anthony Bartlett

FOREWORD BY
Scott Cowdell

CASCADE *Books* • Eugene, Oregon

THEOLOGY BEYOND METAPHYSICS
Transformative Semiotics of René Girard

Copyright © 2020 Anthony Bartlett. All rights reserved. Except for brief quotations in critical publications or reviews, no part of this book may be reproduced in any manner without prior written permission from the publisher. Write: Permissions, Wipf and Stock Publishers, 199 W. 8th Ave., Suite 3, Eugene, OR 97401.

Cascade Books
An Imprint of Wipf and Stock Publishers
199 W. 8th Ave., Suite 3
Eugene, OR 97401

www.wipfandstock.com

PAPERBACK ISBN: 978-1-7252-6418-2
HARDCOVER ISBN: 978-1-7252-6419-9
EBOOK ISBN: 978-1-7252-6420-5

Cataloguing-in-Publication data:

Names: Bartlett, Anthony W., author. | Cowdell, Scott, foreword.

Title: Theology beyond metaphysics : transformative semiotics of René Girard / by Anthony Bartlett ; foreword by Scott Cowdell.

Description: Eugene, OR : Cascade Books, 2020 | Includes bibliographical references and index.

Identifiers: ISBN 978-1-7252-6418-2 (paperback) | ISBN 978-1-7252-6419-9 (hardcover) | ISBN 978-1-7252-6420-5 (ebook)

Subjects: LCSH: Christianity—Philosophy. | Philosophical theology. | Semiotics—Religious aspects. | Girard, René, 1923–. | Sacrifice. | Religion and culture.

Classification: BR100 .B30 2020 (print) | BR100 .B30 (ebook)

Scripture quotations contained herein are from the New Revised Standard Version Bible, copyright, 1989, by the Division of Christian Education of the National Council of the Churches of Christ in the U.S.A. Used by permission. All rights reserved.

Quotation from Ted Chiang's *Stories of Your Life and Others* used with permission of Penguin Random House.

Quotation from Henry Miller, *Tropic of Capricorn*, used with permission of the author's estate. Excerpts from Sandra Schneiders, *Written That You May Believe*, used with permission of Crossroad Publishing.

Image on front cover is the Sinai Christ, sixth century, from Saint Catherine's Monastery, Sinai.

Manufactured in the U.S.A.   11/30/20

To Bethany House Community, 2014–20, which along the road of its individual and group studies provided pressing inspiration for the theoretical work here. And, above all, to my wife, Linda, ever at the heart of the journey.

Neither revolution nor reformation can ultimately change a society, rather you must tell a new powerful tale, one so persuasive that it sweeps away the old myths and becomes the preferred story, one so inclusive that it gathers all the bits of our past and our present into a coherent whole, one that even shines some light into the future so that we can take the next step. . . . If you want to change a society then you have to tell an alternative story.

—Ivan Illich

This is the covenant that I will make with the house of Israel after those days, says the Lord: I will put my teaching in their inmost parts, and I will write it on their hearts.

—Jeremiah 31:33

How was it possible, when I sat down in the parlor at my prehistoric desk, to use this code language of rape and murder? I was alone in this great hemisphere of violence, but I was not alone as far as the human race was concerned. I was lonely amidst a world of *things* lit up by the phosphorescent flashes of cruelty.

—Henry Miller

Contents

Foreword by Scott Cowdell | ix
Preface | xiii
Acknowledgments | xvii
Introduction | xix

1. Eavesdropping | 1
2. Biblical Upgrade | 22
3. Murderous Semiosis | 30
4. The Thread of Deconstruction | 50
5. After Truth: Coming of the Other | 65
6. The Long March of Signs | 80
7. Mountain of the Modern | 101
8. Postmodernity: Semiotic Triumph | 112
9. Ontology: What's *Really* Going On! | 131
10. The Semiotic Gospel | 149

Bibliography | 175
Index | 181

Foreword

IT'S NOT THAT METAPHYSICS is bad, necessarily. It's not even that we need to get rid of it. It's just that a certain sort of metaphysics accompanies and indeed underwrites a bad theology. Anthony Bartlett urgently wants us to get past that bad theology so that we can begin to know and speak of God as God truly is, for the sake not only of truth but also of human liberation.

This problem we have with God has been thoroughly explored by René Girard, whose mimetic theory lies at the heart of Bartlett's ongoing project. Famously, Girard theorizes the joint origin of religion and culture as the fortuitous outcome of cathartic violence, with a functional sacred emerging to scaffold humanity's linguistic, social, and institutional advance. Tactical dissimulation is essential for keeping this foundational violence under wraps, lest it lose its power to suppress further disorder. Hence the augmentation of protective rituals with every culture's prudent insistence on its miscellany of social prohibitions, to which is added the justification provided by an authoritative mythology.

Girard parses the myths of Western antiquity and a range of tribal cultures to unearth the scapegoat victims that stand behind them. He is enabled to do this because the prophetic texts of Hebrew Scripture and the Gospel Passion narratives do what social science has failed to do, by revealing real victims whose actual sacrifice underlies humanity's venerable structures. The Bible offers a different sacred, deconstructing mythology and redefining God in line with Jesus's praxis. Cross and resurrection reveal a God beyond the covert violence of humanity's various sacred orders, releasing a new imagination and a new praxis.

And so we come to metaphysics. Girard regards it as implicated in the larger mythical enterprise whereby we seek to know and inhabit the world as meaningful. He gives qualified support to Nietzsche, Heidegger, and Derrida in their critiques of Western metaphysics. Girard worries about Nietzsche's unstable flirting with the Dionysian, about Heidegger's mistaken concern that Christianity's God is a barrier to properly embracing the lifeworld, and about Derrida's exclusion by *différance* of an elusive but nonetheless real origin of language and culture: the sacrificial victim. But he is certainly amenable to a critique of Western metaphysics. Enter Tony Bartlett.

Our author is chiefly a talented and creative interpreter of Scripture. I'd even say exhilarating. His Girardian hermeneutic shows how text after text, book after book, both in the Hebrew Scriptures and the New Testament, can shed its accustomed readings to reveal a God beyond structuring violence. There is some of that textual engagement to be savored here, but the bulk of Bartlett's biblical exegesis is being saved for a subsequent, companion volume. In the meantime, he seeks to clear the decks of metaphysical blockages so that Scripture can speak out clearly and make its fullest impact. Bartlett's central conviction is that human structures, yoked to the eternal return of violence and its homoeopathically violent containment, are capable of being transformed. The false sacred can be undone, as we see happening at the first Easter.

Bartlett knows that metaphysics must accommodate historical change and that objective reality comes epistemologically entangled with the world as humanly known. But, like Girard, he is enough of a metaphysical realist to insist on real events that were concrete and decisive enough to change the human world, in particular events involving Jesus Christ. Bartlett resists so-called postmodern trends that sacrifice realism for relativism and a perpetual cascade of meanings. The die was cast for these trends in Descartes's early modern split between the world and the knowing subject, which via Kant is perpetuated in modern philosophical accounts of the real. Close empirical attention from the phenomenologists to how we inhabit the lifeworld repositions this characteristically modern problem, though it hasn't resolved it. Bartlett looks elsewhere, to a premodern alternative that has reemerged in a philosopher whom he regards to be truly postmodern, C. S. Peirce. And that alternative is the science of signs—semiotics.

I will not tell the story for him. Suffice it to say that following John Deely, in his magisterial study, *Four Ages of Understanding: The First Postmodern Survey of Philosophy from Ancient Times to the Turn of the Twenty-First Century*, Bartlett pursues a regularly overlooked Latin tradition of logical thought that came to fruition with Descartes's contemporary John Poinsot and then skipped the modern era to reemerge with Peirce.

Rather than objects and signs being arbitrarily related—whereby the modern bifurcation of mind and reality is confirmed semiotically and realism is perpetually problematized—Bartlett favors a more nuanced account involving a shift of metaphysical gravity. We can welcome both the reality of objects and affirm our genuine access to them, while recognizing that those objects are inextricably part of our world as humanly known. Such a shift in metaphysics allows for a real relation between subject and object that is mediated by signs. All signs are perpetually being substituted (e.g., by metaphor and metonymy) and hence they participate fully in a historical, cultural, and linguistic flux. Yet that sense of restlessly shifting connection within the lifeworld need not sever the genuine bond that signs mediate between subject and object.

What Bartlett seeks through signs is an ontology-replaced-by-love—a direct engagement with the real (attuned to Heidegger's being-in-the-world), though expressly in the key of love. His sympathies are with phenomenology and, in accounting for the ongoing fact of human transformation set in train by the Gospel, he is perhaps closest to Jean-Luc Marion's favoring of love over Being in philosophical theology. If we stick to a more static metaphysics, however, we face the risk that Nietzsche, Heidegger, Derrida, and various of their followers have named (albeit controversially for some). And that is to set whichever oppressive status quo in concrete, justifying repressive conditions. Such metaphysics too readily co-opts God in support of human will to power.

Avoiding today's widespread volatilizing of meaning—which for Girard is no guarantee that repression won't be promptly re-sanctified, and which risks Christianity's replacement by neopagan toxicity—Bartlett charts a new course under contemporary philosophical conditions. He bends metaphysics in ways that both streamline his theological mission and support the theological critique lying at its heart. This theological critique takes a messianic, eschatological, eighth day of creation perspective, the proleptic echoes of which are brought to light throughout biblical tradition. This eschatological perspective pivots away from Western theology's overinvestment in protology out of a concern that all origins with echoes in metaphysics are violent. When Bartlett returns to biblical protology, he interprets it as eschatologically oriented protest literature. Here he is in tune with Eastern Orthodox theological insights, along with current Old Testament scholarship. Bartlett's chief aim is to show how it is that all things are being made new in light of an in-breaking future.

It is helpful to remember that dallying with metaphysics is not Bartlett's concern, believing as he does that urgent times brook no distractions. He knows, however, that he can't dismiss metaphysics entirely because we humans make typically slow semiotic transitions, as is evident in our widespread incapacity for too much newness. Myth, ritual, *and* metaphysics can survive as once-occupied shells that new forms of life can nevertheless repurpose and inhabit. Bartlett, like Girard, would not have us take all such legacies of the false sacred too seriously on their own terms. But, suitably deconstructed, they contribute to the semiotic chain leading to the newly emerging thing—perhaps inevitably so.

In closing let me commend this book, which I found stimulating from end to end. It has helped me significantly with my own current work on the relationship between mimetic theory and philosophical theology. And, scholarship aside, as a Christian and a priest I commend Tony Bartlett for the spiritual insight and missional purpose that suffuse his book. I will not be alone among his hopefully many readers in being grateful for this.

—Scott Cowdell
Research Professor in Public and Contextual Theology
Charles Sturt University, Canberra, Australia

Preface

THIS WORK STANDS AT some distance from the central concerns of René Girard, although it puts his name at center stage in the title. Girard never moved to consider the philosophical ramifications of his thought. So wedded was he to the core insight of his career—the historical and prehistorical action of mimetic desire—that he strayed hardly at all into any philosophical framework. All the same, his thinking was powerful and fluent enough to be philosophically aware, and to introduce reference to a philosopher where he thought it fruitful to his ends. He is sometimes compared to the hedgehog in the ancient Greek proverb, "A fox knows many things, but a hedgehog knows one big thing." Perhaps it would be truer to say that Girard was both fox and hedgehog, and he made the fox in him serve the hedgehog and its one big thing. A good example might be found in the book where he gave his mind its freest expression, *Things Hidden since the Foundation of the World*. There he nods briefly at the philosophy of Martin Heidegger, using it to buttress his argument in respect of mimesis and violence. He sees in a flash a clear meaning, agreeing with the German father of ontology that the intrusion of Greek metaphysics into Christian thought was alien to the gospel. The reason is, as he declares, that the Greek Logos, together with its later Heideggerean offspring, is inseparably linked to violence, whereas the gospel Logos is not. That's some conclusion. And it shows vividly the easy crossover of his thought into biblical scripture, while having a tangential, if not averse, relation to philosophy.

I first met Girard in November 1993, at a lecture he gave in the Bird Library, Syracuse University, New York. I don't remember the exact title of his talk, but it was provocative and had something to do with the gospels and anti-Semitism. He never really got around to his topic. He simply explained the workings of mimesis, with passion and panache. There is not the slightest trace of anti-Semitism in Girardian thought, but there is an understanding of the Bible as a workshop of anthropological revelation. That would be its point. After the lecture, there was some hesitance in the audience in asking questions. Even though almost all the faculty of the Department of Religion were present, lined up in a solid phalanx, no one really wanted to engage. It may have had something to do with Girard's evident and elegant Frenchness, and the awe that Continental Theory (predominantly French) seemed to inspire in American academics at the time, with Girard somehow gaining reflected status and authority. Or, perhaps, few wanted to be seen giving him the recognition implied in a question. I think Girard felt the latter, because when I went to speak with him afterward at the podium—where no one else seemed to want to—he remarked that "the thought about scapegoating is itself scapegoated."

There was a sort of *cordon sanitaire* around this man, but to some degree he placed it there himself. In order to establish a discourse that in spirit went back to the ethnological researches of the nineteenth century, and before that, as he claimed, to the Bible itself, Girard was obliged simply to reiterate, over and over, the astringent power of his core concept. Human beings are an unstable construct and they seek to resolve the instability through paroxysms of violence directed at a single or group victim. Not only that, but it is this very feature that brings humanity into being, its cruel logic sitting at the very root of human culture and its formation. Girard showed enormous courage to bring this dramatic thought to recognition, swimming upstream against a prevailing attitude against metanarratives, one favoring by and large abstract intellectualism. The result was akin, in some respect at least, to my first experience: a man alone at the podium.

The present work seeks to knit Girard into a broader tapestry of thought—one that, I think, was always there but that, due to its apparently lightweight and ungrounded character, is not favored by those looking for things more traditionally marbled and secure. But it has the advantage of speaking at deeper levels, and even in fresh tongues, in ways a more dogmatic thought cannot do. Semiotics is the study of signs, their production and function, and Girard had some trenchant things to say about the origins of signs, and therefore how they work. Moreover, the Bible is, of course, a matter of stories and signs, and, therefore, a congenial subject for the discipline of semiotics. Girard seems—at least originally—to place his trust in the web of scripture rather than any structured metaphysics. By making those threads in Girard demonstrable in their original weft, so to speak, I hope both to tie Girard into a fabric of new human meaning and to draw attention to the production of this meaning in its own right.

The man alone in the middle of the room in a New York academic library has since passed on, feted now for the huge impact his thought continues to have, amid the ongoing labor of understanding and developing his legacy. The tapestry I attempt here gives a rightful place to him in the pattern of the cloth, and yet demonstrates that pattern for its own sake, for the revelatory wonder and transforming beauty it alone brings.

Acknowledgments

MY SPECIAL THANKS TO Saorsa Wissman of Union Theological, New York, for spurring the first vision and development of this study; very special thanks also to Dr. Susannah Ticciati of King's College London for encouragement to publish and for introducing me to a wider and more bracing world of semiotic conversation; a heartfelt acknowledgment to Canon Theologian Scott Cowdell of Charles Sturt University, Australia, who helped me separate the intellectual wood from the trees, discover its natural shape, and who gave unofficial Anglican approval to the final product; and, in terms of lifeworld, a shout for Café 407 in Liverpool, New York, a place itself of transforming semiosis, with personal gratitude to the healing vision of its founder, Mary Ellen; lastly, once again, and most of all, gratitude and love to Bethany House community, which continues to struggle generously with these raw hopes and dreams, before they are turned into the form of scholarly prose, and even perhaps ultimately a way of church.

Introduction

THAT LONDON IS A city, dating from Roman times and located on the banks of the river Thames, is a fact. But even as we state the fact there is a wide wash of interpretation which surrounds it. What is a city? Why is London named as one? (It is also called a town.) Who were the Romans? Why are they referenced? What is the function of the river, in particular the one named Thames? Why is it mentioned?

Just like a city on a river any fact needs walls and dams to keep it from flooding, but the very walls and dams which define it are themselves their own cities with their own rivers, walls and dams, and so on infinitely.

This is the starting point of the book. The flood tide of language, its complex, swirling currents which carry humanity onward so effortlessly and yet so mysteriously: a Wittgenstein-style observation. But *the sign* is the book's theme. The human sign which gives meaning is the central component of all human symbolic systems, including language.

It is the subject matter of semiotics, the formal study of signs and their function. It is also the concern of anthropology and, specifically in this book, the generative anthropology of René Girard. It is, moreover, a fundamental topic for theology, although this has not always been clearly recognized. It surely must be the case, however, when, among many similar statements, the New Testament tells us, "Human beings do not live by bread alone but by every word that comes from the mouth of God." By means of this volume theology, with all its words, stakes its claim to be understood semiotically and in a radical way. It establishes theological semiotics as a method and discipline in its own right; and this is the case above all because the biblical tradition has made the human sign *generative* in a crucially new and contemporary sense.[1]

---

1. The tools of semiotics have been applied before in the affairs of theology: as a way

The *sign* has arrived at the point where it becomes a prime theological topic, potentially equivalent in status and impact to Aquinas's *esse*, or Luther's *faith*.

Girard has given us a scientific anthropology of human origins, in which the biblical text and its formative tradition play a pivotal part, both revealing and confirming core findings for anthropology. In which case we have a very unusual—unprecedented in fact—mixture of human science and the material of theology. The sign in this context, therefore, becomes originary or generative in both prehistoric and theological senses. The primordial symbolizing effect of the original murder (Girard) is subsequently inverted and transformed in the biblical tradition into a primordial gesture, a generative sign of love, reaching its conclusive moment in the death and resurrection of Jesus. If this is the case it means that the human system of meaning, its anthropological structure, is revolutionized at its very core, in its most proper nature and function.

Nonviolence is the marker that will return again and again as the most vital descriptor of a revolution in meaning. In the past nonviolence has been treated as an ethical response or a political tool, certainly a spiritual practice, but here it arises as a revelation of truth, of the character of Godself. As such it cannot be a negative (in fact a negative of a negative), but something entirely new and constitutive in the order of reality. If humanity itself is founded in violence an emerging new constitution of human existence will find it difficult to express itself. Nonviolence is perhaps the best readily available term that seeks to give this novum an expression and it does so in the form of a refusal. The heart of the gospel, "the death and resurrection of Christ," is itself a double negative. However, it is one finally affirmed as a transcendent positive, a crossing out that is by no means simply a denial but in fact a cosmic transformation. The sign value of nonviolence is, therefore, in this book infected by the gospel positive. *Nonviolence* takes on the quality and hue of an inbreaking of life.

The alteration in meaning that is announced carries through the work of salvation. "Salvation" has gotten itself a bad name. A contractual scheme that

---

of analyzing literary effect (Geninasca, *Signs and Parables*); or a method of identifying symbolic forms and their role in Christian spirituality (Neville, *Truth of Broken Symbols*). Ticciati (*A New Apophaticism*) perhaps runs closest to the present project, showing how human beings may be viewed as truth-telling signs of God when viewed in a key of transformation, making transformative semiotics a way of reference to a transcendent God. The present study views semiotics not simply as a heuristic tool, but a core philosophical discipline for the understanding of divine revelation. Human transformation is at root semiotic, and so the discipline is central, and not simply an auxiliary to explaining something more truly understood as ethical, spiritual, or metaphysical.

rescues an individual from the miseries of the present world, and worse ones to come, while guaranteeing a fabulous alternative in the afterlife, all by means of supreme violence unloaded on a specially selected victim—something like this cannot inspire human confidence. In a situation of unprecedented crisis for human life on earth a model of such cynicism will less and less commend the Christian religion. The historical fact of this reading of salvation can only be excused on the basis of the generative power of violence redoubling in order to remain in effective control. My book *Cross Purposes* attempted to lay out the historical processes by which this happened. What is being offered now in this present volume is very different.

If the Godself of love breaks into the world, that is not going to happen in terms of a brute transaction which replicates the very cruelest contours of human practice and self-dealing. It has to occur by a means that instills a different mode of existence, a different way of being human, and *therewith* transforms human understanding itself. In a transactional understanding an exchange takes place in one region of being in order to bring you to another. You cannot sit in and possess your new car until part of your own world is handed over (your money). The bank is the mechanism of credit (trust, fiduciary institution) that enables the transfer, that holds the whole order in place while allowing a movement of reality from one space to another. In the transactional notion of salvation (Christ paying a debt/penalty) there must be a bank to negotiate the whole thing. In which case the bank is God and God is the bank, greater ultimately in meaning than a Son or a Father. There is finally, therefore, no grace.

In contrast a transformation in human meaning does not employ a human institution but creates something new, a *sign* that connects to a completely new way of existence. The development of a theological semiotics is a pathway of discovery of a new humanity, employing the cultural roots of the generation of meaning in order to change them entirely.

To proceed critically on this pathway theology has to identify its own most proper term, one linked essentially to *sign*, not to *being*. *Relation* (or the most specific version of this we will arrive at—*hupostasis*) is the term which allows the sign to reach out beyond present being to completely new possibilities. But it does so from within present existence because it is a *real* relationship, made possible by Christ. To understand this involves a shift from "things" and "ideas" as fundamental, to seeing signs and relations as truly constitutive.

Beforehand, relation to a "spiritual" world may have been taken as abstract, otherworldly, mystical or mythical. A semiotic relation, on the other hand, must be concrete, this-worldly, humanly transformative. The veil that lies over the world does not divide it from a true world elsewhere, a Platonic heaven, the translunar *ideal* of a perfect world. Instead as semiotics it opens this world to what it yet will be, known in and through the relation of a sign. Fully to grasp this is to leave behind *being* as the final bank of reality constructed out of the generative power of human violence, and embrace instead *relation* as the real, made possible by the sign of love. And of course, where a transactional arrangement remains within human control—for ultimately, it is we who constitute the bank—relation is something we are drawn into from the outside, from beyond our capital reserve: while, at the same time, it remains something we are perfectly free to refuse!

Because of the several intersecting levels of the inquiry the full argument for these claims must proceed from different starting points. This is where *Theology Beyond Metaphysics* becomes a journey, or a series of journeys repeated on top of each other. As we go forward, we see the question of the sign from different angles, building up a more and more comprehensive picture, including the function and impact of the biblical text. In this way we mark out a landscape with the Bible ultimately at its center, arriving at the territory of theological semiotics in its own right. At which point theological semiotics may be accepted as a field of inquiry in a sovereign sense. It is still, however, an experimental, exploratory journey, and it depends on those who journey with the book whether they too can arrive at this new territory. But I am convinced that there is a profound paradigm shift to be made, allowing the Christian believer to find Christian existence as a real (semiotic) relation to a new humanity.

A general eschatological dimension has always been part of Christianity—the already-but-not-yet. But what is offered here goes well beyond a mere statement of scriptural principle. One of the reasons for the craziness of the contemporary world is the way a verbal signaling from a politician or public representative is immediately countered by its opposite, on mainstream or social media. The intense, inescapable back-and-forth (*twittermania*) conditions actual human awareness and makes a tranquil human life untenable any place where there is Internet connection. In fact, for some the very conflict becomes a way of life—listening to a chosen news outlet twenty-four-seven and becoming infected by chronic anger as a way of being. It's as if the power of the sign brings it to a point where its relation becomes impossible to ignore: it has to be answered at once by an equal and opposite shouting and signaling. This mimetic explosion of the sign makes it a force of destruction. In contrast, enacted signs of forgiveness, peace, community, nonviolence, in conscious juxtaposition to mimetic crisis, become a new and vital possibility of human relation here and now on earth. Christian community is not simply an optional benefit of salvation, it is actual restorative meaning for a manic lifeworld. In this case, a Christian signals with her face, her relations, her practice, an actual earth brought to peace and life. The journey of this book brings the reader to a critical understanding of this truth.

It does not mean that the return of Christ, the *Parousia*, is reduced simply to positive historical change. What it does mean is that Christian existence is a real relation to another human way in the world. It is what elsewhere Bonhoeffer referred to as "the profound this-worldliness" of Christian existence. The preaching of the gospel is theologically and meaningfully uncoupled from its past otherworld alienation, and most of all from a God of retributive violence—something which has distorted the whole historical profile of Christianity through the centuries. Instead, we have the vigor of the gospel sign continually inviting the semiotic species (humanity) into a vital relation of nonviolence, with congruent aspects of justice, compassion, and peace. This is a gospel that satisfies at the deepest level, which transforms the face of the earth even as it teaches human beings the true character of their existence.

As already declared, we begin with the business of language. Because it is so second nature to us as humans—its mystery lived within but never fully grasped—language may serve to set us in motion away from metaphysical truth toward semiosis, the process of making meaning through signs. Language (spoken or signed) is something we inherit effortlessly and necessarily, like the air, like sunshine. To become freshly aware of this awakens in the reader a sensibility that will develop progressively through the book. The opening chapter, therefore, is a meditation which leads us, in a fitting conversational way, into the living world of language. It is the aperitif prepping the palate for more serious, disciplined work afterward. It's there because it too is made of language, and by tasting it and savoring it in its own "poetic" form and function we are made ready to understand language, and its sign value, better.

There follows a transitional chapter, one which provides a second way into the argument at a more academically aware level. If the first chapter was a kind of operetta, setting the stage in a narrative way, the second is the true overture to the study, announcing the major theme and concern of *theological semiotics*. It introduces the context of postmodernism, helping frame the character of the argument against the background of a world which asserts a "constructed" nature to truth. Within this framing we see the Bible as a radically new source of (non-metaphysical) meaning which has entered the human scene. Its new semiosis has both a destabilizing and transforming effect, explaining a lot of the crisis of our times.[2] The overall pattern that emerges

2. For an accent on the destabilizing see René Girard's *Battling to the End*.

provides a compelling understanding of both our contemporary world and the role of the biblical tradition within it.

Some of the work of the philosopher Charles Taylor may be introduced at this point to provide a ready-made horizon for such a large-scale claim. Taking a cue from the reflections of early nineteenth-century German Romantic thinkers, in particular Humboldt (1767–1835), Taylor demonstrates that when it comes to deeper human meaning the "shape of experienced meaning doesn't precede [its] articulation, but comes about through it and with it." "Articulation" is Taylor's word for new verbal expression of meaning. It "alters the shape of what matters to us. It changes us."[3] In other words language enshrines the search for human meaning, spurs it on and answers its need: when a new expression or articulation arises humanity is shifted in its very self. He goes on to argue that storytelling, or narrative, produces these meanings in a privileged way, such that they cannot then be reduced to the synoptic frame of the work or a detached moral teaching. He says the "convincing power" of the work comes from the whole background and telling of the story, bringing a transition of new meaning to the reader.[4] How much more would this be true of the transhistorical, sustained "story of stories" which we call the Bible? Taylor's viewpoint thus corresponds to the argument of semiotic transformation. The difference is that the latter offers a more grounded, less mysterious view of language. The *sign* is never simply a neutral instrument of communication, neither is its power somehow to be more originally explained in and by an "idea" in an intellectual soul. Rather, it has its own generative power, rooted in its concrete prehistoric origins. It is these that are also subject to radical change over the biblical span, bringing with it the potential for human transformation.

It is the thought of René Girard which enables this more explanatory viewpoint, and after the transitional second chapter we dig deep in the tilth of Girardian anthropology. We discover his generative semiotics, while recognizing how they are produced in concert with his own surrounding context of thought. Girardian semiotics are evolutionary and radical, leading away from metaphysics toward the possibility of a semiotic reversal and new beginning. This places Girard in the company of a fellow Frenchman, Jacques Derrida—a strained company, it is true, but one which delivers a substantive fellowship of thought in a key respect. The fourth and fifth chapters cover this parallel story. Derrida was the doyen of deconstruction, but someone whose reflection eventually had more than a biblical tinge, reaching out toward a nonreligious "messianic." In the latter stages of his career Derrida insisted on

3. Taylor, *Language* Animal, 188, 189.
4. Taylor, *Language Animal*, 309–10.

a non-deconstructible responsibility for the arrival of the "other": that is, a human meaning that is not based in preconceived notions but in a radical relation that draws us beyond ourselves. Derrida merits his peculiar place in the present book because, of all the "continental" philosophers who danced at the cliff-edge of the loss of certainty, his writing appears most sensible of and responsive to semiotic transformation.

We could say, in epigram form, that if Girard is the overall climatologist of the human scene, recording major shifts in human patterns, Derrida is the meteorologist, telling us some of the actual weather we are having. Placing Girard side by side with Derrida flows from a semiotic reading of the biblical tradition. It both derives from and reinforces the argument of a profound transformation of meaning going on in the roots of culture by reason of the Bible's potent set of signs.

Where postmodern thought and its underpinnings serve to make the case of a semiotic transformation, John Deely's formidable intellectual labor enables us to trace this process back in time, piloting a way through layers of intellectual development beginning with the Greeks. His *Four Ages of Understanding* is a kind of *summa semiotica*, providing rich material for the argument of semiotic evolution. Its description of the actual progression of intellectual ages and the detailed content, especially of the Latin age, almost cry out for an engine of change such as argued here. Over three chapters, 6 to 8, we cover some of the terrain of Deely's account, leading us step by step and logically into the emergence of full-blown semiotic thought, above all in the writings of Charles Sanders Peirce. The American genius represents a crucial *terminus ad quem*, in parallel to the European postmodernism of the earlier chapters.

Along the way we also encounter the thought of intellectual giants like Aquinas, Vico, Descartes, Heidegger, often following their perspectives deeper on our own account. The effect is to place semiotics in conversation with significant philosophical viewpoints and prepare the ground for a final estimate of semiotic thought in regard to the core philosophical question, the nature of *being*. This is broached in the penultimate chapter 9.

Here the study moves to tie its various strands together into a significant conclusion. If the thought of "signs" has undone our metaphysical universe, leaving meaning as an apparent tangle of threads rather than a schematized whole, it does not say that our actual human relation to the world is any less life-giving or intelligent. On the contrary, it is possible it can achieve its proper function for the very first time. A metaphysical world sets all in order but backed up by structures created out of generative violence. A semiotic relationship offers the possibility of something the "eye has not seen," a world set free from violence. To invoke what "eye has not seen" might seem to suggest an invisible otherworld of an ideal spiritual type, but turning in this chapter to the phenomenology of Jean-Luc Marion reinforces another, much more concrete possibility. Marion's analysis refers to an intellectual or spiritual relationship not frozen in the idolatry of a gaze which returns the human self to itself, as in a mirror. The term he uses for this other, non-idolatrous beholding is "the icon," something which invites the gaze beyond itself into an infinite depth. The icon is itself a gaze which looks back at the viewer, inviting them into the invisibility of self-giving.

This is the invisibility of semiotic meaning. In metaphysics it is the viewer's gaze returned to itself in a dazzling mirror, including the viewer's concept of a heavenly otherworld. What Marion offers is effectively a this-worldly truth that is an alternative to all violent relation. It is a relation which is *hupostasis*, the Christian-era concept of a mode of relation proper to Christ. What is so exciting about this understanding is how it fits with some of Girard's own analysis, among the most trenchant of his entire opus. In the pages from Girard we examine in this chapter the anthropologist shows how the Christian *logos* is radically other than the Greek *logos*, a dramatic break from broad patristic opinion. It was the insight of Martin Heidegger which brought him to this understanding: although delivered in a hostile sense Girard received it positively, and as profoundly true. Heidegger, as we'll see, had sought to liberate a thought of *being* from the control of metaphysics, but in the process had accepted (even celebrated) the primordial violence he found evident in *being* itself. It is the inheritance of the logos of violent being which Girard identifies in Greek thought and from which, along with Heidegger, he completely separates the Christ logos of the gospels.

The engagement with Heidegger, and yet divergence from him, bring us to a word which emerges in the course of the study and can sum up the approach here. It is "semio-ontological" and it tells us that the reality of our world is not given absolutely prior to or separate from human existence and the signs by which it lives. *What is* depends intimately on a relation, or a series of relations, with and through the human. It is the revolutionary semiotic relation just named—the *hupostasis* of self-giving love—that ultimately mobilizes the possibility of a transformative semio-ontology, of a world redeemed from violence by the sign-value of love. In which case semiotics appears as an inherently theological discipline, one now pressing for appropriate recognition and attention.

The book concludes with the demonstration of a biblical-semiotic masterpiece. The Gospel of John essentially selects itself for inclusion in the present discussion. It is this Gospel which explicitly tells us that Jesus worked "signs" (Greek *sēmeia*), while leaving it provocatively open exactly what such "signs" mean. The Fourth Gospel's fairly fraught path toward canonical recognition around the middle of the second century suggests there is something different and even problematic about its manner of address. Despite the apparent simplicity, almost banality, of its language, its elevated references and allusive phrasing made it a favorite of gnostic writers in the early part of that century. But a semiotic reading provides, I think, a much more significant hermeneutic of this language, one referring to the inverse of a separated realm of eternal truths.

The chapter develops a close inquiry into the semiotic constitution of the Gospel, from the Beloved Disciple, through the famous "I am" declarations, to the figure of "glory" shared by Jesus and the Father. The same concept of relation as guided the analysis in the previous chapter is now seen played out over and over in the decisive figures, images, verbal markers, rhetorical devices, and layering of the text. The theme of the icon also returns, this time in comparison to an actual work of painting known as the Sinai Christ. Exceptional features of this iconography provide a basis for a very specific semiotic description of the gospel text, marking it out as generating its own "iconic" function. One particular term is presented. It is "slippage," something which signals an oscillation back and forth between the elevation of Christ and his surrender in the cross. It is this doublet, informing many of the Johannine signs and the movement within them, which opens the semio-ontological space of *hupostasis*, the depth of giving *as* transcendence. The returning gaze of the self-giving Christ into the human realm creates new human meaning as such.

The thought of this chapter leaps the whole biblical progression and focuses only on John's Gospel. It provides a parade case of semiotic transformation, but it implies a preparatory movement parallel to and earlier than the triumphant emergence of semiotics in the Christian epoch. John stands as a kind of evolutionary peak, but the enormous vitality of its composition depends on the energy of earlier writings growing the semiotic values by which such a gospel could arrive. John's Gospel gives a dense account of transformative meaning, based in the experienced novum of Jesus's self-pouring-out for others. But this, in turn, could not be possible without the Hebrew Bible preparing the codes by which such a meaning could be put in place and embraced in the person of Jesus. The present volume must look, therefore, to a subsequent undertaking on the part of this author to present the biblical narrative as an evolutionary semiosis leading to the figure of Jesus.

Ted Chiang's short story, "Story of Your Life," tells a tale of aliens arriving on earth and the task of a linguist, Louise Banks, to learn their language and communicate with them.[5] It was made into a successful film, *Arrival*,

---

5. Chiang, "Story of Your Life," in *Stories of Your Life and Others*.

directed by Denis Villeneuve. The story can serve as a parable of what is being talked about here, about the nature of language and signs, about how they reach into the heart of our actual human reality.

The aliens are named "heptapods" by the researchers and in effect they have two languages, one spoken and the other written ("Heptapod A" and "Heptapod B"). It is with the latter that the most interest lies. While the spoken language follows fairly conventional usage, with the equivalent of nouns and verbs in decodable sentences, the written language has an amazing character of linking everything together simultaneously. The writing does not use phonetic words, as in alphabetic systems, but *semagrams* providing strictly visual meaning. It begins with a single twisting line on a page that somehow goes on to encompass the whole scheme, modifying everything in it. The implication is that the totality of meaning is known at once, from the very outset.

Chiang put a lot of effort into creating the technical plausibility of Heptapod B and it is with the consequence of this highly unusual writing that the payoff of the story occurs. As Louise becomes more and more proficient with the aliens' writing her own mind and actual frame of meaning changes. She begins to see things at different moments the way Heptapod B does, with past and future as simultaneous, whole epochs of time understood all at once. "I experience past and future all at once; my consciousness becomes a half-century-long ember burning outside time. I perceive—during those glimpses—that entire epoch as a simultaneity."[6] The dramatic point is that our own linear, human mode of writing coexists with a linear consciousness of past, present, and future, while a simultaneous form of writing coexists with and then actually serves to produce an understanding and knowledge of everything at once. The effect in Louise is a profound acceptance of her whole life, including the tragedy of her daughter's untimely death. The infection of the alien writing creates a new transcendence of peace within a timeless script of Louise's existence.

The logical conundrums of Chiang's story are not important. What the storyteller is giving us is a fable about written language changing human life. The privileged semiotic status of writing is the view of a certain postmodernism, and Chiang is carrying what is known as its "synchronic" character to a literary extreme, making a whole life synchronous with itself. But the boldness and beauty of his story are themselves an actual event of human writing. They do not depend on the fiction of Heptapod B, but on a signified (written) relation which makes it work.

---

6. Chiang, "Story of Your Life," 140–41.

We can reflect further that the heptapods' writing is something that takes place in two dimensions on a flat surface. Somehow on a flat writing space they make everything appear simultaneously. Meanwhile, *actual* human meaning takes place in a kind of three-dimensional space which we might imagine the brain to be. There are any number of possible pathways of language branching above, below, and around a given neural thread in the mind. But what is being argued in this book is that human meaning actually has four, even five dimensions. It obviously has a depth in time, with words accumulating and shedding meaning through the centuries, but, most importantly, also going back to a distinct, prehistoric point of origin in an act of founding violence. Human language is a deep well and at the bottom there is a singular spring or event. But this event does not simply bring a dimension of time or depth. It holds a sense of the sacred, a pulling together of the whole universe in a single transcendence, and thereby indeed giving everything a sense of the simultaneous, of the *timeless*. Chiang is trading off this sensed dimension or relation of meaning.

But what if the whole construct can be reinvented from a start point of absolute self-giving? A transformed human existence comes when the primitive grammar of human meaning is reconstituted so that the fourth and fifth dimensions begin again in the generative nerve of love rather than that of violence. This would seem very difficult to map in actual neural-semiotic terms, but the writing of the New Testament, and its continual reiteration in preaching, could well claim to carry through in practical and real terms an effect parallel to Chiang's Heptapod B in his little fable.

Is this not a more realistic version of Chiang's story? Would not an absolute effect of love make an individual human simultaneous with everything, in terms of mutuality, empathy, and life, and would that not bring its own timeless sense? Chiang's story is a thought experiment arising from the depth of our human struggle for meaning, bringing a sense of victory over the dissolution of time. The argument of the present book is that the biblical tradition provides a much better chance of his story's semiotic transformation. It is a project and possibility which we only of late have begun to understand, after long millennia of metaphysics.

1
Eavesdropping

How Foreign!

HAVE YOU EVER BEEN close to a conversation in a foreign language, maybe in a café or while traveling on a plane or a train? Maybe Russian, or Hindi, or Japanese? Maybe across the aisle, at the next table, or right beside you, sharing a compartment? The phrases and intonations mean nothing to you, but you know of course they are meaningful to the conversation partners. Maybe you are a little jealous that these people are engaged in such lively communication, while you are left alone. In any case, you are completely aware that those two or three people are meshed together in a world of signs and images. It fills up their minds and hearts, almost without remainder, and makes them wonderfully *human* as you sit there listening.

As you continue to give attention to this exquisite tide of sound you reflect that these people, although right next to you, are really in another world. More than that, they are creating that world even as they speak it. Those strange, so well-formed sounds, and the way they knit together in an endless skein of threads falling from their mouths—it all creates a human experience which is total for those within it. Yes, they have a peripheral awareness of you and the setting you're all in, but while their words pour forth, they may as well be on the other side of the planet.

They are physically in the same location, but linguistically, semiotically, neurally, they are in another universe. That cat's cradle of words, tangling together all the speakers, is like the special-effect holograms you sometimes see in the movies. Suddenly in the fictive world of the movie there is a kaleidoscope of things spinning around the room, and the people looking on are no longer really in the original place, but brought to an entirely different dimension created by the holograms. The only difference is that here the virtual world is not a computer-generated effect in a motion picture, but a product of the ancient power of words, a stream of images and meaning tumbling out from a group's brains and mouths.

So, what are these words? What are these little audio explosions producing this virtual reality? Their effect has to be more or less coincident with the emergence of humanity itself. No power of language or symbols, no humanity as we would recognize it! So, the question goes back to the origins and meaning of humanity itself. To ask about words is to ask about who we are as humans and where we came from. We will return to the mysterious questions of origins again below, but for the moment let us stay with our eavesdropped conversation.

If these people are talking about the price of bread in a store you use, or a sports team you and they all support, then perhaps the idea of a world created by words is harder to accept. It could be argued they are using words as simple signals, with a one-to-one reference to physical events and experiences you all share. The words drop away and become simply pointers to "things themselves" via our thoughts or memories of those things. Which is perhaps what we think about words most of the time: the classic progression of sense impressions, through thoughts, to words. This is the "objectivist" empiricist perspective and it acts as a standard backdrop to any discussion on language. Of course, words refer to real things! How else could we deal with the actual world?

But what if the overheard foreigners are talking about places and events you've never seen, never experienced? It's obvious their words now appear at another level of mystery, much more like free-floating virtual entities with little reference to anything beyond themselves. "Ah, yes," the objectivist would surely reply. "You personally are in the dark here. But the foreign conversation partners are simply accessing their memories, which are a direct record of sense impressions, like photos or videos. It is these impressions which retain the one-to-one reference and all the speakers are doing is applying words in a strict representation of what they see in their 'mind's eye.' Clearly you cannot access these stored impressions, but what you *can* do is get a handy travel guide and foreign dictionary. Then you will be able to translate their words and, following on, access your own sense impressions of the very same things or things very much like them! You will be able to accurately to re-create their world!"

- *What's in a name? A rose "by any other name would smell as sweet"*... *But would it?*
- *There is this thing with a perfumed smell and the English call it a rose, but the Turks call it* gül. *If you hear that sound, g–ü–l, just grab the*

Turkish-English dictionary and you'll find it, a rose! But then does that word smell as sweet as a rose? *Do Turkish roses in fact have (culturally) the same smell as an English rose? There is the classic "English rose," the expression of a particular English climate and beauty. So, do not Turkish roses have a particularly Turkish sweetness? A Turkish friend told me that "gül" is a name used for the prophet Muhammad (pbuh), "The Rose." Ever since, Turkish "gül" is for me is a heady mixture of rose and the founder of Islam. Or a Turkish rose with the scent of a prophet!*

The Always Unscientific Dictionary

However, with the appeal to a travel guide and dictionary the objectivist viewpoint hits a reef. Yes, they may be talking of the afternoon they went boating on a river, or a big city center they spent a day in, and you can go and get the brochure, or just log on to Google Earth, and get a very faithful image of those places. But the words that are used to describe the lived experiences in those places are translated in the dictionary, and by what external measure do we know that the dictionary represents the same personal "image" or personal impression to the English speaker? Even the brochure or Google street view appearing on our screens might have a very different resonance for the speakers who were actually in those places; how much more so the words used to describe them? We certainly believe there is a common world which we all know regardless of nation or culture: we could not live together on the earth without that trust. But isn't that the point? We "believe" there is a common world. And our words are a constant auditory pledge of that trust, and by an order of magnitude specifically their own. Our words argue us into the world—their world—second by second, day by day, throughout our whole lives. We never dream of needing an external measure for dictionary equivalences, let alone checking ourselves. We simply allow one language to carry us over into another and we're done! Language itself does the job for us, using an English-Russian or English-Japanese dictionary, with some basic text-reading ability! Not any system of testing and verification. Why is that? Let's examine this in more detail.

Say, for the sake of argument, that I happen to have a handy lexicon for the strange language I am overhearing in the café or plane, and I manage to spell out a word which strikes me and look it up. If I identify the word correctly in one column, I then trust that the word on the other side, the one in my own language, represents something that is happening inside the overheard speaker's head. We may ask, then, did the English compilers of the dictionary go through each item one by one and have the foreign speaker point directly to the object in question? And did they carry out a strict analysis of any abstract terms to be sure of their meanings? Normally a language dictionary or vocabulary will also give a variety of idiomatic uses for its terms, indicating a range of possible meanings, which further complicates the question. What was the objective check on all these unusual meanings? Look everywhere in the dictionary and there are absolutely no footnotes backing up any of the paraphrases and usages, just as there none for *any* of the translations. The editors felt absolutely no need for references to actual accessed experiences, dated empirical observations, or analytic discussions. At which point the objectivist protests, "And obviously so, because the real world is staring us in the face all the time; our languages know it and correspond honestly and evidently to the fact!" But is this truly simply the case? Do not the different languages have their multiple words—*eau, acqua, wasser, hudōr*—for that wild and wet stuff in the world, because each linguistic community is making its own world, again and again, in relation to that stuff while at the same sharing that stuff in an actual world? Thus, learning that word from a dictionary allows that particular community to engulf you with its cultural meaning before you fully know it or understand it, even as it is also vital to be able to ask for a glass of water!

We must conclude, therefore, that reading a dictionary we do indeed base all our confidence in those who simply speak both the languages, who have mental pathways constructed in, by, and through both language worlds. We are relying on the bilingual brains of the dictionary compilers. So long as they have the established conduits one idiom flows back and forth with another in the power of language itself, flooding human meaning generally and almost insensibly from one arrangement of sound-signifiers to another in the grey matter of the translators.

A foreign-language dictionary is not an encyclopedia; it is really a great series of interrupted conversations by a person or persons who speak both languages.[1] For sure, the person or persons will have shared very many sense impressions (for example, the "rose") and heard the relevant words spoken directly in their original and target language. *But even if they have, they never communicate any of these contexts for their translations, and as readers of the dictionary we never ask for any of this information as criteria of*

1. According to Umberto Eco a dictionary is in fact "a disguised encyclopedia," but that is because he views the encyclopedia itself as an "unrestricted galaxy of pieces of world knowledge," and a dictionary, in parallel, as "a turmoil of infinite accidents." In other words, the attempted definitions of the dictionary are always in fact an effect of interpretation. He is talking about native-language dictionaries, but what he says applies *a fortiori* to the rough-and-ready, free-and-easy equivalences of the foreign dictionary—with their underlying chaos of accidental meanings in each translation. Eco, *Semiotics and the Philosophy of Language*, 68.

accuracy. In other words, there is something about language which carries its own calm assurance when it talks of the world. It's not that an actual flower—"the rose"—does not exist to be pointed to and named, but that language creates its own internal system of meaning and a translator simply introduces us to that system, using the connecting doors of words themselves to lead us from one system to another. How is it possible that the English rose belonging to temperate gardens in Kent or dusty housing terraces in Manchester can *mean* the same thing as an Italian rose competing with the dazzling sun overlooking the Mediterranean?

It is even more striking that we never request any kind of philosophical demonstration for abstract concepts or idioms, any kind of referenced discussion or set of definitions. In the very best lexicons, all you get is a series of phrases and usages in the history of the language carried over into the native language: in other words, it is both languages together which testify to the foreign meanings. The compilers have understood this and simply represented it as fully as they can. Learning a foreign language, therefore, is never a matter of finding precisely the right equivalence. It is, rather, a process of entering the matrix of the language itself, using general equivalences as a doorway. In every case, therefore, a rose is a rose is a rose is a rose, in the sense of *all* the various meanings carried by the word. In truth, therefore, a rose is never completely, simply or absolutely "a rose"!

Italian Interlude

I was blessed to live in Italy for a period. It was in a voluntary community where different people came and went, some staying a brief period, some for longer. When I joined I had only a basic grasp of the language and had catch-on conversations as best I could, looking in a dictionary for strange words when I returned to my room. Sometimes I would forget the word I needed to check, sometimes my brain was just too tired to bother. At other times the word was used so often I felt I already knew what it meant and could get along fine without looking it up. In these instances, it was clearly the language itself that was communicating. I was learning its meaning from the inside. One such word was *impegno*. It was used so often, with so much weight, that I really felt I understood it. It means "commitment" in English and, in a situation where the nature and health of the community depended on how committed people were, the word naturally got a fair bit of play. I picked up its sense from the repeated contexts in which it was used and the warm feelings it generated. I think at some point I reflected explicitly, "This must mean something like 'commitment,'" or I did actually look it up and felt, "Yes, I knew that!" Another word was *frantoio*. It was used a lot in the late fall and early winter and in connection to the olive harvest which many members of the community, including myself, had worked at. One of the members went to the *frantoio* every day and I knew it had something to do with processing the olives; eventually, I was certain it meant "olive press." I don't think I ever looked it up.

Those who take a strict realist approach to language might approach this inner sense of meaning with, paradoxically, a more idealist version. They might say that I already had the "concept" which the Italian word represented and simply fitted the word to the concepts. But this ignores the roots and resonances of a word like *impegno*, the fact that they are different from those of *commitment*: its "concept," therefore, is strictly speaking different. *Pegno* means "pledge" or "in pawn" and is likely related to the word *pugno*, which means "fist"; that is, *impegno* is something like "given over into a fistlike grasp." Meanwhile *commitment* is derived from Latin *mittere*, implying something like "being sent to a destination." Ultimately what I was doing was a personal job of translating, that is, "carrying across" one word into another, merging the meaning worlds of both. They occupied a similar or analogous space or function in each language, but fuzzy-edged, understood in practice and nothing as clear as a preexisting "concept." The very different roots of the two words demonstrates two pathways producing roughly parallel landscapes, but never a self-existing idea. Indeed, I couldn't help feeling that adding the Italian word to my vocabulary introduced a more military or militant feeling to the thought: it put me in mind of honor duties not just dedication. As for *frantoio*, I'd never come across an olive press before in my life, so, essentially, I had to invent the concept for myself out of the Italian.

For the sake of contrast, let's take something very well known, so when it came to a translation I, and anyone else, would presumably understand precisely what was being talked about. People who speak both languages agree that the signifiers of English *mouse* and Italian *topo* represent a small, furry, long-tailed animal which emits a squeaking noise. And yet, as is obvious, I have just used a series of words to indicate the meaning of those single words, and, once again, the direct reference of these further words is taken on trust. If you should press me about the meaning of "furry," or "tail," or "squeak," I would once again have recourse to a series of words to explain what I mean by them. And so on, *ad infinitum*. Words seem to depend on more words for their meaning, and this is the case both in respect of the dictionary-translated foreign language and in respect of a native language too. The objectivist might claim that it is in fact possible scientifically to define "mouse" down to an extremely tight point whereby we can only possibly be talking about one single thing: *Mus musculus*! Yet, although that scientific classification (within biological taxonomy that is itself always undergoing revision) is very precise, we certainly do not *need* it in conversation. Moreover, it is far from "the thing" we normally have in mind when we say "mouse." Using this word people's thoughts much rather fly to cheese, traps, cats, and Disney movies—rather than any strict scientific category.

You see what I mean? Words operate generally on their own self-contained energy or effect, not by definition, and people are perfectly happy to talk in the vague, conventional, free-floating way which words permit. Whatever the sense impressions present in an overheard speaker's head, or in that of a conversation partner, it is the words which effectively tie us together in a field of meaning. As normally used, words are much more like poets than scientists!

The Color Spanish

Here, then, perhaps we may state a general rule: *Words as commonly used have no need for an external check outside the living use of the language itself; words help organize the real world, but they do so in their own mysterious power, without a strict, or even strictly possible, external validation.*

Yes, evidence and fact-checking and logical coherence are all important conditions for rational thought and, indeed, essential restraints on the power of language, but what I am arguing here is a primordial function that we often hardly recognize or give heed to. All the forensic and scientific conditioning of language does not take away the fact that we live within it more than we rationally and functionally control it. It is this fact that, paradoxically, opens the possible space for human transformation. Let us go further with the discussion, continuing to clear the ground for a more dynamic sense of language and its signification.

Our objectivist may continue to press: "You're clouding the issue. You have completely brushed over sense impressions. These must be fully accurate from an evolutionary standpoint, otherwise the natural world just wouldn't work. And words reflect that accuracy. Take color, for example: it is a wavelength of light necessary for recognition in the animal kingdom, etc. Animals don't have words, but they know a color when they see it. I am the same as the animals in physical makeup, so when I say yellow, I mean a wavelength of light measured between 565 and 590 nanometers. Simple as that."

And right there we have the huge conundrum of words. Our objectivist has to be right on the level of sense impressions, but it is their relationship with understanding that has been one of the great puzzles of philosophy.

One of the first things philosophers noticed was that sense impressions can be deceiving. "Am I dreaming?" is a question which can be asked both in and outside of a dream. And so "reason" was taken as the criterion of truth, not sense. Next, alongside the uncertainty of sense, human opinion was contrasted with reason, in as much as it is plural, unreflective, mired in prejudice. And this is just another way of saying you can't rely on words. As Nietzsche pithily put it, *Jedes Worte ist ein Vorurteil* (every word is a prejudice!). Thus, uncritical sense impression and prejudicial words are more or less in the same boat, unsuitable for attaining truth. That leaves philosophy, then, the demanding goal of attaining somehow an accurate and critical—that is, unprejudiced—view of the world of which we speak. In terms of sense experience, we feel, along with the objectivist, that there has to be generally accurate uptake at the biological level, but what about its relationship with articulate meaning, with words? The final answer has to be that sense and words occupy generally separate worlds, overlapping certainly, but working on quite different planes of human information.

Nature is very good at creating codes that warn us instinctively, that is, without words. White spots on red, or yellow and black stripes—these are all pretty convincing aversion signals. Large glittering white teeth say unambiguously, "I want to eat you!" while a vibrant green color says a healthy and honest "Please eat me!" Thus, the objectivist is entirely right: frequencies of light are real and informative, and it is possible to see and name them truthfully and accurately. This kind of conclusion is the companion of hundreds of years of specialized scientific method, involving observation, measurement, hypothesis, and control. Science aims at a disciplined use of observation and words to describe it, but its accuracy is always based in math rather than language as such. If a measurement cannot be made and then replicated there really is no science. And it is exactly that function of numerical precision which cannot be applied to words or used to retrofit them. Words are not numbers; their sense is almost entirely different.

Words in their own natural state are those very human things which secrete their own sense, and that's the issue we're addressing. We can illustrate this by using the term for that precise frequency of light, the color "yellow." If we also present the word in Spanish we take away some of its "natural" resonances in English, and hear it more strictly as a word. Spanish *amarillo* is close enough to English "yellow," yet different enough to allow us to experience exactly what it is capable of doing *as word*.

When a Spanish person uses that word what shades are there of lemon groves in Andalusia, of Spanish yellow rice, of a vivid streak in a painting by Goya? Perhaps I ask these questions because *amarillo* awakens those associations for me, but, in any case, the result is the same. "Yellow" comes with its distinct package of meanings, and none more perhaps than with things Spanish. If we refer again to an empiricist's response it might go something like this: "Everyone gets an identical idea of what 'yellow' means because it is a frequency of light. All else is the effect of local setting, which is generally translatable in the same logical way if we only take the necessary time and effort."

To which I'd have to say that the language realist just missed the proverbial elephant in the room, a yellow one! The "local setting" so swiftly dismissed contains an almost infinite amount of information, going back to childhood days when our Spanish speaker built up a hundred thousand associations with *amarillo*. These include slight geographical effects or modulations on the frequency of light, but most of all they were constructed out of emotional and relational experiences, many of which she is hardly aware of as she speaks, let alone able to communicate them to us. Even if she is referring to the yellow car parked across the road, in a directly indicative sense, immediately she uses the word all these other meanings are waiting in the wings for their moment on stage. All they need is a nod in their direction and they appear. What could possibly be the scientific instrument to measure this numberless, shifting cast of possible characters?

One leading protagonist of "yellow" will be the Spanish flag. The national colors consist of two horizontal red bands divided by a broad yellow stripe the size of the red bands combined, with a coat of arms emblazoned on the yellow part. When Spanish people see this flag, for example at the Olympic games, it will no doubt evoke in them a host of emotions. We say a national flag acts as a symbol for that entire country, so the appearance of the Spanish flag, involving that bright yellow band, will unloose a chain of meaning almost without end (and for some, inevitably, not all positive). The color yellow is a central element of the code releasing this chain and so, reciprocally, when the word *amarillo* is spoken, that entire national code may well be "flagged" somewhere, at some level, in relation to the color.

The term "symbol" has brought an important element to the discussion. It is usually employed for a visual image which gathers into itself a rich field of meaning and is often differentiated from another term, "sign," which is seen as far less potent. A "simple sign" is often understood as a single pointing to something. The street sign with an arrow, giving directions to the city center or the railway station, would be an example. Even more rudimentary would be a number: five, for example—five items, or the pure number five. Charles Sanders Peirce, the great nineteenth-century thinker on signs and semiotics, actually reversed the nomenclature. For him, a symbol was this bare, culturally learned indicator, including arrows and numbers, while a sign had much richer meaning. This latter viewpoint is the approach here, while retaining something of the common usage for symbol.[2] Later we will see how Peirce developed the understanding of "sign" in a very compelling way, one that covers every instance of meaning; for the moment, however, we can allow "symbol" to retain some of its traditional sense for the sake of the broad argument.

So, to consider again the word *amarillo*, we can say, yes, for sure, it may be used in reference to the Spanish flag in a "purely descriptive" fashion. "The Spanish flag is composed of yellow and red bands." But we also see it connects with a dense inner reserve of meaning—it is "heavy with symbolism." Thus, "I saw the yellow flash of the Spanish flag . . ." So, it is that the color/word *yellow* has immensely more possible meanings than simply the spectrum of light, meanings that have also evolved and grown over time. Yes, light has its physical frequencies, but words have their own frequencies too. And they have the ability to lend that frequency to numerous other words, and in turn shape the frequency of those words, in an almost impossibly rich scattering and refraction of allusion and meaning.

Neural Notes

- *Question: If words have their own frequency in what medium does it operate? What is it that vibrates if I say "yellow"?*

Our focus on words will already have hinted to the reader that we're not considering here a Greek mind, the home of a disembodied, immaterial thought. Such a notion must itself derive only from the amazing phenomenon of language, its possibilities of "internal speech," together with its formulation of propositions and ideas. In the past it seemed evident that the only thing that could be responsible for these wonderful events was a separate "mind," an intellectual psyche or soul. Contemporary advances in computer science, however, with micro-processors capable of huge amounts of calculations at lightning speed, have shown us that activities akin to thought can be carried out by machines. With the right programming, using keywords and algorithms, a computer can engage in a conversation with a human and convince that person that it is in fact human. (This is the famous "Turing

2. The concepts "sign" and "symbol" easily spill over into each other, as we can see. Even a number, "five" for example, can gain powerful associations when considered as a word in combination with other words: think "high five" or "five stars." "9/11" is a good example of a set of numbers which is highly significant, or "symbolic" in the conventional sense. Peirce's nearest equivalent to what we are used to naming "symbolic" is something he calls the "icon" (including paintings and photographs). It is telling that the word "iconic" seems to have gained greatly in popular usage over the past several years, perhaps partly displacing "symbolic."

test," which states that a computer which can show enough resourcefulness in conversation with a human to become indistinguishable from a human has in fact demonstrated the ability "to think."[3]) Coming at the problem from the other direction, the discoveries of neural science have provided a credible picture of a "brain machine" similarly capable of processing great quantities of information within a living organism in continual movement and change. The brain is made up primarily of "neurons," electrically excitable cells transmitting data and commands through electrical and chemical signals. The human brain is estimated to have up to 100 billion neurons with the possibilities of several thousand connections or synapses between an individual neuron and others around it. It has been calculated that the brain of a three-year-old child has about 10^{15} synapses (1 quadrillion). The possibilities of multiple communication pathways, as well as permutations that can continually be added, are astronomical in number and byzantine in complexity.

The brain remains in many ways a mystery to science. How in fact do these neurons work in terms of language and thought? How do they store verbal information? How do they retrieve it and increase it by setting problems and seeking new patterns, solutions, and meanings? Despite the profound questions, the basic point at the moment is the obviousness of those 100 billion neurons as the machine that makes language possible. If, for some reason, the machine is damaged, people can quickly lose their ability to speak, remember, reason, be aware. Biological design must always be economical, for evident reasons: redundancy wastes energy and reduces the fitness of the overall organism. By way of comparison, non-ape mammals have a mean of between 100 million to a billion neurons. The great apes have roughly a tenth the number that humans have. (Pilot whales are nearer still, with a third to a half of the human amount, although of course much larger in size.) Thus, humans possess a disproportionate amount of neurons, requiring the necessary energy to fire them, and this has to have a purpose. The prime candidate must be communication and information: sign, symbolism, language, thought and mind. (Interestingly, pilot whales are known for their extensive and complex communication, including squeaks, whistles, buzzes, and clicks!) Thus, the present knowledge of neural science automatically pushes our concept of human thought from the supposed separate and "spiritual" function of mind to the intimately material and complex neural structure of the brain.

---

3. Alan Turing (1912–54), English mathematician, cryptanalyst and computer pioneer, suggested the test.

The flow of language becomes completely plausible as neural communication sequences. We are certainly unable to string together a single sentence without a coordinated sequence of electrical and chemical discharges inside our brains; again, once a brain is damaged, for example by a stroke, language ability is severely compromised. The inference, that those discharges are themselves what carry and make meaning for us, seems increasingly inescapable. More and more it appears that our meaning is fully embodied, that it is entirely *bodily*. So, thinking for a moment about those language discharges, and the thousands and thousands of neurons that are involved each time we make a statement, we might appropriately speculate that the bit of brain code which is the word "yellow" resembles a photographer's flash firing or lighting up a complex of neurons. Together that complex forms a kind of portrait studio with a linked set of associations for the signifier "yellow." Verbalizing that signifier (either aloud or mentally) is a sudden lighting up of pathways inside the brain and indeed the whole body-self. The portrait which flashes up because of it is a loose tableau of stored experience, association, metaphor and meaning, rather than a strict one-to-one representation. And the tableau can shift and change not just from one speaker to another, but over the years for an individual, or indeed from hour to hour. Who can tell what sudden unexpected association, or neural byway of "yellow," will flash up next time I hear that word?

The idea of a "neural studio" made up of a network of associations gives the sense of something both bounded and borderless, precise and marvelously imprecise. It stretches the word's potential meaning over a thousand moments and situations. The exact frequency of light which produces the color "yellow" in the optic nerve and the brain behind it is obviously factual. That frequency must play a real part in the neural studio. But the frequency would never shine so brightly, it would never grip our imagination, if it were not for its presence within words, in symbols, in meaning. Yellow is only really *yellow* when it is spoken as a word!

In which case when I am actually talking and looking for a word in relation to Spain, "yellow" could easily suggest itself: the yellow of its flag, its plums, its *Cuarenta y Tres*, its onions, its sierra grasses and the gold in its cathedrals and palaces. But then, conversely, when the word "yellow" is used for itself, it may suggest a host of other possibilities, things as different as "sickness," "daffodil," "cowardice," "mustard," "traffic light," "school bus," and so on and on, without end. All this takes place along neural pathways lost to any reconstructive geography or map, but known at once and at firsthand by the brain that has (or *is*) its language. All the brain has to do to function is to do a "search" along those pathways and see whatever results. This may be the result of the brain's natural idling, like a motor not in gear but firing continually, without ever turning off. The brain provides a spontaneous flashing up of neural networks, what we might call "daydreaming." But then at any moment, prompted by a question, a conversation, or a deliberate private search, we can begin selectively pursuing certain pathways, using memory and/or logic.

Here is by far the most mysterious of the brain's neural functions: the ability to run in parallel to itself, effectively switching off certain pathways to privilege others. It's as if the brain has learned the trick of its own pathways, functioning somehow in synchrony with them all and able somehow to guide the selection of the studios which will light up. The fact that this is not by any means a certain or clear process—our memories can "fail us," something can be "on the tip of my tongue" and not be remembered, or my logic can easily break down into fallacy—demonstrates itself that we are dealing not with a spiritual self-transparency but with a material-electrical process which can very easily "short out." Fortunately, it is not the task of the present study to investigate this marvelous parallel function. The key point is that it can at least be described, if not fully explained. There is indeed a crucial gap in understanding, but the vital thing from the perspective of this book is that no matter the failures of memory or logic, language continues; *it* never fails! Indeed, in the instance of trying to remember something the asking of questions and the use of other words seem almost always to provide the catalyst in recalling something to mind. For example, "What is your very first memory?" will set in motion a train of images and sensations from early childhood; but without those words, or something like them, it's highly unlikely those very early sensations would come to the surface. And, certainly, in regard to logic, it is impossible to pursue an argument, including "in our heads," without rehearsing it in words. Thus, it's very possible that the search function of the brain is the gift of language itself: to prompt a journey along neural pathways you have first to employ words as the trigger and continue to do so in the use of logic. Even in a situation where memories freely associate in our heads it takes words to identify them, to give them a formal and recognizable meaning. We can therefore conclude that the actual electrical impulses that light up the successive neural pathways of thought have their main control and relay apparatus in language.

- *We have come to the core perspective of this study, without so far having turned to specialized thought on linguistics or philosophy of language. The use of language is the human function, second to none. And it's the very open-endedness of language, its ability to change course, to follow a different path, that opens to us the possibility of one day arriving at truth. These "semiotic shifts" must be capable one day of opening to us the horizon of meaning for which we have always been searching!*

Once unleashed words work their magic with happy abandon, conjuring up different worlds like Aladdin's lamp. And so, our overheard conversationalists in the train are in a true sense creating their world as they speak, or their words are creating the world for them. The speakers are of course using whole sentences, which are statements about situations, past, present and future, and there is therefore an intentional element in what they are saying. Their statements propose meaningful truth, one way or another, something generally speaking we can call an "argument." This activity is itself a specialized (and extremely important) function of our neural repertoire, using logical functions, things like "the whole includes the part," "for an effect there must be a cause," "a thing cannot both be A and non-A," etc. But, as already noted, the control is never perfect, no matter how fluent or intelligent the speaker. Questions or retorts can be made, jokes and puns too; there is room for misunderstanding or simple non-understanding. This is a major reason why there is conversation at all. And it is certainly the reason why there are arguments as actual *altercations* between speakers. The shared words may be taken in numerous different directions, including diametrically opposed notions of the world. But it is always the words which allow this possibility, a genetic openness in and to the world. The speakers have their language in common and apply conventional senses to the words, but at the same time they do not and cannot tightly control the pathways the words will generate. It is this natural polysemy or porosity of words that constructs an actual conversation—a free-floating exchange of experience and meaning in many ways produced by the words themselves.

The semi-independent existence of words is what in fact makes a foreign language, or indeed any conversation, intelligible. If words had a strict one-to-one relationship to the thing experienced, then there would be no way to learn that word, unless I too had encountered that single selfsame thing. Everything in fact would be a proper name, and just as I can have no idea of what a speaker might mean by a certain "John Smith" whom I have never met, every word would be similarly individual, single and opaque. It is the "neural studio" and its fuzzy-edged repeatability from brain to brain which allows humans to have common names and general ideas. It is not the "thing itself" (*the* rose, *the* mouse, *the* color yellow) which produces universals, it is the words. Once again, that does not mean there is no such thing as a genus of flower called *Rosa*, or animal called *Mus*, or frequency of light called yellow. But we would have no sign-making access to this "reality" if it were not for the amazing neural networking of words, their loose, rather free-floating, inherently creative connection to the world.

All of which leads to our final lesson from our overheard foreign conversation in the café, the train, or the plane. As we described it above, the listener is on the outside of the language world. Yet, precisely because she is human and shares the neural pathways which enable humans to converse, the overheard conversation can never be completely lost. Even as she sits listening, very much in the dark about what the group is saying, there is also something happening within her. Very slowly, and probably unwillingly, her eye, ear, and brain are looking out for meaning, for body states and gestures alongside the sounds and cadences, with the remote possibility she might pick up something and recognize significance in what they're saying. Obviously, if they all get up and leave the café, or the flight comes to an end, then absolutely nothing will be learned. But if for some reason she were to be plunked down in the group's native country for a few months, then almost inevitably this process would continue—to the point where she would begin to understand and even speak some of their language.

In these circumstances the listener's behavior cannot be very different from that of an infant as it begins to pick up the words and syntax of the surrounding speakers, spontaneously, as a matter of imitation. Of course, a handy dictionary and a plan of study in a school (consciously rehearsing and practicing the language) would speed things up for the adult listener. But none of that would help unless she was also tuning into raw conversation, and little by little making it her own. Everyone who has been in the situation knows the exciting moment when they find themselves "thinking" in the new language: it is the point where they have successfully made the transition into a new set of semiotic pathways, a newly constructed suite of "neural studios." No amount of vocabulary and grammar lessons can make this transition. Ask any school pupil who has "done six years of French"; they never arrive at this point. But after six months in a foreign country, simply by paying constant attention and seeking to replicate what it has learned, the brain gets to the level where it is making meaning in the new language. The listener in the café or on the plane is, therefore, already in the stream of meaning in which the foreign speakers are swimming. She is swept along by their current of words, whether kicking and screaming or bathing willingly.

But this is also true in a continuing way for speakers of a native language. New words, expressions, and meanings are always being learned and appropriated. And as these new meanings are taken in, is not our actual humanity subtly changed? Perhaps linguistic shifts were noticeable in every era, but they are clamorous in our time. The Internet has powerfully affected language, both in terms of its own special vocabulary ("email," "memory stick," etc.) and the mushrooming of "digispeak" on texting devices, things like the near-universally recognizable "lol" or "bff." In this instance it's as if an electronic machine has the effect of reducing written words to a residue, a skeletal trace marking verbal conventions as fragile and evanescent as the binary code underlying them. So by assimilating to the level of the electron, is not language shaping or modeling a certain impermanence around and within relationships? This is a rhetorical question, and there are certainly many restraining, more traditional forces at work, but you see the point! Language and its forms, its media, can help model and mediate concrete human changes. The final purpose of this book is to point to such a change, but at a level that has profoundly more impact than smartphones or computers. This one works not on the surface medium of technological innovation, but grows imperceptibly under our feet, over the course of centuries, even millennia, shaping the generative sources of human language as such. It is of course a huge claim, but once we have admitted the possibility of change on the surface, why not at more radical levels? In the following chapters we will seek to unpack a more theoretical view of the roots of language, of how they can be affected, and why this idea of semiotic change is a vital human consideration. For the moment, let us continue our first brushstrokes on one further canvas, getting what might be called our artist's impression of one last astonishing possibility. We are asking, what is the cultural agency that is shaping our meaning from the inside and below, such that our collective conversations have swung in a certain, irreversible direction over the course of the modern era?

Beginnings

It's astonishing that the first three chapters of the Bible do not explain the origin of language. They explain just about everything else: the origin of land, sea, animals, gender, desire, law, temptation, transgression . . . but not language. It's as if the very presence of a human being in the story necessitated the given feature of language, its *already-there* quality. And the fact that the first parents attach names to all the animals hints at this, broadly telling us that language is a distinctly *given* human feature, tied always already to human existence.

The Bible is a written account, and it achieves some of its authority from its assuming fixed form in manuscripts and their being faithfully copied over the years. It does not tell us how language came about, but neither does it attempt to downgrade language and its crystallized form in writing. In contrast, Plato, through the mouthpiece of Socrates, has a critique of writing.

He tells how Theuth, god of the arts, mathematics, and astronomy, also invented writing. He went to the great god Thamus to present his discoveries, telling him that writing would be of mighty use to the Egyptians, as an aid to memory and wisdom. Thamus disagreed, saying it would actually lead to forgetfulness through reliance on writing and actual disuse of memory. It would bring "not truth, but only the semblance of truth; [because its practitioners] . . . will be hearers of many things and will have learned nothing."[4]

Socrates seconds the opinion of Thamus, arguing as he does, for philosophical recollection of eternal things, something that should belong to each soul as birthright. In effect, Socrates is fighting the fissile character of language in favor of eternal truth, but this happens via Plato in and by *writing*, and so he (or Plato) involves himself in something of a contradiction. As a classic philosophical teacher, you can only establish the memory of eternal truths through writing!

It seems that the Bible is much more at home in the world of language, taking it as a necessary human starting point, beginning with Moses's writing down "the words of the LORD" (Exod 24:4) and going on to embrace a manuscript tradition which preserves both the law and the words of the prophets. The Bible starts *in medias res*, in the midst of the human situation and its open-endedness. So, can it help the human situation through its writing?

Another thing the early chapters of the Bible do not explain is sacrifice. At the beginning of chapter 4 of Genesis we have the (in)famous sacrifices of Abel and Cain. But God in the story never said he wanted sacrifice, nor made any provision for it. Even more mysterious is that God prefers Abel's sacrifice to Cain's: Cain is simply fulfilling the God-given vocation inherited from his father, Adam, to be a tiller of the soil and grower of crops, so how could he be in the wrong? There are gaps in these accounts, and those gaps are as significant as what is clearly present and accounted for.

It's as if the book of Genesis deliberately leaves some questions up in the air—as if it is telling us there is more road to be traveled for a full, definitive, in-depth revelation of the human condition, while pointing strongly in that direction. A perspective of the complete biblical road—its gradual, dynamic and overall transformative pathway—is the grand project of this book, but not in the usual religious or churchy sense. Signs or semiotics are the thought at the heart of this study, with the argument that the biblical tradition has a radical and pervasive effect on their deep structure. There

---

4. Plato, *Phaedrus* 275a (Jowett, 75).

are significant gaps in the biblical account, but significant for precisely what they leave out. There are also significant inclusions, matter that has not attracted much attention in the past, because it was all incorporated under overarching themes of fall, sinfulness, legal redemption. But there are in fact clear indications of "violent origins" and with them the possibility that our very human world of signs goes back to the same source. We see that the book of Genesis, in chapter 4, strongly suggests it was out of founding acts of murder there arose the totality of human culture. After Cain kills Abel—and God's basic compromise with violence, giving protection for Cain's life through the threat of further violence—Cain becomes the founder of the first city. After him his descendants are, pointedly, the inventors of the range of human culture, including music, animal husbandry, and metallurgy. This, in itself, is a startling perspective, but why not go the whole way and include language among the human inventions?

Someone who did just that was the French scholar and theoretical anthropologist René Girard, a pivotal thinker of the twentieth and twenty-first centuries. Girard argued that the collective victim of primitive hominid violence produced the first moment of cognitive transcendence. What does that mean? It means that the event of killing a family or clan member in the primitive band of protohumans—an act of violence brought on by intolerable rivalry in the group—gave birth to specific human attention. The intense shock and its sudden branding into a raw but advanced neural network produced the first condensation of abstract awareness, separating itself out from the mist of immediate sensation and instinct. This dramatically new perception came intimately tied to a sound, a vocalization, a cry that captured the catastrophic moment. Out of the intensity of the event, therefore, comes the first "word," and with that, eventually, religion, rules, and developed language. We will lay Girard's thought out in more systematic detail in chapter 3, but we have come directly to the central point. The reason is because we have by no means forgotten our eavesdropped conversation in a foreign language and the general problem of language's imprecision and yet vibrant living force. In answer to the conundrum of language we can say at once, with marvelous and liberating daring, that from the very birth conditions of language derive its endless doubling and substitution, the way one thing can stand for another, and may do so without end. To understand this let us trace once again the electric contours of the primary scene.

Tensions in a primitive group (through hunger, disease, natural disaster, or simple jealousy between rivals) produce conflict and soon these escalate to violence. Each one is enraged, the enemy of the other, with blows and cuts falling, terrifyingly, indiscriminately. Suddenly, out of the mayhem one individual stands forth (through weakness, or for some reason already marked as an odd one out) and that individual becomes the focus for all the group's explosive hatred, the one "blamed" for the whole crisis. All the lethal blows descend in a lightning storm on this figure until he or she is dead. Then instantly, miraculously, the tension evaporates and the atmosphere changes to uncanny peace. The world is gathered into one; a sense of meaning and wholeness which was not there before is expressed in an original cry wrung from the participants. It amounts to a totally new transcendence of immediate circumstances, and with that the simultaneous birth of language and the sacred. Only something "divine" could have done this, or, rather, this new revelatory impact *is* "the god," the source of both all evil and all good. It is the sense of the divine or the sacred which counts, not the memory of the actual crisis, and indeed this memory is pushed to the margins, so it is only *mis*remembered in the form of myth. If an accurate memory were preserved, rather than a distorted one, then the hostility and rage would be renewed rather than the (obviously much preferable) uncanny peace.

So it is that the first word, the first story, is *already* a substitute for something else, a displacement of an event that the group cannot afford to remember lest the violence "contained" in it should break out anew. As Umberto Eco says, a sign is anything that can be used to tell a lie![5] Lying is built into the very fabric of language. At the same time the word has difference running right through it, the difference between "evil" and "good," yet both somehow gathered into one. Thus, the primordial cry wrung from the murdering crowd contains all that is needed for language: a systemic unity producing "the world," and yet in its very bones a primary difference, *yea* and *nay*. The basic misrecognition lies behind it all, but that doesn't matter because the meaning, the "story," is so much more important than the facts. Human existence is up and running and its semiotic power (the power to give and shape meaning) is unnegotiable. Proto-language has the built-in ability to extend itself, because once sacred meaning exists then everything in the world can have meaning: *this not that, here not there, now not then*. The rest of the world shares, by displacement, in the meaning brought by the sacred, and progressively—through metonym and difference—there can be a name for everything. The invention of actual sounds (words) is wholly secondary to the first essential event of meaning. But once the event of the victim occurs group vocabulary follows. Perhaps it takes a very long time, with many false starts and failures, but ultimately, as the factual languages demand, vocabulary is put in place, the lexicon is born.

---

5. Eco, *Theory of Semiotics*, 58–59. "The possibility of lying is the *proprium* of semiosis . . ."

As just mentioned, all this will be set out in systematic detail below, but suffice for now to get the summary, revolutionary picture of the extraordinary fact of language. Girard's thesis fits the nature of the case, giving us a plausible origin while explaining the intimate mutability of words. At the same time, part of the theological fascination of Girard's thought is the fact that it works in a feedback loop with biblical scripture. Girard uses many evidences from outside the Bible, but he finds in the Hebrew and Christian Scriptures a unique source of revelation that enables us to see through the murk of misremembered and misrecognized violence to the devastating truth of violent origins. (We have just seen this powerfully evinced in the story of Cain, but it tracks forward inexorably to the crucifixion of Jesus.) Indeed, the Bible and its message represent a singular power in bringing the world to the knowledge of itself. And it is in this effect that the Bible produces its potentially most extraordinary result—the gradual re-creation of human language and meaning itself.

The revelation of violent origins of human language must necessarily bring with it a destabilization of meaning in the world, but by the very same token it introduces a totally a new meaning—the inverse of violence. Love is the revelatory engine bringing us the truth of the human condition, but that is exactly the point. It is divine and human love which shows us at one and the same time the dysfunction *and* the transformation of the *anthropos*, giving us together human reality misspoken, and human reality re-spoken and remade.

And so once again we are back with our observed conversation, the animated little drama of a world produced in common by a group of "foreigners" on a plane or a train. How stable or unstable is their language? How permeable to change? What if the biblical story could slowly and almost imperceptibly introduce into their conversation the seed of a thoroughly radical change of meaning? What if the forgotten victim at the source of human culture should be revealed and simultaneously this intolerable truth be shown as one of immeasurable compassion and forgiveness? What if the very thing we absolutely cannot behold should, by beholding it through the Crucified, become the source of a completely new humanity?

Our overheard conversationalists are creating their world as they speak, or, rather, their words, their whole fabric of language is creating the world for them. But the claim of this book is that certain elements of their language—themes spread throughout the world by the biblical gospel—are re-creating their language itself, and therefore their humanity with it. It's as if the sea which we humans swim in, the sea of words, has been permeated by a salt that we did not know existed, one that can bring life to everything. Or, perhaps better, the sea has been touched by an entirely new current or tide which, little by little, is pulling everyone with it to a destination we can barely envision but which becomes more real the more the tide gathers its force. So, our conversationalists are partaking whether they know it or not in a huge and vital evolution: a change in the very meaning by which they understand, grasp, and realize their world.

No doubt this is very different from traditional theologies of law, grace and eternal destiny by which the work of the gospel has been understood. And the kind of proposition I am making here is open to attack from two sides: on the one by those who might think it "humanizes" what is essentially a supernatural mystery, and on the other by those who might see it as a new form of Christian absolutism. Elements of defense against either of these accusations should appear progressively in the rest of the book, but, essentially, they consist in the fact that the linguistic argument stands up for itself and a humanizing effect cannot (and should not) be denied. And if its outcome tends necessarily to nonviolence and welcome of the other, who could wish otherwise? Right now, my response is to assert how these thoughts fit within an anthropological and semiotic scheme calling out unquenchably for a future of love. Although it might claim also to be Christian theology how can this be other than a desirable human destiny?

But let us begin once more. We transition now to the more critically located argument of this book and we do so with a short chapter developing further the understanding of the Bible just given. At the same time it situates the hermeneutic within the broad context of postmodernism, and so creates a seam between our conversation about imagined conversation and the current intellectual and cultural context. Most importantly, we lay out the full schematic of theological semiotics, the vision of human transformation which unfolds through the rest of the book.

2
Biblical Upgrade

In the beginning was the word . . .

Postmodern Violence

POSTMODERNISM AND THE MARK of the postmodern may be summarized as the "constructed" nature of human truth. There is an implied violence in our truth claims, enforcing as they do an order that is in fact "non-natural," not metaphysically grounded because metaphysics itself is groundless. We build our castles in the air and they are the castles by which the world is protected and held together. But now, precisely as we understand that they are built in air, they are starting to collapse. There is a decided shakiness to the various forms of our psychological, political, and philosophical identity. For example, "white," "male," "heterosexual," "Western," "civilized," etc., all of these denominators, in the past so seemingly solid and unshakeable, are now open to question, in particular from their binary others who were rendered subordinate and invalid—"colored," "female," "gay," "Oriental," "savage." These thoughts are not unknown to any of us. Even without following the philosophical journey that has brought us to them, one would have to be living on a rock in outer space not to have some sense of a shift in the times. And once again, in all of it there is the implication of violence at work. Violence here remains largely on the level of thought and attitude, in erecting the privileged categories. But actual violence never seems far away, whether in past or possible future events, defending a necessary line-in-the-sand identity.

Moreover, the situation has now also developed beyond the original categories, in as much as the attack on privileged certainties is itself seen as a form of privilege in its own right. This in turn leads to a further reaction which in its upside-down way mirrors the initial demotion of cultural exception. "Progressives" can now be characterized, in an Orwellian reversal, as an oppressive elite. In which case the postmodern scene degrades into an endless angry search for the subordinate or "victim" status which alone grants power.

One contemporary thinker has gone beyond mere sensibility to metaphysical privilege and has provided a compelling theory of actual human violence. The thought of René Girard has already been sketched in relation to language, and we saw there the primordial role of violence. Girard's analysis is also able to explain the phenomenon of desired victim status, on the basis of the actual historical revelation of the victim. Today, according to his argument, we all recognize and affirm the victim because of a deep cultural process mobilized, essentially, by the Bible. A core element in the human landscape has shifted; the victim not the oppressor has the most powerful status, and this is preeminently the result of biblical revelation. We, therefore, involve Girard once more in the discussion, but this time in a frame of the present intellectual and cultural setting. Doing this allows us, in turn, to lay out the argument of biblical semiotic transformation more incisively and in principle.

Girard's thought is an astonishing example of high Enlightenment reason which conceives a scientific basis and role for religion. He sees human religious practice as a vital source of truth, and, in particular, the revelation given in the Jewish and Christian Scriptures. Revelation here is not to be taken in the usual theological sense of the nature and actions of God (although it does not necessarily exclude that). Rather, it is a disclosure of root human relationships. In this understanding *the Bible reveals an anthropology, the generative way we structure ourselves as human beings in and through violence.* Girard is a different kind of postmodern thinker, because he produces a claim to actual hard knowledge, not uncertainty. However, because this knowledge exposes violence at the heart of culture it necessarily takes its place as a parallel form of postmodern sensibility. How can we trust cultural forms if they are founded in violence? All the same, his thought remains traditional in a pivotal way. His claim that the Bible plays a unique role in unveiling the violent origins of humanity gives dramatically new tenor and meaning to this religious tradition. It suggests an evolving, transformative dynamic within the scriptural tradition itself. In other words, it is an argument about semiosis, about the production of human meaning, and one that has a biblical nature.

In the following chapter we will look at Girard's work in more bibliographical detail, but here we have an immediate broad principle crucial for the present study. The Bible in the past has been interpreted almost exclusively as a source of religious information, about the character of God and God's dealings with his chosen people. Now rather it is shown as a tool for grasping the generative source of human culture, including language. Necessarily included in that disclosure is the possibility of a revolution in the very source of meaning. This is a point that is not underlined by Girard but is cardinal to the present study. How would the hidden, violent spring of human culture be revealed unless something new had entered at that primitive level to suggest an alternative? In normal experience awareness of objects is given against a certain horizon or background by which we know clearly what they are. For example, a chair appears in a room different from the floor and the table, because of the light falling on it, the distribution of objects, and the context of use to which they are put. But what about the very machine of meaning itself, the generative source of culture, language and linguistic thought? To identify this at its source, and know it as originally violent, then surely a background or horizon must have appeared that is entirely different in nature? You cannot grasp the dark outline of the land unless the glimmer of dawn has appeared above it. Similarly, you cannot grasp the dark secret of original murder unless the light of compassion and forgiveness has shone across it and through it.

This is the entry point of love. Where does the solution lie to the endless "waterwheel" of the victim when the millstream is the force of anger and resentment and each bucket seeks to come out on top by first going under at the bottom? Is it not a transformation, whereby the stream becomes forgiveness and nonviolence, and the bucket joyfully surrenders to the stream so that what comes after may also be filled?

A Biblical and Human Process

The picture above is something of a greeting-card image, but it gives the strict thesis of the present book, based in a rigorous anthropology and semiotics. Postmodern revelation of violence, including the death of metaphysics, would not be possible without the irruption of an alternative principle within human existence. And if this principle arises in the Bible it does so by a slow, painful reprogramming in which the alternative cannot become plain all at once. If it had arrived suddenly, fully formed, it would certainly have been so alien as to be unrecognizable. It would have been impossible for anyone actually to embrace it, given it is so contrary to actually existing humanity. As it is, we know the books of the Hebrew Bible took more than a thousand years to be written, and the Christian Scriptures, arriving late in time (or a "fullness of time"), were themselves about a hundred years in the making. The sole compelling explanation for such an extended rhythm of revelation is precisely that such a profoundly new principle of human meaning can only emerge step by step, as and when human beings can appropriate it.

We stand, therefore, before the semiotic miracle of the Bible which is the nerve of the whole way of thought here. The word "bible" signifies a series of writings—*ta biblia* in Greek is plural, meaning "the books." So, the name itself entails the possibility of scripture as a conversation with multiple contributors, sustained over a very long period. But what is the point of keeping up a many-sided conversation for more than a thousand years unless it is reaching continually toward a new level of articulation and understanding, rather than repeating the same thing over and over? The argument then is definitely not that the Bible somehow achieves a transparent intellectual idea, or a set of ideas, but rather that it intervenes in the root structure of signs and meaning itself, diverting the river of human semiosis from its original spring or, in fact, providing a new one. This is a much more challenging claim. The Bible builds on the fluidity of human meaning, arriving finally at a form that is genuinely radical and new.

Words do not simply have fuzzy borders, they have a deeply shady evolutionary origin, one with which Christ engaged, shifting that obscure beginning into entirely new possibilities of construction. Cutting against the long grain of established meaning it is only over the course of centuries that this shift has become both possible and visible. But now, such is the subversive power of the process, human meaning is experiencing a real destabilization, the breakdown of privileged meaning accelerating in the ways we have described. The "center cannot hold," and it is apparent, as we have noted, in the cyclical, mutually defeating attempts to claim "most authentic" victim status. The old order of violent certainty, frayed to extremes, seeks desperately to reassert itself, but it is able to do so, as Girard makes clear, only by use of the revelation of violence itself and a cyclical taking the side of the oppressed, the victim.[1] We do not require much insight to see how doomed this effort is. How much more promising, then, is a new human meaning of compassion and gentleness, arising precisely as the revelatory backlight exposing our old humanity and expressing itself at the heart of our language? It's as if our speakers in the train or plane are being taken by the very words they share to a completely unexpected human destination, and little by little they themselves are becoming aware of it.

Does all this sound at once outrageous and ridiculously naive? Maybe it sounds that way at first, but, as far as Christian faith is concerned, what I am

---

1. This situation is really the latest "terminal" point in the anthropological odyssey Girard has pursued for us. It is presented most fully in his last book, *Battling to the End*. Many of his other books laying out the essential prior stages of his thought will be introduced in the next chapter.

stating is really no different from the first line of John's Gospel: *In the beginning was the Word*. In the past this phrase has been understood metaphysically. The "Word" communicates at once a divine and philosophical principle, the Second Person of the Trinity as an eternal entity which gives all things their existence and truth. The shocking thing in John's prologue is that it goes on to identify this principle with the person of Jesus, a human individual in time. Immediately, therefore, the whole thing gets turned upside down. What should be eternal is suddenly historical. The absolute beginning has entered history to provide a fresh beginning there. Theological shorthand of this is "the incarnation." In the past we have understood this, again, as a metaphysical claim—an event producing some type of metaphysical change in humanity, visible ultimately and only on an eternal plane. But isn't the logic of "the Word made flesh" the other way around? If the Word is "made flesh" it is unavoidable to take it also *as* flesh, that is, as actual human word and speech: a dramatic new beginning of signs and their meaning. What is eternal becomes temporal, so that whatever is "truth" is now manifest in the fleeting but atavistic, spoken but inherited, discourse of humans. And, thereby, the very meaning generated by their laryngeal fluctuations of breath is changed from within? The logos is incarnate for the sake of the flesh, not so that flesh may be swallowed up by eternity. And the human quality *par excellence*, the language of the language animal, now becomes the privileged vehicle of divine identity. Isn't it likely even that the author of John's Gospel had the courage to claim an extraordinary bursting-in of the divine in humanity precisely because an unquantifiable newness had already been experienced in the actual signals of meaning that were produced by Jesus?

We are dealing, therefore, with a superlatively human process. What may be understood from one side religiously—as the result of a divine intervention—may be seen, on the reverse, as something completely human. When I first explained the content of this book to my eldest son—whose thought is a filial brand of atheism—he exclaimed, "Very nice, very humanist!" A process of semiotic transformation based in the Bible can be assumed as a contingent anthropological event, desirable and affirmable, but not needing the agency of God. Nevertheless, it seems eminently possible to view it from a faith perspective: a transcendent semiosis of love cannot break into and overturn generative violence without a power beyond the human. Thus, we have the New Testament confession that "God is love," proclaiming that a new humanity of love can only be brought about by the divine. Thus, I believe, it is possible to make the argument of this book both from a humanist perspective and also from one profoundly indebted to theology. Indeed, this double valence reflects the deep project of humanization intended precisely by the God of the Bible. It also corresponds closely to Jesus's parables of the leaven in the batch of loaves, and the mustard seed and the birds of the air which come to rest in the branches its bush produces. What on the one side looks like a natural historical process can be read on the other as a divine plan. Meanwhile, there is no need to demand passports from the birds of the nations as they find a home among the branches of God's kingdom; just as little as bread supplied to the hungry has to come with a papal *imprimatur*!

The Semiotic Interpretation

We now have our fingers upon the deep pulse of the book. The Word-made-flesh is a change in flesh itself, which includes most critically the quality of information by which our "flesh" is held together as meaning. In order to bring about that change it would never be adequate to drop an abstract idea on humanity from above, telling everyone simply how to see, believe, and behave differently. Even if this were possible it would be effectively to change the creature all at once into something entirely different, equivalent to a super-brainwashing. From the perspective of human freedom this is, of course, intolerable. And in scriptural terms it is otherwise than the case. "All the scriptures" spoke of Jesus, but it was exactly this meaning that had to be explained to the disciples by the Risen One in person over the course of a leisurely walk to Emmaus (Luke 24:13–35). The signals had to be interpreted by the person of Jesus in his reality as an entirely new kind of human being (in the role of "interpretant," as we will see later). And before that he himself, in his historical existence, had to grasp those signals in an unprecedented act of practical synthesis. Luke, wisely, did not write down Jesus's explanation, because in a way he had just attempted to do so, over the course of the whole Gospel. But, more crucially, he avoided a formal catechesis because the space had to be left open for the continuous and progressive semiotic interpretation that would ultimately allow us (and everyone else) to catch up with the meaning of Jesus.

I do think in fact that at this latter stage of things it would be a valuable project to reconstruct some version of Jesus's revelatory conversation that Sunday morning; from the perspective of twenty-one centuries of experience and scholarship we would surely be able to attempt a semiotic account. In one respect the present volume offers a theoretic sketch of this, given its central motif of Bible-inspired semiotic change, and then, especially, in its ending with a semiotic reading of the Gospel of John. But a thoroughgoing account of the Bible and its transformative metanarrative will have to wait for a further volume dedicated specifically to that. What is urgent here is the general theoretic of semiotic change and how this can be seen to play out in overall Bible terms ending in Jesus. In John's Gospel we read that the Word of God is the one who "is close to the Father's heart" (1:18). He thus makes directly available to his followers—and the whole world—the new meaning of God and humanity he represents in his one, singular life. But, at the same time, he depends on "everything written [about him] in the law of Moses, the prophets, and the psalms." He himself is the product of a millennium-long semiotic labor. If we don't read the Bible in this way it reduces the preparation of the Old Testament to a kind of magic legalism, and there is absolutely no reason why "Jesus" should not have occurred a thousand years before. As it is, Christian theology has always done "exegesis." It has read the New Testament by a kind of "reverse engineering" which leads you very quickly to core elements of the Old Testament/Hebrew Bible. Then going forward again we get to Jesus and his dramatic condensation of the semiotic themes necessary for redemption, for a new way of human life that brings life, not death. The final chapter on John shows this playing out in almost mathematical terms and so completes the arc of the argument. The hope is that the whole thing can have a compelling value as a program of human "re-meaning." Meanwhile, the overall process may be diagrammed as follows, giving the full picture at a glance. The Christian message is entirely one of meaning change, prepared in the OT, reaching its generative point in Christ, playing out afterward in cultural change, and continually "re-read" and internalized by Christian disciples. It works as follows.

- standard human programming: *humanity is born in the "thickness" of violence as the source of its meaning; we cannot emerge into a free space, as we have no other way of constructing who we are.*

  - narrative preparation: *the story of God's people is one of long struggle with this root programming, of being led step by step to letting go of old humanity for the sake of something dramatically new, and writing the story of change in sequence.*

    - rebirth of human meaning in Jesus: *the prophet from Galilee embraces the transformative meaning of his scriptures and becomes in person the new human; by definition this is also intimate relationship with his Father/Mother who has always intended this change.*

      - slow percolation of this meaning at semiotic level: *because Jesus represents a semiotic revolution he is taken up by culture in an implicit process, not the same as doctrinal belief; little by little the issue of violence and its victims is brought to light because of Jesus's revolutionary suffering rather than retaliation.*

∽ reading the transformative pathway theologically: *Jesus's religious meaning was formulated largely within established metaphysical frameworks, but now because of what we understand semiotically his new meaning is creating its own conditions for communication, leading to transformative nonviolent theology.*

What is being offered is in its way close to what used to be called a "spiritual" reading of the Old Testament—connecting the meaning of one part with another by overarching spiritual themes, above all with and through Christ. But where this was done largely through use of literary figures, especially typology and allegory (making, for example, the exodus a figure of baptism), what is suggested here is something entirely more structural and organic. There is a theological process at work in the actual language, changing our whole way of framing and knowing reality. The redemptive effect can be expressed in legal-metaphysical categories (viz. "divine adoption," "regeneration," "salvation," etc.) but that way largely misses a real-world transformative impact: the completion of the work of physical creation intended by a life-giving God. Indeed, none of these traditional categories can have any identifiable reality (short of some speculative, beyond-time-and-space afterlife) if they are not encapsulated in transformative events of meaning in living human beings: if they are not in fact located in an actual process of the meaning-making human brain reaching into its deepest constitution and finding there a new core relationship. As already mentioned, the process can have progressive transformative value for any who encounter it through the cultural diffusion of the gospel. It has theological value for all who embrace it in faith, as God's way of bringing about the divine purpose of life and love. We are reading the text backwards semiotically, from Christ, but forwards too: forwards from Abraham to the point where Jesus was able to embrace the revolutionary meaning of the Old Testament. From that point then it makes perfect sense to see how Jesus's intervention would continue fundamentally to impact and shape real historical human meaning.

Within this horizon we are now able to launch fully into an investigation of semiotics, beginning with our key thinker, Girard. We will pay close attention to the background of his thought, something shared in parallel with another key contemporary thinker whom we will consider in sequence. We will then move progressively in succeeding chapters to an expanded grasp of the broad Western tradition that has got us to this critical point of semiotic awakening.

3

Murderous Semiosis

The thought of René Girard was introduced in the previous chapters, a little abruptly and somewhat casually, but perhaps that is the best way. It seems most fitting for a set of ideas which represents such a drastic break with the metaphysical universe in which we have so far lived. Rather than ideas and truth arriving somehow naked and pristine from a superlunary sphere of intellect, they come to us poorly washed and clothed following terrible crises of human desire in both our primitive past and our current world. This present book is about semiotics, the science and study of signs, and it turns now formally to the work of Girard because his thought gives us a rational hypothesis about the origin of our world of signs. It presents what might accurately be termed a *generative semiotics*, and clearly it is these Girardian semiotics which are the root of this study. Once we have understood this, we will turn to other connected treatments to see how Girard's thesis can be integrated within a broader understanding of signs. We will be following a circling pathway, working our way out from Girard to other thinkers with whom he is to be associated—figures without whom his thought would, in some instances, not be possible, and, in general, not intelligible. Thus, we will be able to situate Girard convincingly as a semiotic figure. In the meantime, we continue to keep in mind how Girardian semiotics are, in their own quite peculiar and radical way, biblical semiotics.

Girard's Structural Breakthrough

To reflect on language is always in fact to go around in a big circle, or in many overlapping circles, like the rings of Saturn. Yes, there must be strong objective references: as an evolutionary phenomenon language would be useless unless it enabled humans to navigate the world successfully. Furthermore—and of course—scientific language carries through an extremely precise and successful response to physical reality. Science's presumption of a real physical order with accessible rational structure is a bedrock of contemporary culture. Nevertheless, once we begin to examine actual language and its use, we enter a boundless well of human meaning, with a life somehow entirely its own. How could we possibly tell lies if it were not for the strange semi-autonomy of language? How would politicians deceive us, or propagandists, ideologues and religious leaders prompt our thinking for us, including in the most counter-evidential ways? Or, how could we be tone-deaf to ourselves, or simply plain ignorant of what we're talking about, if language was not able to carry us along on its own irresistible wave without ever feeling the need to explain itself thoroughly?

As we have seen, Girard's thought offers a deeply consistent postmodern inquiry arguing that language emerged from original and misremembered acts of human violence: it is as such congenitally a scheme of deception. At the same time, he has told us that the Bible uniquely unmasks the deceit, and therefore somehow cuts across the grain of signified falsehood. Girard's anthropology supplies, therefore, an evolutionary semiotics whose substance, over the space of two millennia, has profoundly affected the course of human meaning. Girard, however, toward the end of his career seemed to think as if the biblical revelation—including his own analysis—was too little, too late. In a personal note to me he commented on a piece I had written, one which suggested we were on our way to the discovery of our true humanity. He replied, "But is there enough time?" My view is that if Girard thought we were at the end of the possibility of a peaceful civilization we are in fact more likely at the beginning. If the semiotic tools for the full human recognition of both violence and forgiveness have only lately come to light, then surely there needs to be enough time for their assimilation? And if we do not think that in terms of the foresight of divine providence, we must surely not discount human beings' celebrated ability to adapt dramatically when, and only when, things have reached a point of crisis.

The three basic stages of Girard's thought have been rehearsed many times, and because much of their detail will emerge in what follows there's no need to go through them again in pedantic detail. Mimesis, scapegoating, and biblical revelation of the victim make up the grand sweep of his hypothesis. The three topics take us from the core human faculty for imitative desire, through the crisis of violence resolved by the collective victim, to the Bible's textual vindication of the victim as innocent. This shocking, three-layer archeology of humanity both attracts and repels by its simplicity. In a less frightening and frightened time it perhaps would not have been given a hearing, but any thought coming in the aftermath of the twentieth century would not warrant much attention unless it reckoned with man's annihilating violence. As it is, at the threshold of the third millennium Girardian anthropology makes steadily gathering strides as the single most persuasive reckoning with human violence—and this is the case both despite and because of its organic link with the biblical narrative.[1]

Violence and the Sacred is the book where Girard left behind his previous concentration on imitative desire identified in key works of literature and plunged deep in the undergrowth of ethnography and anthropology.[2] He established there the principle of the surrogate victim (or scapegoat) present at the basis of archaic—and thus all—human culture. However, one of the characteristic things about its argument is the way it gathers evidence not just from traditional ethnography but from other areas of the humanities, thus building a raft of evidence. These areas include sociology, literature, psychology and, at an implied level, semiotics. The inspiration of semiotics is in fact an essential root of *Violence and the Sacred*.

In the ninth chapter Girard examines the anthropology of Claude Lévi-Strauss, the hugely influential thinker in the middle of the twentieth century who introduced the framework of structuralism to ethnographic research, moving it decisively away from "natural" or biological explanations toward what seemed like purely formal relations. Girard derives from this understanding a key piece for his own puzzle. There is in fact no way Girard could have arrived at the anthropological layer off his thinking without the discoveries made by Lévi-Strauss. Reading the latter's *Elementary Structures of Kinship*, and others of his writings, you get a sense of how Girard's insights seem to be bubbling just under the surface. What is of intense interest for our

---

1. See Michel Serres, French philosopher and, with Girard, member of the Académie française, who called Girard the "new Darwin of the Human Sciences." McKenna, "Darwin and Girard," 3.

2. Girard, *Violence and the Sacred*. His book on literary criticism was *Deceit, Desire and the Novel: Self and Other in Literary Structure*. In this, his first book, he showed how great works of literature came to the realization that desire is "mimetic," or imitative, rather than spontaneous. Key protagonists are shown to learn their desire by following the eye of another gazing on its object. Thus, there is always a triangular structure to desire: model, object, subject. It is also important to underline how these insights came from reading literature, what might be seen as a form of pure semiotics: the signs having no direct reference to a life-world but linked only to each other and thereby creating a "meaning" which may or may not affect the actual world, depending on the inner response of the reader. As Charles Taylor says, storytelling or narrative is a privileged way of giving a new articulation to the world, one that does not depend on the world as previously constituted to and by the reader (see p. xxiv above, notes 3 and 4). What Girard identified in these networks of signs was a very precise mode of human relationship—mimetic desire. In other words, these rich semiotic clusters, called novels, of themselves produced the concept at the root of his thought.

purposes is the way linguistics, and specifically what is known as structural linguistics, were, *in their turn*, crucial for the development of Lévi-Strauss's own insights. Structural linguistics are recognized to have begun with a Swiss thinker named Ferdinand de Saussure, a man seen as a progenitor of the modern science of language and signs, and his work profoundly influenced Lévi-Strauss by his own admission.[3] From Saussure Lévi-Strauss borrowed the revolutionary method of regarding relationships between terms as primary, not the terms themselves. In sympathy with this approach he understood relationships between kinship groups as a form of language, rather than belonging to some eternally set ontological or biological order.

I will circle back again to Saussure's thought below, in order to show its parallel influence on another key thinker in our inquiry. But to reconstruct at once the line of influence to Girard I may summarize Saussure's viewpoint as follows, introducing one of the standard articulations of contemporary semiotics.[4] As a matter of common observation there is no repeatable, conscious thought without words. But the phonemes (basic sound units) of a language have a nonessential character, that is, the sounds of our words have no intrinsic relation to the concepts they carry. The sounds of words are not an auditory snapshot of their objects, otherwise all the languages of the world would exhibit a sound-similarity to each other when referring to the same concept. Therefore, words can only work within a string of links and differences held with other sounds/signs around them in a particular language tradition. Thus, it is the *relationship* between signs which actually produces functional meaning, not discrete or ideal units of information. And the relationships themselves are actually made up of differences, between and within signs. We might compare this understanding to seeing

---

3. Lévi-Strauss, *Structural Anthropology*, 20.

4. See Saussure, *Course in General Linguistics*. Saussure's own preferred name was "semiology," and there is some confusion between the two terms. Strictly speaking, semiology is applied just to language and does not include the world of natural signs (tracks in the snow, red sky at night, etc.). Saussure in fact saw all signs under the heading of language: "Signs that are wholly arbitrary realize better than the others the ideal of the semiological process; that is why language, the most complex and universal of all systems of expression, is also the most characteristic; in this sense linguistics can become the master pattern for all branches of semiology although language is only one particular semiological system" (*Course in General Linguistics*, 68). As we shall see, some want to reject Saussure as a semiotician because of this unwarranted primacy of language (and the supposed arbitrariness of signs that goes with it). However, since the 1960s "semiotics" has come generally to be used to cover all reflection on signs, including "semiology." In the process the subject of semiotics also refocuses the question of the truth-value of signs, and this will become much more urgent as we go forward. Meanwhile, Saussure's accent on arbitrariness decisively highlights a certain violence at the roots of human signs, and this evidently helps explain Girard's own line of thought.

a house, and naming and thinking of its parts as things in themselves and separate from each other. But walls and roofs, floors, joists, boards and nails only have meaning in relation to each other. What is a nail without a piece of wood to drive it into? And, in fact, what is a house without people to live in it, a street or a field which it occupies, a city or province where it is located, and so on without end? Indeed, a wall or a house is only "a thing" because we name and distinguish it that way. In reality, it is a set of relationships and differences, and our name for it presupposes, includes and holds in the background of our minds the virtually endless set of relationships that compose it, all themselves made up of words (signs)!

Lévi-Strauss applied this structural principle crucially to the social norms or structures governing families linked by marriage, or, as they are called, "kinship structures." He argued that these structures did not belong to some supposed ideal order, as had previously been thought (i.e., the "elementary family" of man, wife, and children, around which everything else orbits in bands of lineage and marriage, as you find in kinship charts). Instead he saw that external relationships between separate family groups were the basic anthropological structure, and this was the crucial thing. As he says, "[I]t is not the families (isolated terms) which are truly 'elementary,' but, rather, the relations between those terms."[5] Specifically, the relationships were a live system for exchanging marriageable women among groups, and everything pivoted around the variations of positive or negative attitude between the main players in the scheme. There were in fact four key roles spread over two generations: sister (wife in another family), brother (uncle to her children), father, and son (husband to another woman/sister); and as there was a positive relationship between one pair there was a corresponding negative relationship between another. For example, a close, familiar relationship between father and son was paralleled by a relationship of rigid taboo between brother and sister; or this could be inverted, with a familiar relationship between brother and sister, and a strict or rigid one between father and son. It is not necessary to go into or even comprehend all the specific details. What is of the essence is that for Lévi-Strauss kinship emerged as a symbolic system in which pairs of oppositions control other pairs in an endless series of correlations and inversions. In this system the relational attitudes of actual persons while noted are of no inherent interest. The only important focus is the structural balance and abstract symmetry of the whole edifice. As he says, "A kinship system does not consist in the objective ties of descent or consanguinity between individuals. It exists only

---

5. Lévi-Strauss, *Structural Anthropology*, 51.

in human consciousness; it is an arbitrary system of representations, not the spontaneous development of a real situation."[6]

It is vital to grasp this overall framework in order to understand the emergence of Girard's thought, and its implication in a theory of language. Not only does Lévi-Strauss derive his thought from linguistics, he believes, as just said, that kinship relations are themselves a form of language. In a provocative phrase he explicitly compares the currency of kinship relations to the currency of language, that is, words. He says, *"The women of the group . . . are circulated between clans, lineages, or families, in place of the words of the groups, which are circulated between individuals."*[7] In a nutshell, Lévi-Strauss unmoored culture from metaphysical presuppositions and set it adrift on a sea of purely semiotic relationships, that is, a kind of language; and, yes, this language was as mobile and uncertain as the sea itself.

Girard then used the structural insights Lévi-Strauss had derived from Saussurean thought to reach his own dramatic and very different breakthrough, that of foundational violence. It was only a matter of scratching just below the surface of the positive/negative pairs to detect the smoldering threat implied: kinship relations are not bloodless mathematics, they involve desire and intense danger. The incest taboo is a universal human rule and Lévi-Strauss considered it to lie at the center of symbolic relations, the pivot around which the exchange of women revolved. "The primitive and irreducible character of the basic unit of kinship, as we have defined it, is actually a direct result of the universal presence of the incest taboo. This is really saying that in human society a man must obtain a woman from another man who gives him a daughter or a sister."[8] Lévi-Strauss never took this beyond the symbolic level—a code which has a crucial role but is never explained apart from an idealized social benefit. "The prohibition of incest is less a rule prohibiting marriage with the mother, sister or daughter, than a rule obliging the mother, sister or daughter to be given to others."[9] Girard, in contrast, argued consistently that the taboo and its results come from the intense need to prevent violence at the heart of the human unit: the taboo results from primary crises (between brothers/fathers/uncles) for access to an available female, the terrifyingly murderous results, and the resulting sacred boundaries created to prevent their reoccurrence. It is as part of these boundaries that the external exchange system results. "Positive exchanges are merely the reverse of prohibitions, the results of a series of maneuvers or avoidance

---

6. Lévi-Strauss, *Structural Anthropology*, 50.
7. Lévi-Strauss, *Structural Anthropology*, 61, italics original.
8. Lévi-Strauss, *Structural Anthropology*, 46.
9. Lévi-Strauss, *Elementary Structures of Kinship*, 485, 480.

taboos designed to ward off outbreaks of rivalry among the males. Terrified by the fearful consequences of endogamous reciprocity, men have created the beneficial reciprocity of exogamic exchange."[10] In one dramatic blow Girard breaks through the abstract computations of kinship and exchange to discover the bloody faces of human rivalry. So, instead of a philosopher or mathematician at the dawn of human systems of thought, there is the human community and its terrified devices to prevent further killing.

Arbitrary but True

In this way Girard forces through the structuralist surface. As he says, "Structuralism constitutes a negative but indispensable stage in the discovery of the sacred [generative violence]."[11] Earlier he proposes "to carry the Lévi-Straussian critique . . . a little further than Lévi-Strauss himself has chosen to do."[12] It is the very existence of a structure alongside the absence of a metaphysical order which leads Girard to his remarkable insight: that human meaning has violent, nonrational origins. This truth seems indeed to have been hovering just beneath the surface of structuralism, and it did not take Girard much effort to plunge through. However, Girard also wants to take the analysis of origins in a simultaneously different direction, one that will move quickly to establish rational process. He will claim that an order brought by violence provides the conditions for the emergence of symbolic meaning together with empirical observation, and therefore a paradoxical degree of rational truth. It will be this claim that will set him decisively in a class of his own among the poststructuralists. The existence of this rationality will also lead him to posit the concrete origin of language in the event of foundational violence. These claims will make for a constant tension, in the possibility of return of rational truth, borne back on the very random tides of uncertainty on which it was first lost. The connection to violence, however, will continue to revert language itself to that remarkable, indeed violent flux at the birth-pangs of human culture.

If we continue to examine this paradox in Girard's work it gives us other verbal clues that connect Girard to structural linguistics, but also always jumping beyond to rational truth. You might say that Girardian analysis is always a matter of core human communications, or the linguistics of human existence: something simultaneously violent and rational. In *Violence and the Sacred* he comments on this explicitly: "The origin of symbolic thought lies

---

10. Girard, *Violence and the Sacred*, 239.
11. Girard, *Violence and the Sacred*, 242.
12. Girard, *Violence and the Sacred*, 226.

in the mechanism of the surrogate victim . . . It is a fundamental instance of 'arbitration' that gives rise to the dual presence of the *arbitrary* and *true* in all symbolic systems . . . To refer to the origin of symbolic thought is to speak as well of the origin of language."[13] In these succinct remarks Girard makes plain his understanding that human language and meaning begin with the arbitrary victim of original violence. But he makes the immediate point that both arbitrary meaning and actual truth arise from this amazing system. This is then Girard's characteristic ground: the simultaneous possibility of an arbitrary system and objective scientific truth. For Girard "symbolic thought" is initially no different from what Lévi-Strauss means by the term, that is, the differential conceptual forms by which the world is structured. But unlike Lévi-Strauss he is seeking a clarification of an objective, identifiable source behind the differences. By playing on the possible senses of the word "arbitration" he suggests both the fact of arbitrary difference and yet the possibility of correct "arbitration," or judgment, about a real world.

Lévi-Strauss also transferred the structural principle to the understanding of myth: he concluded that the various different versions of a myth acted themselves as a form of language, communicating different meanings by their variable structural choices. This meant there was no single overall meaning, simply different variations obtained by holding oppositions in tension as binaries or pairs. The key object of study was always the way in which binaries could be inverted or interchanged with others.[14] Essentially Lévi-Strauss again followed Saussure, shifting the accent from fixed points to the relation between them.

But consistent with his claim to truth Girard goes well beyond Lévi-Strauss's concentration on differential mythological structures, stressing instead a fundamental triad of "myth, ritual and prohibitions." It is a threesome of anthropological practice, all equally constant, valid and real in forming a bulwark against violent origins. Myth is the misremembered record of the original crisis and its solution. The events are told as strange, often illogical "stories of the gods" in which the benefits of the original murder bring peace and meaning to the community, but always described in oblique, opaque ways.[15] The triad also begins the long labor of actual human knowledge. Repeated ritual together with the maintenance of attached prohibitions allow for temporal measuring, predictability and quasi-scientific inference. One example for Girard would be a recognition of the connection between

---

13. Girard, *Violence and the Sacred*, 235, italics original.

14. See, for example, "Structural Study of Myth," ch. 11 in Lévi-Strauss, *Structural Anthropology*, 206–31.

15. Girard, *Violence and the Sacred*, 64, 87.

the sex act and becoming a parent: prohibitions—strict relations between a man and a woman to limit violence—make sure only one man had sex with a particular woman. Then after a certain measurable period, in a time frame marked out by ritual, a baby arrives![16]

Despite the arbitrary roots of thought and language in violence there is, therefore, a real accumulation of human knowledge. This comes about first of all because, as I have indicated, effective signs and standard rules and structure allow space and time for true connections to be made. But Girard also strongly suggests that today we have a special language, one that is steadily arriving at a fundamental human truth. There is "something more than mere chance . . . linking the indubitably real progress of the so-called human sciences with the slow but steady progress of knowledge toward an understanding of the surrogate victims and of the violent origins of human culture."[17] He does not elaborate but "something more than mere chance" must surely include the revelatory power of the Bible to unmask the victim. In his following book, *Things Hidden since the Foundation of the World*, he will demonstrate how the Bible joins with the human sciences to bring a specific scientific knowledge in its own right: the knowledge of the victim.

First Signs

Things Hidden is a transformative book, emerging at the apex of Girard's thought.[18] Structured as a dialogue between Girard and two other conversation partners, it allows the anthropologist to comment freely and expansively, giving his mind its freest rein in the wide areas his theory touches. Not surprisingly it provides the most comprehensive statement of generative semiotics, and at the same time the book draws profoundly from the well of biblical revelation. The two themes are not consciously linked in the text, but there seems to me to be a powerful implicit connection. The whole middle section of the volume, Book II, is titled "The Judaeo-Christian Scriptures," and it represents an enormous transition of meaning, from generative violence to something altogether different. The very fact that Girard is talking about a distinctive text as the agency of anthropological change demonstrates that we are fully in the area of generative sign systems. Before we get to this, however, we must pay attention to Girard's detailed investigations in the area of language itself.

Book I provides a compelling description of the primary scene, the famous founding murder at the heart of Girard's anthropology. The full

---

16. Girard, *Violence and the Sacred*, 226.
17. Girard, *Violence and the Sacred*, 240.
18. Girard et al., *Things Hidden*.

discussion given to this matter also brings Girard head to head with structuralism, and we can see how he now comprehensively departs from its barren framework of binaries. Although Girard's semiotics also demand binaries (not this/but that) he goes well beyond them, and following him down this path leads us to the most vital questions of the present study.

Girard starts in fact with the birth of "meaning" at a point prior even to the production of the signs or symbols. It amounts to an astonishing moment of pure awareness. We can see here the full quantum leap that Girard's hypothesis takes beyond Lévi-Strauss's formal constructions. I reproduce it here in full because of its extreme critical relevance.

> [E]ven the most elementary form of the victimage mechanism, prior to the emergence of the sign, should be seen as an exceptionally powerful means of creating a new degree of attention, the first non-instinctual attention. Once it has reached a certain degree of frenzy, the mimetic polarization [of all against all] becomes fixed on a single victim. After having been released against the victim, the violence necessarily abates and silence follows the mayhem. The maximal contrast between the release of violence and its cessation, between agitation and tranquility, creates the most favorable conditions possible for the emergence of this new attention. Since the victim is a common victim it will be at that instant the focal point for all members of the community. Consequently, beyond the purely instinctual object, the alimentary or sexual object of the dominant individual, there is the cadaver of the collective victim and this cadaver constitutes the first object for this new type of consciousness.
>
> To the extent that the new type of attention is awakened, the victim will be imbued with the emotions provoked by the crisis and its resolution. The powerful experience crystallizes around the victim. As weak as it might be, the "consciousness" the participants have of the victim is linked structurally to the prodigious effects produced by its passage from life to death, by the spectacular and liberating reversal that has occurred at that instant . . .
>
> There is no need to assume that the mechanism of awakening attention works right away; one can imagine that for a considerable period it produced nothing at all, or *next to nothing*. Nonetheless, even the most rudimentary signifying effects result from the necessity of controlling excessive mimesis; as soon as we grant that these effects can be in the slightest degree cumulative, we will have recognized them as forerunners of human culture.[19]

19. Girard et al., *Things Hidden*, 99–100, italics original.

We have here a full-blooded evolutionary account of human meaning- and sign-making, unparalleled in the simplicity and immediacy of its concept and, at the same time, its cultural shock value. There is no smooth inner evolution of the grammatical "wiring" of the brain resulting little by little in universal nouns and verbs, or—viewed externally—some sort of behavioral continuum multiplying the signals of smart primates all the way up to human language. Rather, Girard's picture has all the abruptness and pain of a birth, or, more accurately, of a fearful death in a dramatic tragedy. In a later book, *Evolution and Conversion*, Girard accents this point and leaves less sense of prolonged reaches of time. He calls the event an upheaval or "catastrophe," implying the etymology of the word, a dramatic turning point often associated with a death or a sudden violent change.[20] In consonance with the feeling of theater, we should notice how the product of the moment is an event of *attention*. Girard uses this word twice, as well as "consciousness" twice. He is saying that something completely out of the ordinary happens in the awareness of the protohumans or "hominids," a bolt out of a clear blue sky constituting a "meaning." This must necessarily be a neural event, something that happens in the grey and white matter of the brain. And it would be here that the repetition of the event would presumably continue to lay down pathways that could be progressively accessed and strengthened.

This would also have to happen among a plurality of individuals in a group, so that together they will recognize and communicate their awareness. The protohumans are conscious—at least dimly—of the event happening with and to each other. This collective awareness may in fact include only a core and lack two or three others of the primary group. But once it had happened in a critical mass it meant that human meaning, or "rudimentary signifying effects," had begun. The fact that this plural awareness perhaps did not happen in the first event of group victimage—or even the third or tenth random event—could account for those initial stages in the emergence of meaning that are "the longest in human history."[21] But for the breakthrough finally to occur there must have been some real accumulation of neural programming in the brains of the hominid group, until at some point along the line, sooner or later, the dam is breached and real signification—a sign—occurs.

Following these remarks one of the dialogue partners, Jean-Michel Oughourlian, questions Girard directly about the role of binary signs, which, as we have seen, was the dominant intellectual context in which Girard worked. Girard had already had implicit recourse to binary oppositions to

---

20. Girard et al., *Evolution and Conversion*, 109.
21. Girard et al., *Things Hidden*, 100.

present prohibitions (... *that* is not permitted, this is ...). Oughourlian refers to the general viewpoint, saying, "Any beginning ... requires at least two signs that signify one another." He then asks how Girard's thought "will engender the binary opposition of structural linguistics." Girard's answer demonstrates how he has used the intellectual currency of his time to arrive at a completely novel viewpoint, and he is now decisively shutting the door on that previous discussion. He rejects the binary scheme and proposes instead "a simpler model that is uniquely dynamic and genetic ... the model of the exception that is still in the process of emerging, the single trait that stands out against a confused mass or still unsorted multiplicity."[22]

Girard abandons the binary model for the sake of a singular event. From a structuralist viewpoint, it could at once be objected that there is, all the same, still a binary here—the exception/confused mass, where the one implies the other. And, obviously it is true, in order to signify what he means Girard does indeed employ a binary. But in the whole dynamic of his thought we also understand that he is talking about a qualitative eruption which is decisively new even if it takes time. He speaks of "the exception ... in the process of emerging," which means that a novum has arrived and is still in fact arriving. We have to imagine a space of human attention and consciousness where, before, attention and consciousness simply did not exist. Furthermore, that element of meaningful attention had the power to grow progressively.

To understand the circumstance more fully, we need also to remind ourselves that what we are reconstructing is itself the event of the sacred, the strange mixture of terror and peace which is so powerful and so determinative that it is felt as the work of a supernatural being, a god. It is the primal moment of religious awe, and as such it is necessarily unitary and synthetic, not differential and analytic. Girard goes on to say something which is an explicit challenge to the dominant thinking of his time. He claims that the victim functions as the "transcendental signifier." And the "transcendental signified" which it bears "constitutes all actual and potential meaning the community confers on to the victim and, through its intermediacy, on to all things."[23] These terms had a thunderous resonance in poststructuralist thought, and so does Girard's statement. As we shall explain more fully through the next major thinker, the thought scheme of structuralism had itself evacuated the world of transcendent meaning. If everything is an endlessly variable set of oppositions, then there is already nothing that can make a claim to actual self-representing truth, and it was poststructuralism that

22. Girard et al., *Things Hidden*, 100.
23. Girard et al., *Things Hidden*, 103.

clearly declared this. Here is the famous relative truth ("undecidability" or "truthiness"!) of postmodernism. Girard instead bluntly asserts an identifiable evolutionary source of human significance—one soaked in blood and horror, but nevertheless a clear and competent evolutionary basis of human meaning. We must ask ourselves shortly about the peculiar status of this meaning. Girard offers a scientific demonstration of *how* meaning comes about, *how* something acts as a transcendental signifier, but not that it really *is* so, that there *is* metaphysical truth. For the moment, however, we need to continue to focus on the semiotic value of Girard's claim.

The original murder of the victim produced the conditions necessary for a new group attention, one of extreme density and generativity. This original attention was all-encompassing, what might be termed "contemplative" and "holistic." At the same time, it held within itself the possibility of dividing things up, of producing binary opposites, and so of a world of reason and difference. Girard now goes on to say this explicitly, declaring the surrogate victim to be the original matrix of a differentiated world.

> Because of the victim, in so far as it seems to emerge from the community and the community seems to emerge from it, for the first time there can be something like an inside and an outside, a before and after, a community and the sacred. We have already noted that the victim appears to be simultaneously good and evil, peaceable and violent, a life that brings death and a death that guarantees life. Every possible significant element seems to have its outline in the sacred and at the same time to be transcended by it. In this sense the victim does seem to constitute a universal signifier.[24]

Thus, Girard fully recognizes the binary function in the construction of meaning—a series of opposites. But he is able to hypothesize a holistic source for this human ability. He is able to answer the poststructuralist question of transcendental meaning, and to do so in its most natural sense, that is, a religious sense. Religion prehistorically gives rise both to itself and to all other fields of meaning. Girard frequently insists on this in his work: the foundational role of religion for human culture, and at this point in the argument, it closes the circle of his thought about the origin of signification.

Meanwhile Girard makes some illuminating remarks in relation to actual signs and words, and we need to note these in order to underline that he is indeed providing an integral semiotics. At the end of the same chapter of *Things Hidden*, he argues that the killing of the surrogate victim is repeated on multiple occasions because of the felt benefits of reconciliation

---

24. Girard et al., *Things Hidden*, 102.

in the community. The repetition is the beginning of human ritual and with that, at once, the beginning of actual signs. "The imperative of ritual is therefore never separate from the manipulation of signs and their constant multiplication, a process that generates new possibilities of cultural differentiation and enrichment."[25] In the subsequent book, *Evolution and Conversion*, he expands on this insight. He talks of the repetition of the original event as a form of staging where there is a kind of "knowing" renewal of the original event. "The victim is no longer presumed responsible for the crisis, but it is both a *real* new victim that has to be killed and a *symbol* of the proto-event; it is *the first symbolic sign* ever invented by these hominids. It is the first moment in which something *stands* for *something else*. It is the ur-symbol."[26] In this later reflection Girard is saying that the first sign is actually the repetition of the proto-event, and this indeed makes fuller sense. The original group victim creates, as it were, the mental space of an event, but it is the "intentional" repetition or staging which is the true first "symbolic sign." Girard does not bother to define symbol and sign in distinction from each other, but here we get the impression that the symbol does gather a rich field of meaning into itself, in this case the "proto-event," and attach most closely to its whole content. It is then out of the event and its ur-symbol that signs or signifiers multiply step by step, especially through ritual. *Every possible significant element seems to have its outline in the sacred* . . . The signifiers are all attached to the event, but they diversify readily into time, place, movement, sound, dress, priest, people, etc. Girard adds that the emergence is "what philosophers used to call a 'totality,' so those things within the totality can refer to each other, and therefore acquire meaning through indexation and through analogical, metonymical and metaphorical connections between elements in the totality."[27] We will return to this critical notion of totality again later in the book, because it suggests a totalized field of meaning which, although highly diversified within itself, must surely retain traces of its founding trauma/terror. What could be the power to break open this meaning to something other?

For the moment, however, we should stress the way in which signifiers diversify out of the event of the sacred. In other words, it provides the single source for the indefinite multiplication of meaning. From this starting point, signification or language is systemic and alive; it can be acquired and renewed, constantly shifting and growing across a more or less infinite plane

---

25. Girard et al., *Things Hidden*, 103.
26. Girard et al., *Evolution and Conversion*, 107.
27. Girard et al., *Evolution and Conversion*, 104.

of experience. Girard's description is so concrete that we can almost begin to hear the process of language construction. He comments,

> Articulate language and the exchange of words, like all other kinds of exchange, surely must also have its basis in ritual, in the screams and cries that accompanied the mimetic crisis and that must be reproduced in ritual . . . It seems possible, during the ritual around the victim, that cries at first inarticulate should fall into a rhythm and become ordered like steps in a dance, particularly since in ritual centered around the sacrificial act a spirit of collaboration and agreement pervades the enactment of all aspects of the crisis. There is no culture on earth that does not hold its sacred vocables or words to be primary and fundamental in the order of language.[28]

So, sounds wrung from the participants during the first-time and restaged experiences of anger and peace—parallel to but still much more primitive, visceral, and uncanny than the cries perhaps made during the experience of sex—are the very first words, and naturally they have a religious meaning. As illustration we might imagine the name of *Zeus!* as a primary vocable, its intense sibilant sound suggesting something evil and hated and at the same time extremely powerful. Or, *Ea!*, an Akkadian god of water: the pure vowel sound seems to echo a powerful emotional release. Not all divine names have such simple structure, and perhaps even these examples are fanciful and already too refined, but Girard's general point only has to hold at the earliest stages. As Pierpaolo Antonello comments, echoing the sense of original catastrophe, "[M]imetic theory assumes that at the origin of the cultural order there must be a form of radical upheaval that literally projected the human onto a different cognitive level, allowing for the symbolic to emerge."[29] Once a sound with "total" meaning is made, recognized, and repeated, then a differentiated, generative center for further sounds in relation to that "first word" has arisen. Speech sounds (*phones*) could then multiply by a quasi-intuitive metonymic process once the principle of "meaning," or "standing for," is established with the primordial vocal symbol. As Girard says, signs—and therefore gestures and sounds—for "before and after, evil and good, inside and out" all become possible once the transcendent signifier is in place. Perhaps it was enough just to shout out *"Ea!"* in the primary group and there would already be a sense of time—time since the primary event, and possibly looking to a

---

28. Girard et al., *Things Hidden*, 103–4.

29. Antonello, "Maladaptation, Counterintuitiveness, and Symbolism," in Antonello and Gifford, *How We Became Human*, 66.

future of the event's renewal. It would be easy to imagine basic sounds for "(be)fore" and "aft(er)," almost choosing themselves once the possibility of crucial added-on or linked meaning was experienced.

The story of Helen Keller can offer a present-day parable of what we are trying to describe from an immemorial past. Keller was rendered deaf and blind by a severe illness when she was not yet two, and although she belonged to a comfortably off and loving family, she was near feral in her violent reaction to her condition. At their wits' end, her parents hired the services of a young woman, Anne Sullivan, herself partially blind and educated at a school for the blind in Boston. With patience and persistence Sullivan broke through into Keller's semiotic nothingness by continually signing the words for things on her hand. The movie made of the story, *The Miracle Worker*, presents an indelible image of the dawn of human meaning in her soul: Sullivan spells out the letters of w-a-t-e-r on her hand directly under and over the sensation flowing from the garden faucet; suddenly the young Helen understands, and she runs around her garden in a frenzy of recognition, getting the names of as many things as she can. She describes her seven-year-old pre-language condition as follows: "Have you ever been at sea in a dense fog, when it seemed as if a tangible white darkness shut you in, and the great ship, tense and anxious, groped her way toward the shore, with plummet and sounding-line, and you waited with beating heart for something to happen? I was like that ship before my education began, only I was without compass or sounding-line, and had no way of knowing how near the harbor was."[30] Then, at the first experience of the word, "somehow the mystery of language was revealed to me. I knew then that 'w-a-t-e-r' meant the wonderful cool something that was flowing over my hand. That living word awakened my soul . . . Everything had a name, and each name gave birth to a new thought."[31] Did not our distant wordless-but-brain-developed ancestors also live in a "tangible white darkness," until one day the mystery of *Zeus!* or *Ea!* broke in on them with all the weight of collective violence followed by world-founding peace? *Meaning* had been born, the event horizon of abstract truth. And, slowly at first, but then with more and more babbling confidence, did they not race around their evolutionary Eden, giving similar names to everything?

---

30. Keller, *Story of My Life*, 14–15. For the movie: Penn, *Miracle Worker*.
31. Keller, *Story of My Life*, 16.

Mysterious Intervention of the Truth

Having gotten to this point in the Girardian semioverse (universe of signs and meaning), we now have to underline forcefully and paradoxically that none of this demonstrates anything real. On the contrary, the sacred, for all its power, is non-real. Girard's generative semiotics tell us that our ancient category of "god" and all it represents are an epistemic fiction of colossal proportions. It is a mechanism of survival which creates a protective shell of deceit around the extremely volatile creature known as human. It is a falsification of a real event which, in today's terms, boils down simply to group murder and a kind of misrecognized foundational PTSD implanted in the collective hominid brain. There seems no way of getting around this within the terms of the event itself, unless, somehow, we superimpose a metaphysics which themselves have always been composed verbally from the original sign system of the sacred.[32]

The sign system is an infinite series of banknotes printed to enable us to trade, but the gold reserve that is meant to underpin it is essentially missing, a bankruptcy hidden behind high walls of prehistory. Necessarily, therefore, Girardian theory of language is a pure semiotics, enabling us to deal with a real world but with signs that are transcendentally non-referential, enclosed within a system of ultimately false significance. It is not an easy point to grasp, especially as Girard, as we have seen, insists on a real world and the possibility of genuine scientific reason about it. What we have to keep in mind is the fact that science enables us to manipulate the world, with a reasonably accurate relation to it. But this is a relation of use, not of ultimate meaning. Just because we can manipulate atoms and electrons does not tell us they are anything more than a random set of events we encounter on a good day when

---

32. We can hypothesize that Keller's "white darkness" is already some kind of transcendence, a totally unformed yet experiential "absolute" and "beyond." But we must remember that Helen was surrounded by a loving, language-speaking family who would have communicated some sense of repetitive order and truth. In comparison it's very hard to imagine our pre-language hominids experiencing anything other than terror when confronted by the monstrous "beyond" at the heart of the group. Later, after the beginning of culture, the order and tranquility of nature, especially the heavens, could have communicated its own sense of meaning, or at least mystery. This had to be a powerful prompt to metaphysics. But it would have always come with its cognitive lining of terror, given that the first transcendental structure is the attention focused by the victim of a murder. Despite nature's powerful phenomenality it did not and could not provide an independent source of first cognition. It would be unable to cancel out original violence in our construction of *meaning*. Moreover, we have to bear in mind the Kantian critique of metaphysics, the way it shows the speculation of ideas producing endless contradictory results ("the antinomies of reason"). Kant's *Critique of Pure Reason* stands as the angel with a flaming sword barring our way back into the paradise of metaphysics.

the world seems to work. The original "Girardian" awareness of the world was, on the contrary, a divine event which fixed meaning in place. This had an ultimate effect of enabling humans to organize their world in a regular way, but now we understand that the divine event was and is a fiction. It's as if our primitive ancestors were given the "training wheels" of religion in order eventually to ride the bike of reason, but once we learned to balance in thin air those grounding wheels are discarded as pointless.

Or, to offer another (tangentially more biblical) metaphor, we can say Girardian semiotics are truly arbitrary in a philosophical sense, using an evolutionary trauma to create ultimate meaning, using it as a garment of abstraction to throw over, separate out and verbalize a genuine physical reality. But now this magical garment has lost almost all its own sacred quality in our twenty-first-century everyday language. Nearly all the deep nap of the divine is worn off: only the threads, the tensile warp and woof of language remain, as they continue to perform effectively in their residual function of providing a system of signs.

To leave things here would amount to an extremely bleak foundational anthropology. By taking the human sign system back to violent origins, we would not only be left with an ultimately groundless system of signs, but there would be a surrounding aura of essential brutality about our highest cultural achievements as humans. Girard's thought would give grounds for the deepest Schopenhauerian despair. But the audacity of *Things Hidden* is that it skips from generative violence to its cultural inversion and transformation, without missing a beat or pausing for breath. Book I ends with a question about the source of the demythologization of human culture. In answer Girard says the following: "I propose that if today we are capable of breaking down and analyzing cultural mechanisms, it is because of the indirect and unperceived but formidably constraining influence of the Judeao-Christian scriptures."[33]

Immediately we are in the domain of the Christian religion and the God of revelation, so no space is given for a gap in meaning, for a world of despair. Earlier in the context of the same discussion Girard remarked in connection to the transcendental signifier fabricated out of the victim, "I am not saying we have found the *true* transcendental signifier. So far, we have only discovered what functions in that capacity for human beings."[34] In other words, there is implied a Christian signifier at work in the world: its truth arrives like a bolt of lightning out of a clear blue sky. However, it must also be noted exactly what Girard says in the key words linking the two

---

33. Girard et al., *Things Hidden*, 138.
34. Girard et al., *Things Hidden*, 103, italics original.

sections of the book. He does not, at this moment, refer to God or to truth; he talks about "the formidably constraining influence" of . . . scriptures. Otherwise stated—and strikingly so for the subject of this present book—we are still dealing with signs, with words, with writing. The redemption offered to semiotic despair is itself a semiotic one!

Generally speaking, we can be confident that Girard intends a claim to the truth of Christian revelation. Throughout his work he makes absolutely no secret of his Christian faith. It is also of exceptional interest that he offers an explicit apologetics for Christian belief by reason of its effect in exposing the long conspiracy of foundational human violence . . . rather than by rational proofs of God's existence. "What [Christ] brings us cannot come from human beings, and therefore can only come from God . . . the thought that underpins the Gospels must stem from a reason more powerful than our own."[35]

The mechanism by which this reason works is certainly not an infused vision, a Platonic ideal truth. Instead, it belongs to the long travail of the biblical scriptures. In particular, it is the writing of the gospels and the rest of the New Testament over the latter part of the first century CE which counts as anthropological revelation, including afterward their continuously being broadcast and read around the world for the best part of two thousand years. Girard effectively declares the Bible to be a regenerative semiotics, one that changes historical human meaning. And we have to underline this as the technical character of his argument. It is from within the biblical system of signs that truth is found, by reason of the quality of the semiotic reversal itself.

"No one has ever seen God, but the one and only Son . . . has made him known" (John 1:18). With Girard a verse like this cannot be simply a dogmatic statement but a matter of Jesus fully revealing the victim and showing God on the side of the victim, as the love that overcomes original violence, and as a revolutionary semiotics in all these aspects. The revelation takes place against the grain of human culture and so it must come from "outside" that culture. By the same token it can only take place painfully and slowly, through the stories and signs of the gospels invading and deconstructing a human system based on blaming and occluding the victim.

As I suggest, in the transition from Book I to Book II the ontological status of this semiotic apocalypse is never discussed, that is, the issue of whether there is indeed a real nonviolent divinity actually behind this change. It is somehow assumed. Or, rather, it is an implied inference from transformative anthropology, a mysterious, incarnational inference working itself out on the level of signs. We will return to this as a key question

---

35. Girard, *When These Things Begin*, 92–93.

in the penultimate chapter on ontology, but for the moment it is possible to say in short order that it is exactly the semiotic shift that Girard presents which makes the whole thing work. It is precisely as a semiotic reversal of the sacred that the biblical reading is introduced. And thus, the very existence of the shift—its textual and semiotic dynamic—"creates" the meaning of a nonviolent divine.

Girard does not have to provide any kind of philosophical argument for the shift from a violently fabricated sacred to one that is nonviolent and authenticated by its nonviolence, because the shift does the work for him. Girard steps lightly, like Peter Pan himself, over the greatest chasm in the history of human meaning, and it was the biblical text which put the necessary spring in his heel. Whatever we might prejudge intellectually about the ontological status of either violent or nonviolent divinity, the change in human meaning worked by the biblical text is effective in its own right. The importance of this cannot be overstated. We are in the presence of a semiotic revolution and, therefore, at a second and vital stage of reflection, we can say it is semiotic revolution which *is* the character of Christian faith. This in a nutshell is the argument of the present book.

We turn now to other accounts of semiotics in order to flesh out the meaning of the discipline, and to place what I have characterized as generative semiotics in a wider context which can help solidify and illustrate its crucial importance.

4

The Thread of Deconstruction

Collapsing the Temple

AT THE SAME TIME Girard was developing his scandalous version of human language, another thinker was producing a commentary on language with a capacity to scandalize all its own. The two thinkers meet amidst the ruined arches of human truth, but where Girard found a span reaching down through the rubble, able to carry him away to the God of a new creation, the other remained in place, faithfully documenting each broken pillar and pediment, while awaiting the coming of an impossible reconstruction. Jacques Derrida was a Francophone Algerian Jew, growing up under French colonial rule. His liminal status on all these counts contributed greatly to his uniquely fractured vision of human meaning. To include a discussion of Derrida here is as natural as our introductory scene-setting of a contemporary air-flight and its overheard foreign language. Of any public intellectual at the end of the twentieth century and the beginning of the twenty-first, Derrida most clearly represents the open linguistic borders of our modern world, the way in which it has broken down the safe, secure boundaries of native tongue, identity, truth. Placing him here both corroborates Girardian semiotics of violent origins, showing how language continues to store violence in its natural workings, and reinforces the process of disclosure going on in our time. Derrida unquestionably participates in the transformation of signs happening all around us and among us. To understand his work a little helps us widen and deepen the context in which we understand the Bible as semiotic transformation.

To talk of an encounter of Girard and Derrida is also factually true, and in a highly intriguing way. In his early career Girard was a professor at Johns Hopkins University, in Baltimore. In 1966, as chair of the Romance

Languages Department, he organized a symposium, "The Languages of Criticism and the Sciences of Man," with the intention of bringing some of the bright new lights of the French intellectual scene to the US. The roster of speakers included people like Roland Barthes and Jacques Lacan—and, at the last moment, a young Jacques Derrida, who was largely unknown in the US up to that point. The paper Derrida presents is entitled "Structure, Sign, and Play in the Discourse of the Human Sciences," and his remarks have an astonishing effect, to the extent that they change the course of the conference itself, leading the occasion to be renamed "The Structuralist Controversy." As one of the participants said, "I hadn't realized that he [Derrida] was going to be the Samson to tear down the temple of structuralism."[1]

We have already introduced some of the content of the epoch-making paper—in relation to that phrase with an attitude, "transcendental signifier." It was Derrida's employment of it in his presentation that upset the philosophical apple cart and announced the age of poststructuralism. We have just seen how Girard's intellectual journey necessarily encountered the concept, relating it to the founding victim. We now see where he perhaps first met the thought and how his journey is intertwined with Derrida's.

Derrida clearly and forcefully lays out what he sees as a chronic essential *lack* in the Western philosophical tradition, one which has lately been laid bare through the work of the human sciences and in direct relation to language.[2] The lack in question is of a metaphysical center, a fixed point of meaning upon which any argument must depend. In its place language substitutes a succession of terms which masquerade in the role of absolute meaning or self-presence. In the Western tradition, for example, there is *essence, existence, substance, soul, subject, beginning (arche), end (telos)*, terms which produce in a piece of writing the effect that there is indeed a fixed point, a final center of truth. But that effect is a metaphysical illusion. What is Derrida's evidence for this? It can be found in the discipline of ethnology—and once again it is that crucial figure, that presiding thinker we have encountered with Girard, Lévi-Strauss, who provides the key. Lévi-Strauss's work represents a critique of ethnocentrism, dislocating philosophical thought outside its traditional European cultural homeland toward supposedly less important cultures, and that could only come about at a moment "contemporaneous with the destruction of the history of metaphysics."[3]

1. Richard Macksey, cited in McCabe, "Structuralism's Samson." See Haven, *Evolution of Desire*, ch. 8.
2. Derrida, "Structure, Sign, and Play in the Discourse of the Human Sciences," in *Writing and Difference*, 278.
3. Derrida, "Structure, Sign, and Play in the Discourse of the Human Sciences," in *Writing and Difference*, 282.

Derrida goes on to illustrate from Levi-Strauss's own writing the conscious lack of center, and with that the necessary function of what he calls the "supplement." He comments, "The *overabundance* of the signifier, its *supplementary* character, is thus the result of a finitude, that is to say, the result of a lack which must be *supplemented*."[4] A supplement is something added on, and yet it also carries the sense of *supplying*, of providing for what's missing. "The supplement" thus becomes a linguistic stand-in or surrogate for the fixed center and a key term for Derrida. The word or signifier carries with it the sense of some "real truth" which, in actual fact, it is only supplementing or substituting for. Moreover, this implies there is always another sign or signifier waiting in the wings to make an entrance: because the one before can never quite give us the presence it claims to give, but must wait for a further supplement to help out. And so on, indefinitely! Derrida's own intellectual career is consciously demonstrative of this. Rather than make any of his own terms fixed and metaphysical, he went on to develop a long list of metonyms, terms which are deliberately signaled stand-ins for the same supplementary function of language or texts. We shall look at one or two of these below, but for now we can note Derrida's consistent attempt at making an argument about metaphysics which might avoid constructing his own. By means of Derrida's efforts, therefore, our world of signs suddenly jumps from a very secondary, neutral function, to something much more primary and dynamic. It goes from having a walk-on-walk-off part to being the main protagonist—from being a servant upstairs to being the mistress and master downstairs.

At the same time Derrida is conscious that the old repertoire of metaphysical concepts does not simply disappear. Indeed, he continues to use them even as he asserts their illusory qualities. Unless we do this, there is a chance of a false naïveté (of having no metaphysics) which simply falls back into covert metaphysics. Derrida gives the example here of the sign itself.[5] Just to say everything is a sign does not avoid metaphysics. It becomes rather its own kind of metaphysics. What we can say is that to realize everything is a sign—or, at least, that the sign conditions everything we claim we know—can separate us from a too immediate or dogmatic immersion in a concept or a text. It enables us to retain a profound openness in terms of meaning, and in fact we will see this develops into a key aspect of Derrida's thought as it progresses.

4. Derrida, "Structure, Sign, and Play in the Discourse of the Human Sciences," in *Writing and Difference*, 290, italics original.

5. Derrida, "Structure, Sign, and Play in the Discourse of the Human Sciences," in *Writing and Difference*, 281.

Here, at the moment, however, is the key passage, the percussive shock which undermined the temple pillars—the announcement of how "language [had] invaded the universal problematic." That is, the very nature of language now told against the standard philosophical pieties. Girard's founding murder and its primary vocalization could not be more undermining. Derrida declares first that the discovery of "the structurality of structure" has brought a decisive rupture, because it destroys the presence of a center (or the center of a presence) in the text. From that point on,

> It became necessary to think both the law which somehow governed the desire for a center in the constitution of structure, and the process of signification which orders the displacements and substitutions for this law of central presence—but a central presence which has never been itself, has always already been exiled from itself into its own substitute. The substitute does not substitute itself for anything which has somehow existed before it. Henceforth, it was necessary to begin thinking that there was no center, that the center could not be thought in the form of a present-being, that the center had no natural site, that it was not a fixed locus but a function, a sort of nonlocus in which an infinite number of sign-substitutions came into play. This was the moment when language invaded the universal problematic, the moment when, in the absence of a center or origin, everything became discourse—provided we can agree on this word—that is to say, a system in which the central signified, the original or transcendental signified, is never absolutely present outside a system of differences. The absence of the transcendental signified extends the domain and the play of signification infinitely.[6]

Saussure Again

With these words we hear the thunderclap of a literary and philosophical climate shift, one which Girard fully inhabited. The common filiation of Girard and Derrida back to Lévi-Strauss demonstrates the conditions of an age. But behind this, as we have noted, there lies the linguistic "vortex" of Saussure. The figure of Saussure demonstrates how language, or semiotics, had shaped the key questions. Derrida will turn expressly to his work, and we shall look at this at once, but in order to grasp these common lines of descent we must first turn in greater detail to the thought of the Swiss

6. Derrida, "Structure, Sign, and Play in the Discourse of the Human Sciences," in *Writing and Difference*, 280.

semiotician. Saussure's famous book, his *Course in General Linguistics*, was not published by its author but produced from lecture notes taken by two of his students and published after his death. Although his work is considered possibly dated in some quarters it remains foundational for postmodern linguistics, semiotics, and anthropology. As has been remarked, research in this area is either pre-Saussurean, post-Saussurean, non-Saussurean or Saussurean. Focusing now on his pivotal ideas will serve thoroughly to ground our understanding of how language has invaded the philosophical problematic, as well as help further clarify the semiotic implications of both Derrida and Girard.

There is no doubt Saussure made a key breakthrough establishing language in its own right as the bearer of meaning without dependence on a pure priority of thought. Rather than seeing language as the sign or copy of pure thought, Saussure was able to demonstrate the intrinsic relationship between linguistic signs and meaning, at the core of thought itself.

Saussure proposed that signs should be understood not as a simple name or label given to a thing. Rather, they had their own internal composition, consisting of two parts, "signifier" and "signified." If we were dealing with words these elements would roughly speaking be the sound (signifier) and the concept (signified) which it carries. But Saussure also specifies that the signifier is not simply the sound or phonic element; rather, it is a "sound-image," meaning it carries some kind of echo or signal in our heads. The proof of this is that we can talk to ourselves without moving our lips, or we can recite a poem mentally. Saussure in fact went on to declare, "[T]he linguistic signifier . . . is not phonic but incorporeal—constituted not by its material substance but by the differences that separate its sound-image from all others."[7]

The feature of difference is absolutely crucial. Meaning is not made up of pure, discrete ideas. It arises from differences between signs bound together in a chain. Here is the well-known statement: "[I]n language there are only differences . . . a difference generally implies positive terms between which the difference is set up; but in language there are only differences *without positive terms*. Whether we take the signified or the signifier, language has neither ideas nor sounds that existed before the linguistic system, but only conceptual and phonic differences that have issued from the system."[8] For example, the morphemes c-a-t create a signifier different from those of c-u-t, or c-a-p. These differences, along with other surrounding

---

7. Saussure, *Course in General Linguistics*, 118–19. By "incorporeal" Saussure does not intend some otherworldly "spiritual" event, but an effect within the invisible mental processing of language.

8. Saussure, *Course in General Linguistics*, 120.

differences, create the conceptual meaning. Meaning is achieved by the differences. Thus, the signifier "cat" will also take on specific values depending on whether neighboring terms indicate a domestic situation, a thoroughbred show for tabbies or calicos, a jungle setting, or a vehicle with continuous tracks. Saussure continues, "The idea or phonic substance that a sign contains is of less importance than the other signs that surround it. Proof of this is that the value of a term may be modified without either its meaning or its sound being affected, solely because a neighboring term has been modified."[9] "Value" here is the overall meaning of the term in the phrase or sentence. For example, the value of the term "cat" changes completely from "the cat asleep on the rug" to "the big cat asleep in the jungle."

The final step is in consequence of the first two: the sign has an essentially arbitrary character. There is nothing in the actual signifier or set of phonemes intrinsically tied to the concept. If you think about it, this is already a very natural conclusion. The existence of multiple spoken languages, with a vast variety of sounds for signifieds, gives conclusive demonstration. So, for example, *dog, chien, perro, hund* are all signifiers for the four-legged friend of humankind, and they sound nothing alike. However, this evident fact assumes a considerably greater urgency in connection to Saussure's theory. A signifier can be of any quality of sound or vocalization: it means something only within the system of differences of the given language. Thus, the arbitrary character of the sign ties into the whole nature of language, to its mysterious self-enclosed, self-authenticating character made up of internal difference.

Language suggests many possible illustrations of the internal dynamic of difference. A great display of the absence of positive terms, and yet presence of meaning, is the "Buffalo sentence." It was taught to me by my younger son, who claimed that you could make a sentence out of one identical word repeated seven times, to which I roundly declared, "Not possible!" But he was totally right (and hereby I atone for doubting him!). The added benefit of this example is that the internal differences are incorporeal and formal, demonstrating that the function of difference reaches into the level of the concept, not simply sound.

An initial reading produces absolutely no distinction between the seven words, and so no meaning. "Buffalo buffalo buffalo buffalo buffalo buffalo buffalo!" But then if we "hear" the implied difference between the various "buffaloes" suddenly it all falls into place. The first and sixth use is adjectival (i.e., from Buffalo, New York.) The second, fourth, and seventh involve the normal sense of a "bison." The third and fifth have the verbal

---

9. Saussure, *Course in General Linguistics*, 120.

sense of "to bully or intimidate." Finally, there is a silent "that" between the second and third uses, signaling a relative clause. Read in this way everything makes sense, but it is not because anything has changed in the sound of the terms themselves. Rather, a string of "incorporeal" differences has inserted themselves in the sentence. They are inaudible and invisible, but they happen in the sentence because we read it while "hearing" (or even seeing) those differences. The meaning thus results: "Buffaloes from Buffalo that bully other buffaloes bully buffaloes from Buffalo." The differences are grammatical (i.e., nouns, adjectives, verbs), but according to Saussure, grammatical forms are not in principle separable from difference in general.[10] They are simply another mode of the same thing. A continual string of homographs in the same sentence can only be differentiated by the internal, inaudible differences in the string of signifiers themselves, implying other signifiers and further differences until the sentence is complete. Normally the conceptual differences among words is signaled both by their form and clear grammatical status, and so we do not notice how difference enters fully the conceptual level. But the "Buffalo sentence" alerts us to how difference at the level of the concept is also essential for meaning.

Another good example of how language functions can be taken from this extremely garbled yet still intelligible sentence, something which became a meme on the Internet: "*Aoccdrnig to a rscheearch at Cmabrigde Uinervtisy, it deosn't mttaer in waht oredr the ltteers in a wrod are, the olny iprmoetnt tihng is taht the frist and lsat ltteer be at the rghit pclae. The rset can be a toatl mses and you can sitll raed it wouthit porbelm. Tihs is bcuseae the huamn mnid deos not raed ervey lteter by istlef, but the wrod as a wlohe.*" But what does it mean to read the word "as a whole"? In fact, it's not the "whole" the brain reads—it does not pause painstakingly to untangle and recompose every letter into the correct word. There is no essential character to the sign—an exact spelling of a word without which the concept would not appear. The brain simply picks up enough clues of difference within the words and between the words in the sentence to differentiate the sign and read the piece effectively. Thus, differences in language create meaning, and they cover the spectrum from the sounds and consonants, through grammar, to contextual clues and usage.

On the basis of these reflections derived from Saussure we can pivot effectively to a better grasp of Derrida. No one's thought comes in a vacuum. Indeed, it only arises in a function of difference from what has come before.

---

10. Saussure, *Course in General Linguistics*, 135.

Original Writing

Derrida's first three books, *Writing and Difference*, *Speech and Phenomena*, and *Of Grammatology*, were all produced in one *annus mirabilis*, 1967, shortly after the feted Johns Hopkins symposium. The centrality of language is evident from the titles, and with their publication Derrida announced himself as an exceptional voice in the area of philosophical semiotics. Girard's *Violence and the Sacred*, from which we quoted above, was published in 1972, and their common debt to Lévi-Strauss, and behind him, Saussure, signals, I think, an intellectual era rooted and bound together in semiotics. Pursuing Derrida's work helps us delve deeper into an essentially common trajectory and its consequences for human meaning. As we engage in Derrida's work, we also bear in mind that his style of writing is specifically geared to his thought, full of fractures and fissures, parentheses, dashes, synonyms, italics, foreign words, etc., to such an extent that it is sometimes very difficult to recognize an intelligible sentence. This is by design—we are strategically reminded again and again of the differential character of every word and phrase, so that what is normally carefully narrowed to achieve self-identical meaning is blown up to demonstrate a dynamic chain of signification from which we forcibly (if not violently) isolate a sentence. Reading a text by Derrida is very often like being in a hall of mirrors where we have to concentrate very hard to find the "original" shape of the room!

In a framing essay of one of those 1967 books, *Of Grammatology*, Derrida gives an extended discussion of Saussure, whom he offers as the seminal figure shaping the direction of the science of language in the twentieth century.[11] Derrida sets out what will become a signature viewpoint—that there is a massive prejudice in favor of the spoken word as the first point of meaning. Writing is seen as a secondary, derivative doubling, the "sign of a sign," as Aristotle and subsequent philosophers deemed it.[12] Saussure himself follows in this tradition, confirming what Derrida calls the "phonological" or "logocentric" orientation of linguistics. Derrida seizes on telling phrases of Saussure, such as saying that writing is "unrelated to [the] . . . inner system" of language.[13] Derrida protests this prejudice as an arbitrary separation of "inside" and "outside." Rather, for him, "Writing in general covers the entire field of linguistic signs."[14]

11. Derrida, *Of Grammatology*, 27–73.
12. Derrida, *Of Grammatology*, 11. "Spoken words are the symbols of mental experience and written words are the symbols of spoken words." From *De Interpretatione*, 1, 16a 3 (Ackrill, 43).
13. Derrida, *Of Grammatology*, 33, 44.
14. Derrida, *Of Grammatology*, 44.

He demonstrates that Saussure's own position already implies the breaking of the hierarchy. If spoken/aural signs are conventional, or arbitrary, there can never be any essential "natural" priority, and thus everything is writing. Derrida appeals directly to Saussure. Despite the latter's relegation of writing to a secondary role, he is forced eventually to declare explicitly the role of difference as primary, regardless of any ideal thought. Derrida quotes the passage we have already noted. "The linguistic signifier . . . is not [in essence] phonic but incorporeal—constituted not by its material substance but by the differences that separate its sound-image from all others."[15] The quote then continues, as also given above: "The idea or phonic substance that a sign contains is of less importance than the other signs that surround it."[16] If we were to try express this in neural terms, we could perhaps say that the neuron consisting of "cat" is really a quasi-spontaneous combination or linking of many neurons, including the sound signifier: none of which on its own is essential "c-a-t" but an array or cluster of fairly random associations which contrasts with other material around it in and for an instant. It is the contrasting—the difference—that produces the "cat" in the instant. It seems obvious that the sound signifier—something that belongs to words, and then the spelling out by which writing renders words—has a core role in searching and finding the array and "switching off" everything else. All of this happens of course in milliseconds, but it tells us that the mental concept—the signified—is itself always the child of the signifier and the difference that produces it.

On this point Derrida is adamant. If in language there are only differences, then this must affect the signified (concept) as much as the signifier (sound).

> [T]he signified always already functions as a signifier. The secondarity that it seemed possible to ascribe to writing alone affects all signifieds in general, affects them always already, the moment they *enter the game*. There is not a single signified that escapes . . . the play of signifying references that constitute language.[17]

Concepts, therefore, can only be read/understood in their oscillating difference from other concepts. In which case, the hierarchy of thought/speech/writing is disrupted at its core.

These are momentous conclusions: subverting and inverting the traditional order of concept/sign/writing and plunging all meaning into the play

---

15. Derrida, *Of Grammatology*, 53, Derrida's brackets.
16. Derrida, *Of Grammatology*, 53, from *Course in General Linguistics*, 120.
17. Derrida, *Of Grammatology*, 7.

of signs referencing each other. Of course, this runs deeply counter to any secure metaphysics. As he remarks, "[T]he system of language associated with phonetic-alphabetic writing is that within which logocentric metaphysics, determining the sense of being as presence, has been produced."[18] Logocentrism is to take the (spoken and written) word at its word and insist there is solid real presence within it and behind it. Metaphysics jumps from the word on the page, claiming a self-presence that hangs between the reader and the book, and then beyond in the universe. But really it is only a result of the chain of signs operating in the reader's brain and semiotic systems, always pretending a fake externality and reality.

With these arguments Derrida inaugurates the age of "deconstruction," demonstrating the way in which a text can assume and impose metaphysical realities (e.g., here, "real/mental," "outside/inside") and make the reader assume them within the written construct. By showing up the process—in a kind of sidelong glance at the text, rather than straight on—we get to see the hidden contours by which an order or hierarchy is established and thus the world is shaped before us.

Once deconstruction commences, the world seems to dissolve into a mist, a mist made up only of text and its signifiers. The apparent arbitrariness of the sign led to a kind of a frenzied dogmatism of deconstruction in liberal arts and university humanities departments, especially in North America. I remember all too clearly one of my graduate colleagues leaning across the table prior to a seminar and intoning, "There is nothing you can tell me which I can't deconstruct!" However, Derrida was well on his way by this point to mapping his own alternative path to meaning, one that depended on the very fractures in language he had opened up. At the same time, a certain biblical sensitivity pervades his thought, suggesting that the breakdown of metaphysics is somehow also a biblical project. The "road to Derrida" may perhaps, therefore, be also associated with Girard's "formidably constraining influence" of the biblical scriptures. Arriving at Derrida's secular sense of the "messianic" may in fact be part of the transformative semiotic effect of the Bible, its generative power or leaven within human culture.

Différance

What then is this strange writing that constitutes our world of meaning in every sense? Derrida answers with two other terms, "trace" and "différance." These two words are probably the marquee examples of a whole special vocabulary that Derrida developed to describe something inherently

18. Derrida, *Of Grammatology*, 43.

60   THEOLOGY BEYOND METAPHYSICS

indescribable: to suggest both the absence of a presence and yet a connection to a total system which leads us forward while always entailing the deficit of the full sign to come. It is both this absence and yet its suggestion of presence which produces meaning.

Derrida's term *différance* is the French word for "difference," but with an *a* in the last syllable rather than an *e*. The change cannot be heard in the spoken language, as the French pronunciation is the same, but the written effect is powerful. It puckishly draws attention to the written form, once more subverting the supposed privilege of speech over writing. At the same time, it plays on the French verb *différer*, which means both "to differ" and "to defer," in the process creating a new semantic value, one of "difference plus deferral." Différance becomes the most powerful instrument in Derrida's box of tools, assuming an almost mystical significance in the depth of its application and the impossibility of pinning it down in strict referential terms. In consequence some people claimed that, paradoxically, it held the role of "transcendental signifier" in Derrida's thought, but this is to misunderstand the nature of the argument, viewing it from the outside (metaphysically), rather than in its own terms. Although the function of différance is strategically pivotal in Derrida's overall philosophy, it belongs most aptly to the never-ending work of meaning in human language. Adding the element of continual postponement to the thought of semiotic difference, and doing so in one word, creates in a single stroke a figure of indefinite movement in the creation of meaning.

> [T]he *a* of *différance* also recalls that spacing is temporization, the detour and postponement by means of which intuition, perception, consummation—in a word, the relationship to the present, the reference to a present reality, to a *being*—are always *deferred*. Deferred by virtue of the very principle of difference which holds that an element functions and signifies, takes on or conveys meaning, only by referring to another past or future element in an economy of traces.[19]

Difference is thus spread through time, characterized by a waiting and anticipation which always declares an absence at the same time as the illusion of presence. This is a philosophical advance, but Derrida also has an astute semiotic awareness, and in coining this neologism he cannot help hinting at a wider significance than just the linguistic union of "difference" and "deferral." He says, in respect of the *a* instead of the *e*, that it cannot be heard "beyond the order of understanding. It is put forward by a silent mark, by a tacit monument, or, one might even say, by a pyramid—keeping

---

19. Derrida, "Semiology and Grammatology," in *Positions*, 28–29.

in mind not only the capital form of the printed letter but also that passage from Hegel's *Encyclopedia* where he compares the body of the sign to an Egyptian pyramid. The *a* of différance, therefore, is not heard; it remains silent, secret, and discreet, like a tomb."[20]

This is an image, a metaphor, but it slips effortlessly into the zone of archeology and connected anthropology. While forswearing anthropology and sticking to texts, Derrida will more than once signal the tone (if not the claim) of a founding murder. Différance is "literally neither a word nor a concept,"[21] and its role is to subvert the metaphysical tradition by its semio-ontological destabilizing effect.[22] But an accompanying effect of his descriptive language puts us in the area of the foundational victim and a hint of original violence. According to Girard, the pyramid got its shape from the original pile of stones heaped up over the target of a group stoning. And it is of course the tomb of a quasi-god. Hegel likened the body of the sign to the pyramid, and now Derrida says his transformative *a* is a sign like a tomb. An open tomb, because even if it is not heard it is read, and, therefore, something hidden comes to light. Here Derrida skates close to a generative semiotics, suggesting that the exposure of the differential mechanics of the sign—a deconstruction of its metaphysics—contains an inevitable revelation of the victim. He comes at it from the opposite end to Girard but arrives at something near the same place. Once you demystify the sign (abandoning the self-present concept) you necessarily draw close to some actual origin of the stream of signifiers. The physical body of the sign seeks a birth and the great tombs of history gather in our minds as primitive semiotics. It seems inevitable that thinkers like Hegel and Derrida should go there for the first A.

Trace

"Trace" is translated directly from the French *trace*, which means both *track* and the vanishing *remainder* of an element in some given substance. It shares

---

20. Derrida, *Speech and Phenomena*, 132. See Hegel, *Hegel's Philosophy of Mind*, para. 458.

21. Derrida, *Speech and Phenomena*, 131.

22. I use the word "semio-ontological" here and in following chapters without introducing it in a systematic way. This will take place in the penultimate chapter of the book, because in many ways the systematic space of that chapter depends on all the foregoing. But for the sake of its use here I can give a preliminary meaning: "semio-ontological" refers to the way in which the reality of our world, and with that *being* itself, is not given absolutely prior to or separate from human existence; rather, it depends intimately on a relation, or a series of relations, with and through the human sign system.

the same borderline nature as différance, neither a word nor a concept, without essence, yet of immense import. Along with the spatial sense of a track it has the same temporal structure as différance. In fact, it can be considered as itself the temporal structure of différance, by right of the hints or traces of past and future in the supposed verbal present. The following gives both the essential relatedness of all signification and the way it is structured through (and as) time: its name as such is trace.

> Différance is what makes the movement of signification possible only if each element that is said to be "present," appearing on the stage of presence, is related to something other than itself but retains the mark of a past element and already lets itself be hollowed out by the mark of its relation to a future element. The trace relates no less to what is called the future than to what is called the past, and it constitutes what is called the present by this very relation to what it is not . . .[23]

In following these remarks, we have to caution that Derrida is not advancing a theory of language as such. His arguments delve into the roots of Western thought and its metaphysics, an investigation in which he is deeply influenced by the content of reflection of the earlier twentieth-century philosopher Martin Heidegger. The questions at stake belong to the whole tradition of philosophy as such, while following the seams of language in its philosophical usage all the way to the pre-Socratics. When Derrida is describing the "trace" he is following a discussion of the "history of being" first set out by Heidegger which declares that key features of the meaning of being have been forgotten in Western metaphysics. These include "the trace of difference," something lost and forgotten, but nevertheless leaving its traces![24] Here we arrive at the dark materials of philosophical inquiry into the nature of being itself, and at this juncture we have to be aware of not pursuing this particular aspect of the discussion. A lot of it will resurface in the following chapters, and especially the ninth chapter. By that point I hope we will have built up enough credit, so to speak, to be able to tackle the question thoroughly from a semiotic perspective.

Meanwhile, it remains obvious that the question of sign and signification play a huge part in Derrida's project. It is even possible to recognize that Derrida's technique is essentially semiotic, creating linguistic devices (différance and trace) as types of anti-sign that allow us to go "upstream" in language, viewing it in an analytic direction language would prefer to resist. The result is a remarkable set of intellectual algorithms, as it were,

---

23. Derrida, *Speech and Phenomena*, 142–43.
24. Heidegger, *Holzwege*, 336; English in Derrida, *Speech and Phenomena*, 156.

that help us view language against the grain. At the same time the Western tradition is undermined. The monuments or pyramids of metaphysics are empty, providing only a simulation, a trace of a trace.

> The trace is not a presence but is rather the simulacrum of a presence that dislocates, displaces, and refers beyond itself. The trace has, properly speaking, no place, for effacement belongs to the very structure of the trace. Effacement must always be able to overtake the trace; otherwise it would not be a trace, but an indestructible and monumental substance.
> . . . In this way the metaphysical text is understood; it is still readable, and remains to be read. It proposes both the monuments and the mirage of the trace, the trace as simultaneously traced and effaced, simultaneously alive and dead, alive as always to simulate even life in its preserved inscription; it is a pyramid.[25]

Even so we detect Derrida's radical purpose. The trace is the uncontrollable movement or deferral of language otherwise embalmed and entombed in metaphysics. At the same time, as suggested, the idea of metaphysical language as a monument containing a death masquerading as life is so very close to Girard's foundational victim.

In Other Words

Derrida has given us an anti-language that subverts philosophical nostrums, but does it successfully represent human language the way it is actually used? Asked another way, do Derrida's linguistic devices refer simply to philosophical questions, or do they tell us at all about the natural use of language? Derrida would answer that it is impossible to draw a rigid line between the two areas. Différance and the trace belong not just to a narrow philosophical tradition but to the human constitution of speech itself. Otherwise we would fall back into the phonological prejudice which gives purity and authenticity to speech and not to writing. So, no matter the somewhat mystical nature of the terms there must be a practical linguistic reality which Derrida is addressing. We can underline, therefore, what we have already presented along these lines: because speech/writing is made up of a string of words and sentences which are in principle never ending, meaning is composed of a track/trace which leads us ever forward, away from its past, and so entails

---

25. Derrida, *Speech and Phenomena*, 156–57.

the absence of the fulfilled sign to come. It is both this absence and yet its invocation of presence which produces meaning.

We might also view the question in the following light. Because the "trace" is not simply a passive physical pathway but an active function, it may also be conceived of as the join (or the fold) between signifier and signified, and between signified and signified. It allows a sound to become a thought, or a thought to become another thought. In this role it is necessarily invisible and unrepresented. It tells us, therefore, that no signifier and no signified can ever be fully contemporaneous, or indeed one signified contemporaneous with another. Thus, past and future always divide the present: the concept in fact is both past and future even as it is spoken, and a spacing of time and difference enters even our most urgent and certain declarations. Thus, full presence of "truth" is never possible, and all our statements are approximations. Language is like a dog chasing an unseen rabbit down a trail. The dog has a good nose, and we all trust its path and the fact that the dog is pointing to *the* rabbit, but the dog never actually catches the rabbit!

Indeed, if we say that language is always about an absence and the simulacrum of a presence, we must admit that the dog is also a fox and we are always being, at least to some degree, foxed! Part of Derrida's genius is to make the fox and the trace appear for what they are, so as to unmask the magic of language. He makes us see there is something definitely fantastic and unreal about the activity of language in the very moment that it produces a "reality." In the later chapters we will follow the trajectory of another thought on semiotics, one that decisively sheers away from any final absence at the heart of our signs. For the moment, however, it is imperative to accompany deconstructive thought to its term. The full reasons will soon become clear, but from our engagement so far one aspect is already manifest: it would seem intellectually hidebound not to recognize in Derrida a clear companion discourse to one of violent origins.[26]

---

26. See McKenna, *Violence and Difference*. McKenna, who studied with Girard, already identified the clear parallels between the thinkers, underlining the anthropology of the scapegoat as echoed in Derrida's text.

5

After Truth: Coming of the Other

Intellectual Cousins

GIRARD HIMSELF HAD LITTLE patience for what he called the "merry-go-round" of commentary known as "Continental Theory," with Derrida as its fashionable avatar.[1] It was Girard's fate to swim in the same bedazzled waters as the generation of French intellectuals known, with not a little self-congratulation, as "incorruptibles." He belonged, however, to a very different class of creature from the darting swordfish by which he was surrounded: he was, instead, something of a slow and steady grouper, gathering into himself all available sedimentary evidence. Nevertheless, we can see by now that Girard and Derrida moved in the same overall current which took its source in an abyss of arbitrary difference. Out of this Derrida shows us the transcendental signifier is unreal; Girard shows us very much the same but makes explicit the violence that both created the problem and formed a solution—at least the appearance of one. For both, truth is deferred—for one it is always already so, for the other it can be traced back to an original murder, one congenitally denied. But in both cases violence is always a crucial part of making the whole ramshackle world of "truth" work in the first place.

Derrida is explicit on the question of violence, at least from one angle. Talking of deconstruction, he tells us its function is to undo "violent hierarchy":

> On the one hand, we must traverse a phase of overturning. To do justice to this necessity is to recognize that in a classical philosophical opposition we are not dealing with the peaceful coexistence of a vis-à-vis, but rather with a violent hierarchy. One of the two terms governs the other (axiologically, logically,

1. Haven, *Evolution of Desire*, 124.

etc.), or has the upper hand. To deconstruct the opposition, first of all, is to overturn the hierarchy at a given moment. To overlook this phase of overturning is to forget the conflictual and subordinating structure of opposition.[2]

This is of course the moral appeal of deconstruction. Its ethical goal is to overcome social oppression enshrined in hierarchy. Derrida is dealing with language and its hierarchies, but social hierarchy is maintained in language and to deconstruct it there is to destabilize it in real terms. Derrida has no comment on how this type of violence gets established in the first place, only the imperative to reverse it. The concern to overturn hierarchies fits readily with Enlightenment and modern critique. Such thinking generally fails to reach back radically to origins; to do so can itself be seen as a will to (re)establish some kind of hierarchy. However, as we have already noted, Derrida is almost obliged by the nature of his inquiry to give hints of violent origins. A famous essay of his, "Plato's Pharmacy," actually used the structure of the *pharmakon* (a Greek word meaning both remedy/poison) and its intimate link to the *pharmakos* (a ritual scapegoat in ancient Athenian history) to provide another metonym for writing or the trace.[3] On the annual feast of Thargelia, a pair of aged outcasts chosen for their ugliness and poverty were driven from the city, sometimes to their death. Derrida reads Plato, especially the *Phaedrus*, as treating writing as a *pharmakon*, as a remedy/poison. It is poison because it lacks the soul's true "memory," so it cannot speak genuinely for itself and sow seeds of truth in others. However, Plato of course writes extensively, and Derrida suggests that ultimately Plato uses Socrates's death as a way to establish his own doctrine of the soul's innate memory of immortality. Derrida points out that Plato does not use the related word *pharmakos*, even though Socrates drank the poison hemlock (*pharmakon*)—following the city's death sentence—on the actual feast of Thargelia. Effectively, according to Derrida, Plato uses Socrates as the *pharmakos*, driven to his death in order to overcome and yet, at the same time, establish the "poison" of his (Plato's) writing.

By this means he elides the writing, publishing in its place the purity of a doctrine (the soul's immortality). The endless trace of writing is masked and denied by the remedy, the "presence," of the sacrificial death. Thus, Derrida clearly recognizes the historical efficacity of the scapegoat while maintaining his focus on the ambiguous role of writing in creating

---

2. Derrida, "Interview with Jean-Louis Houdebine and Guy Scarpetta," in *Positions*, 41.

3. Derrida, "Plato's Pharmacy," 63–171.

metaphysical "truth"—something seemingly alive but really the monument of a death—the monument of the trace.

To bring these two things together—physical scapegoating and metaphysical violence—is to collapse the separate worlds of anthropology and philosophy. But Derrida never broke that wall, at least not in the sense of recognizing Girardian anthropology. This would have left him, I think, with a severely weakened philosophical position.

In contrast, in a later book in his career Girard does give some recognition to Derrida, and in a telling way. Referring to semiotic communication and its self-referential structure he remarks,

> Can this level of self-reference be unfolded without a center from which meaning emerges? I feel very strongly that only through a center is it possible for the various elements of the totality to communicate with each other. Even if the center eventually disappears, once communication is established, they keep on communicating with each other. As a matter of fact, the center should disappear, so that communication might be developed through increasing levels of complexity . . . A symbolic system functions in this way. It can be decentered, but it is originally centered. That is why I don't agree with Derrida when he says that structures are *always already* decentered.[4]

Here Girard acknowledges that a semiotic system functions by trace and deferral. How could the violent center "disappear" without the effacement which is the work of the trace (*is* the trace); and how could the system without its center continue toward ever greater complexity, if it does not continually operate a "deferral" away from that original center? In other words, does not the language system always look back to that beginning, even as it progressively moves away from it? Girard accepts the semiotic system and its inherent movement; he simply adds that it has a real beginning. At the same time the disappearance/effacement of the center tokens a basic freedom of the sign. This last point will be of huge importance if we are to think ultimately of a transformative semiotics, of a new generative meaning where freedom from violent ontology resides in the sign. In the meantime, however, Girard takes Derrida to task for failing to acknowledge the original center.

We have come to a crux of the discussion, a crossroads between original victim (*pharmakos*) and a system of semiotic effacement (of writing, i.e., the *pharmakon*). Our interest is in showing the powerful overlap between the two systems, because a full semiotics requires both a synchronic

---

4. Girard et al., *Evolution and Conversion*, 107–8, italics original.

viewpoint (i.e., the perspective of the present and its simultaneous relationships) and the diachronic which shows genetically how things got put in place. The synchronic approach was made popular by de Saussure and Lévi-Strauss as a way of bringing attention to the critical concept of relationships between terms. But evolutionary diachrony is also essential if we are to avoid lapsing again into a mystification: without an understanding of historical emergence a synchronic system seems to have dropped out of the sky or arisen like Aphrodite from the depths. This can only result in another form of metaphysics.[5]

To write the collapse of metaphysics is to promote the emergence of semiotics as first philosophy and *at the same time* participate in the revelation of the victim. One cannot come without the other, because the roots of metaphysics must share the roots of all human culture. Directly subsequent to Girard's words in *Evolution and Conversion* quoted above he goes on to say that after an initial period of communication by the center there in fact follows "the dissolution of the center, in the fashion of the forgetting of rituals [forgetting of the actual crises that necessitated ritual] and the emergence of institutions."[6] In other words, with official priesthood, king and law, the original proximity to the center is dissipated, and "natural" or naive metaphysics (god, authority, justice) take its place. Girard does not speak of metaphysics explicitly in this connection, but if we follow through with the parallel Derridean perspective we see how this is inevitable. Derrida has a highly apropos comment in the seminal 1966 essay we introduced above: "The history of the concept of structure must be thought of as a series of substitutions of center for center, as a linked chain of determinations of the center . . . The history of metaphysics, like the history of the West, is the history of these metaphors and metonymies."[7] Derrida includes such examples of *arche* and *telos*, *ousia*, etc., and of course he is thinking in terms of metaphysical concepts. But the inclusion of "like the history of the West" suggests, necessarily, concrete institutions and history. These can never be

---

5. The interpretation theory of Paul Ricoeur stresses what he sees as the dialectic between an *event* of discourse and its meaning, between the temporal message (diachronic) and systematic code (synchronic). See his *Interpretation Theory: Discourse and the Surplus of Meaning*. He recognizes it is essential to maintain the two aspects, but it remains mysterious how the two elements happen together: "The suppressing and the surpassing of the event in the meaning is a characteristic of discourse itself" (*Interpretation Theory*, 12). The Girardian account gives a satisfactory explanation of event (original violence) together with meaning (the sacred and, through it, exponential signification).

6. Girard et al., *Evolution and Conversion*, 108.

7. Derrida, "Structure, Sign, and Play in the Discourse of the Human Sciences," in *Writing and Difference*, 279.

far away from the frame of metaphysics. Metaphysics generates institutions, just as institutions enshrine metaphysics.

It seems to me that the only way out of this common source and genesis is to say there is an entirely separate genetic thread for metaphysics coming down, again, from the skies. And, of course, that is the classical attitude, a metaphysics of Platonic remembrance. The sad thing about a lot of Christian theology is that, whatever Girard's admission about the transcendental signifier being the victim—and hence proto-cognition being the product of violence—it gives its intellectual Greek bride of two thousand years a free pass every time. It tells us with magisterial confidence that the Greek metaphysics it has embraced is pure and true and not dependent on violent origins. I recall a meeting of Girardians in which a prominent Girardian disciple of the time told the gathering, without irony, that he personally had asked Girard whether there *was* an immortal soul, to which Girard solemnly replied, "Yes." The very fact, however, that the disciple felt moved to ask the question shows Girardian anthropology had thrown the concept into doubt.

But shouldn't we perhaps refer to the Greeks themselves, just like everybody else—including Girard—seems to do? Heraclitus of Ephesus was there at the dawn of philosophy, in the sixth century BCE; he is famous for his obscurity but also enough pithy insight to maintain respectful attention to his thought. The fragmentary sayings that have come down to us refer, among other things, to "the logos," a figure destined for enormous later success both as a philosophical and theological concept, and generally understood philosophically as the principle of rationality and organization in all things. However, "logos" can also simply mean "word," and in Heraclitus it could basically mean his own language or discourse used to communicate to his hearers. Thus, he says, "This *Logos* holds always, but humans always prove unable to understand it, both before hearing it and when they have first heard it. For although all things come to be in accordance with this *Logos*, humans are like the inexperienced when they experience such words and deeds as I set out." But if, on the other hand, *logos* is indeed a principle of being, another fragment comes to relevance, one given prominence among Girardians: "War is the father of all and king of all, and some he shows as gods, others as humans; some he makes slaves, others free." This goes along with yet a further saying: "It is necessary to know that war is common and justice is strife and that all things happen in accordance with strife and necessity."[8] So, *if* logos is to be seen as a universal principle it would seem to share an essential provenance

---

8. Fragments B1, B53, B80, in Diels-Kranz numbering; translation from McKirahan, *Philosophy before Socrates*, 112 and 120, italics in original. For Girard and Heraclitus, see chapter 9 below.

with war and strife in that role. At the headwaters of the Greek intellectual tradition there seems absolutely no protective membrane between transcendental signified and violence: their organic unity is fully proclaimed by Heraclitus, even celebrated.

But this has not been recognized in the Christian tradition, indeed until Girard himself. Instead, there has been perfect metaphysical confusion. The grounds for the confusion was helped enormously by the headline use of "logos" at the beginning of John's Gospel—"In the beginning was the Word"—where word/logos merged easily with a philosophical sense. It then settled progressively into a formal mindset from the second century onward, with Christian apologists seeing a feature like Heraclitus's use of the logos as an actual anticipation of gospel revelation.[9] Later on, toward the end of this volume, we will show how Girard fully undoes and reverses this identification, and the final chapter will consist of a thoroughgoing semiotic reading of John, underpinning and illustrating this reversal. However, the takeaway point at the moment is how the two pathways of metaphysical deconstruction, anthropological and philosophical, cannot be kept separate. Violence leaks through the seams of each, and Girard and Derrida are cousins in thought while separated by an ocean of language and method.

Yet, this is not the only reason to pursue the track of deconstruction. In the second half of his career Derrida made a further aspect of his thought clear, one that, more strangely than ever, again parallels Girard's. This time it is the biblical semiotic patrimony that will offer to Derrida also the hope of a way forward . . . or at least the ghost of one.

Trace of the Other

According to the Derrida of différance, the fate of human meaning appears lost in linguistic uncertainty, in mists of metonymy. However, in the latter part of his career Derrida began to extract from those mists an opening and possibility which seemed to add a new concreteness and actuality to his trademark calibrations of language. Yet the truth is, Derrida's striking shift toward a more socially conscious and political kind of commentary still belongs authentically to his deconstructive approach. It still maintains his characteristic lack of tangibility and vanishing essence, but, more to the point, it can truthfully claim that concern for "the other" stems from the fundamental alterity at the roots of deconstruction itself—the trace which is always "of

---

9. For example, Justin Martyr (c. 100–c. 165 CE), *First Apology* 46 (*ANF* 1:178): "Those who lived reasonably [*meta logou*, according to the Word] are Christians, even though they have been thought atheists; as among the Greeks, Socrates and Heraclitus."

the other." What is of crucial importance for our own argument here is that his way forward appears through an analysis of certain privileged signifiers which hold an undeniable biblical reference. We cannot overlook that it is exactly in these areas that there appears a form of semiotic change or "meta-semiosis" in Derrida's treatment, one that offers some kind of human hope. In advancing a thesis of transformative semiotics based in the Bible Derrida's developing frame of thought is of exceptional interest.

At a conference in 1993, at the University of California, Riverside, Derrida was invited to give the main address. The conference was organized to respond to the recent collapse of the Soviet Union and, with that, the existential question hanging over Marxism. Derrida's lecture, delivered over two evenings, comprises the content of a book, *Specters of Marx*, published in French the same year and in English the next.[10] Derrida used the first line of *The Communist Manifesto* (1848), penned by Marx and Engels, as his point of departure: "A specter is haunting Europe—the specter of communism." Derrida exploits the image of a specter or ghost to depict the concern for human justice as a kind of wraithlike meaning haunting our world, a spectral demand that can never properly be fulfilled but which summons us still to respond.

Derrida's method of approach is critical. The Communist project worked from the political base of the organized working classes and was mobilized by a philosophy of historical struggle and the revolutionary violence it involves. Anybody who lived in the era before the fall of the Berlin Wall and was in any way politically concerned knows exactly what this means. Derrida tells expressly of his own left-leaning politics and how, for him, the whole project was always coming to an end, well before the events of '89. He uses this new moment, and what he sees as the celebration by "latecomers" at "the end of history," to reflect on what a struggle for justice might now mean, and indeed perhaps what it has always meant. Instead of talking about a determinist theory of history, he uses the first line of the *Manifesto* as a bridge to a single play by Shakespeare, *Hamlet*, and its drama of a ghost which appears and calls for vengeance. He turns to a piece of literature and from its text derives a powerful sign of the demand for justice: a haunting, a ghost that won't go away, a deep "abysmal" claim that the eponymous Hamlet might refuse but that he can't escape from.

The demand can surely result in violence, as indeed is the case in the final act of Shakespeare's play—the stage is littered with corpses. But Derrida wishes us to understand that in haunting the violence is not thematically or necessarily coded, while the demand is. Is this not the point of Hamlet's

10. Derrida, *Specters of Marx*.

endless havering and hesitation in respect of what he is actually going to do, his famous self-doubt? The demand that the ghost awakens is something that lies deeper than sheer rivalry and the reactive move for revenge. In Girardian terms it might correspond to the irrepressible revelation of the victim, the fathomless outcry of the blood of Abel. The important thing for our purposes is how Derrida extracts this or isolates it within Marx, and so changes the specter of Marx to a nonviolent demand, or at least one stripped of its necessary revolutionary arms.

Derrida makes clear this disconnection of justice from reactive violence by underlining the essential difference from restitution, from law itself. He finds a key to this in the thought of "disjuncture," repeating Hamlet's lament, "The time is out of joint." This is a description not just of the particular situation in a fictional Denmark but of the very character of human beings facing the other's claim to justice. Before the other's claim to justice we are rendered out of sync with ourselves, dragged into the "time" of the other where the only valid meaning comes from her cry for another future. Disjointing is "not for calculable and distributive justice. Not for law, for the calculation of restitution, the economy of vengeance or punishment . . . Not for calculable equality, therefore, not for the symmetrizing and synchronic accountability or imputability of subjects or objects, not for a *rendering justice* that would be limited to sanctioning, to restituting, and to *doing right*, but for justice as incalculability of the gift and singularity of the an-economic ex-position to others."[11]

We see clearly from the piled-up negations regarding restitution—what we could call *quid pro quo*—that Derrida is stressing a demand for justice which has nothing to do with any settling of accounts between equals (between mathematical factors reducible to each other in an equation). As he says, the relationship is *an-economic*: it does not belong in any economy of exchange. The reference to "the gift" directs us also to another work by Derrida, from shortly before *Specters*. *The Gift of Death*, published in French in 1992, is a commentary on death and the role it plays in philosophy, especially since Heidegger and Levinas.[12] It is a remarkable book which manages in its few pages both to synthesize and spring apart some really central themes in Western thought and imagination, and not least in regard to Christianity. It offers a developing reflection on death *as a gift*, something that of course has

---

11. Derrida, *Specters of Marx*, 26, italics original. The influence of the Jewish philosopher Emmanuel Levinas is evident here. Levinas developed a thought of ethics as "first philosophy," the self as trace or substitute of the other, and responsibility as constitution of the self. The very next sentence after the quotation here Derrida himself quotes Levinas: "The relation to others—that is to say, justice." Levinas, *Totalité et infini*, 62.

12. Derrida, *Gift of Death*.

a powerful Christian resonance. The New Testament theme of "grace" is very close: the classic Christian gift without a frame of recompense or exchange. However, where Derrida prefers to focus his own thought is in the claim of the other as absolutely incommensurable, requiring a response in the self that is indeed a kind of death, one without horizon of recompense. What we get, therefore, is a language of ethics, of responsibility, not a theology of grace or love. The figure of Abraham becomes a paradigm, called by God to sacrifice his son, Isaac, without explanation. The gift that Abraham can give in this frame is that of death, of his son, Isaac, but also of himself in as much as he resides within an incommunicable secret of what he is called to do. Derrida uses Kierkegaard's seminal commentary on Abraham's sacrifice, *Fear and Trembling*, as a key resource. Kierkegaard does not look at the story from a historical critical viewpoint, but as a terrifying parable of Abraham's "faith" which does not answer to any human calculation. Derrida derives from this an ethical ideal, even though it is paradoxically irresponsible.

> Abraham's decision is absolutely responsible because it answers for itself before the absolute other. Paradoxically it is also irresponsible because it is guided neither by reason nor by an ethics justifiable before men or before the law of some universal tribunal. Everything points to the fact that one is unable to be responsible at the same time before the other and before others, before the others of the other. If God is completely other, the figure or name of the wholly other, then every other (one) is every (bit) other. *Tout autre est tout autre* ... [W]hat can be said about Abraham's relation to God can be said about my relation without relation to *every other (one) as every (bit) other* [*tout autre comme tout autre*], in particular my relation to my neighbor or to my loved ones who are as inaccessible to me, as secret and transcendent as Jahweh.[13]

This is an ethics of impossible responsibility, because every "other" makes an incommensurable demand—in the philosophical space or role of God—thus relativizing all the other others who nevertheless make their own incommensurable demand! So it is that Abraham is a supreme ethical model because of his absolutely singular responsibility. This is the secret, the ethical ideal in the face of the other who is in the place of God—but not in the face of all the rest of the others. This absolutely singular situation creates the secret of the true gift. "Abraham himself is in secret, cut off both from man and from God."[14] It is the nature of the gift, its incom-

13. Derrida, *Gift of Death*, 77–78, French and italics original.
14. Derrida, *Gift of Death*, 79.

municable singularity—that is, not belonging to any continuity of further life, which is the gift of death.

Death or Grace?

Over against this is the Christian continuum of grace. Derrida recognizes in Christianity another kind of economy, or at least an attempt at one, and his thought here is highly relevant to our central concern with transformative meaning. In the last chapter of the book he carries through a commentary on the Sermon on the Mount from Matthew's Gospel. He notes the promise of "reward" for actions of giving done in secret, without public recognition, but seen in secret by the Father. This is similar to the secret of Abraham's gift, but then also quite different. The teaching of the Sermon

> always presupposes a calculation that claims to go beyond calculation, beyond the totality of the calculable as a finite totality of the same. There is an economy, but it is an economy that integrates the renunciation of a calculable remuneration, renunciation of merchandise or bargaining [*marchandage*], of economy in the sense of a retribution that can be measured or made symmetrical. In the space opened by this economy of what is without measure there emerges a new teaching concerning giving or alms that relates the latter to giving back or paying back, a yield [*rendement*] if you wish, a profitability [*rentabilité*] also, of course, but one that creatures cannot calculate and must leave to the appreciation of *the father as he who sees in secret*.[15]

He goes on to question whether this supposed new economy really does escape the economy of exchange or whether it is only a simulacrum and a bluff, one which will always be called out by a cynical world. In other words, is it possible to give anything back to Abraham, without destroying the gift's integrity in the first place? Or, in contrast, may it be possible to preserve the giving without recognition, without payment, a giving in truth, by means of a "reward" that is true only in relation to the gift's own self-exhausting character? Does Abraham in the abandonment of his secret meet the very spirit of his giving coming back to him? My own response would be that it is not strictly necessary to come to a conclusion here. The very fact of a discussion about the gift at this level and in these terms opens up a progressively open-ended sense of giving. The semiotic space around and within both Abraham's secret and the Sermon on the Mount breaks open the

---

15. Derrida, *Gift of Death*, 107.

possibility of another human way of being, simply by being articulated—the space being opened by being articulated. Is the possibility perfect in itself? Is it true all the way through? This indeed is a secret. It is a secret because it is an imperceptible communication between the language and the possible effects of being human learned from the language.

Derrida would be the last to say that the discourse of the secret could not be contaminated by that of grace, and, of course, vice versa. In either case a semiotic understanding always leads to the possibility of a different ethics, or better stated, a different world. Semiotic shifts bring with them possible new behaviors as the intimate repertoire of human meaning expands and deepens. There is no guarantee that a response of gift or grace will be chosen, but neither is there a certainty it won't once the pathway is created in the neural self. Who can tell in advance whether an individual will not, when the day comes, fully enter the territory of grace? In this understanding ethics is a human journey rather than a template, rather than a pure philosophy. The historical reality of human behavioral change produced by real semiotic change is presupposed because of the integrity of the body-self; that is, there is not a separate "spiritual" intellectual self which "the body" consistently refuses and denies. Rather, there is a deep imponderability about how options of human meaning are chosen and acted on in the reality of an imperfect world; but this undecidability does not at all mean that those options are not really taken up in moments when semiotic pathways become actually available and insistent. In historical terms, one semiotic transformation depends on the real uptake of a prior one, since, by definition, semiosis is a living network and one cannot expect human change to take place by sudden transfusion, rather than nerve-by-nerve construction. Nevertheless, the very organic nature of this process seems to promise human transformation, despite reactive setbacks experienced on the road. Derrida's own philosophical pathway suggests this, traversing the fractured landscape of Western thought to come to a place of *messianic* justice.

The Messianic

The volume *Specters of Marx* is probably the key writing in Derrida's oeuvre demonstrating his participation in a transformative drama. And it is by no means accidental that there is a distinctive biblical character to the language and motifs he uses. Not only does the call for justice have intimately prophetic overtones, not only does the mention of the gift echo the Abrahamic paradigm of responsibility, the book goes on to introduce the crown jewel of biblical transformative signs, the theme of the "messianic."

Derrida first brings it up, most tellingly, in relation to overcoming the shadow of vengeance lurking in the law. "If right or law stems from vengeance, as Hamlet seems to complain that it does—before Nietzsche, before Heidegger, before Benjamin—can one not yearn for a justice that one day, a day belonging no longer to history, a quasi-messianic day, would finally be removed from the fatality of vengeance? Better than removed: infinitely foreign, heterogeneous at its source?"[16]

This is deeply poignant. It gives a specific human content to the messianic, while being at pains to exclude religious markers. Derrida wants the messianic to be without any of the traditional, doctrinally understood content of Judaism, Christianity, or Islam; but it must involve the end of violence ("fatality of vengeance"). The messianism he is talking about is a "desert-like messianism (without content and without identifiable messiah)," a "desert in the desert," meaning an absence of the specific religious traditions which all began in the desert.[17] At this point Derrida flirts with something like a transcendental structure, a possibility built in to the very condition of human existence or being. Here he would be moving away from semiotics toward a kind of messianic ontology.

> If the messianic appeal belongs properly to a universal structure, to that irreducible movement of the historical opening to the future, therefore to experience itself and to its language (expectation, promise, commitment to the event of what is coming, imminence, urgency, demand for salvation and for justice beyond law . . .), how is one to *think* it *with* the figures of Abrahamic messianism? Does it figure abstract desertification or originary condition? [An abstract human longing or a one-time revelatory breaking-in?] Was not Abrahamic messianism but an exemplary prefiguration, the pre-name [*prénom*] given against the background of the possibility that we are attempting to name here? But then why keep the name, or at least the adjective (we prefer to say *messianic* rather than *messianism*, so as to designate a structure of experience rather than a religion) . . .? Can one conceive an atheological heritage of the messianic?[18]

The problem here is that if Derrida opts for some kind of absolute structure of human being which is then only *exemplified* in the historical religions, he is repeating a gesture already made by Hegel and, in his own way, by Heidegger. In other words, he would render philosophical and

16. Derrida, *Specters of Marx*, 25.
17. Derrida, *Specters of Marx*, 33.
18. Derrida, *Specters of Marx*, 210–11, italics original.

abstract something immediate, urgent and human. He would effectively exorcise Hamlet's ghost and its call for justice. Furthermore, he could be seen to betray his own master concept of *différance*, whereby meaning appears by chains of signifiers in which *the* final truth is always deferred and never *really* present. The statement of a "universal structure" does not seem to fit that condition. He asks, on the other hand (and almost in desperation), whether there can be an "atheological heritage of the messianic." This, in one way, seems to be factually indisputable—once the messianic has entered the semiotic repertoire, first through the religions of Judaism, Christianity and Islam, and then through its secular appropriations (Marxism), it belongs to the legacy of what it means to be human. But to claim an "atheological" *source* of the messianic is a bridge too far. In another setting Derrida says as much, and I give another extended quote because of how effective its expression is for our argument here.

> The problem remains—and this is really a problem for me, an enigma—whether the religions, say, for instance, the religions of the book, are but specific examples of this general structure, of messianicity. There is the general structure of messianicity as a structure of experience, and on this groundless ground there have been revelations, a history which one calls Judaism or Christianity and so on....
>
> That is one hypothesis. The other hypothesis—and I confess that I hesitate between these two possibilities—is that the events of revelation, the biblical traditions, the Jewish, Christian, and Islamic traditions, have been absolute events, irreducible events which have unveiled this messianicity. We would not know what messianicity is without messianism, without these events which were Abraham, Moses and Jesus Christ, and so on.[19]

Derrida hesitates because a semiotics of transformation depends on a concrete tradition: on that of the Bible, on its stories, people, losses, and times—times of struggle, yearning, suffering and hope. An abstract messianicity simply would not have enough compelling force to mobilize the coming of the other which Derrida envisages, and envisages precisely through iconic stories like those of Abraham, Moses, Jesus. In contrast the power of Marxism belonged to a historical moment, especially the threat of the organized working classes in the industrialized societies of Europe, and then, of course, the circumstances of the Bolshevik Revolution in Russia during an apocalyptic world war. The end of this moment in time in the last

---

19. Quoted in Caputo, *Prayers and Tears of Jacques Derrida*, 136–37; from a round-table discussion at Villanova University, 1994.

years of the twentieth century is the situation to which Derrida was directly responding in *Specters*. The book, therefore, is testimony to a specific and limited frame of history and its violent array of forces. In contrast, a semiotic transformation works essentially at a level of nonviolence, so it survives with ease the collapse of a violent political energy.

Derrida's left-leaning discourse enjoins an ongoing messianicity after the collapse of Marxism, one that is atheological, while he knows it cannot survive semiotically without the biblical traditions. He says both the democratic promise and the communist promise must preserve the "absolutely undetermined messianic hope [they have] at heart." But they must do so neither with the structures of religion nor with any definite ontological structure to give their hope substance. Rather, Derrida's deconstructive messianic hope is an "awaiting without horizon of the wait, awaiting what one does not expect yet or any longer, hospitality without reserve, welcoming salutation accorded in advance to the absolute surprise of the *arrivant* [one who arrives]."[20] This is an intensely (un)spiritual, (un)relational position, the arid heart of a monk-without-a-gospel waiting in a desert waste for a visitor who likely will never come, and cannot even be imagined coming. How can Derrida suggest this to your average Western mind without a hidden imitation of the biblical tradition, without an unseen but seamless appropriation of its rich semiotics? Derrida has a name for such schemes of thought which trade in a barely hidden way on the legacy of biblical meaning. He calls them a "nondogmatic doublet."[21] He would certainly not deny the same thing in his own thought—he expressly admits it in retaining the term "messianic." The only thing that separates him from the other thinkers he lists (in the last note) is the way his thought so powerfully demonstrates a semiotic debt connecting him to biblical meaning.

Thus, the force of semiotics in general and of biblical semiotics in particular is confirmed out of Derrida's deconstructive philosophy of the other. We have followed a pathway from Girard to Derrida because of a common pedigree of thinkers influencing them, a pedigree which amounts to semiotic origins in both of their conceptual worlds. Girard has given us

20. Derrida, *Specters of Marx*, 81.

21. Discussing a type of discourse where Christian themes are identifiable but "without reference to religion as institutional dogma," he says there are several contemporary philosophies of this type. He mentions Levinas, Marion, and Ricoeur, then comments, "But in the final analysis this list has no clear limit and it can be said . . . that a certain Kant and a certain Hegel, Kierkegaard of course, and I might even dare to say for provocative effect, Heidegger also, belong to this tradition that consists of proposing a nondogmatic doublet of dogma, a philosophical and metaphysical doublet, in any case a thinking that 'repeats' the possibility of religion without religion." Derrida, *Gift of Death*, 48–49.

a primary scene with the birth of language out of a crisis of murder. The brand-new cognition made possible by this event produces the framing for every subsequent act of naming and meaning. The reality embedded in language is always already a deferral from and toward the sacred victim, a way of seeing constructed in and by violence. Derrida's attack on the metaphysics of presence works in parallel to this insight. His understanding of language enables us to see the framing force of metaphysics, and at the same time the destabilizing force of the "other" in our words and writing—a second parallel insight, this time (in Girardian terms) in respect of the victim revealed. In every case a "logocentric" viewpoint ("a rose is a rose!") is blind to the semiotic functions Derrida describes, just as "misrecognition" in Girard refuses to see the way that original violence has shaped all our stories and our thought. Meanwhile, a transformative semiotics is currently at work: in Girard it is directly found in the biblical narrative, and with Derrida it is an atheological language that cannot escape the Bible. Is it possible to see the Bible as such an instrument, as something which over the slow course of the years has changed the very substance of our sign systems, opening up "the absolute surprise" of an entirely other human way of being? If this is the case, then the "nondogmatic doublets" of Christianity emerging from so many philosophies are but a consistent recognition of its transformation of discourse. A claim of this nature could perhaps be dismissed as rhetorical excess or maybe, at most, some kind of epiphenomenon. But that seems to me a willful denial of the weight of evidence. We are dealing with some of the greatest thinkers of the Western tradition: how is it possible for them to be led to incorporate structural elements of biblical meaning (in some cases profoundly so) unless there is an inner dynamic that functions for them in its own right?

Our next thinker will provide a corroborating thesis, and one with explicit intent. A long view of philosophical history can show us a steady shifting toward semiotics in Western thought, one that carries profound and thematic biblical effects. At the same time, it proposes a sense of the sign which is much less enclosed in itself than the Saussurean kind, one much more tensed toward the object and the real. The discussion will, therefore, connect us to other thinkers in history, leading us to some of the ultimate issues related to the sign. In the last analysis semiotic possibilities of transformation cannot be divorced from questions of ontology, of the final character of what is, of the thought of what we call "being."

6

The Long March of Signs

Silk Road

SOMEWHERE AT THE BEGINNING of the second quarter of his monumental, masterful tome on the history of Western thought read from a semiotic perspective, John Deely suggests that the general notion of the sign (Latin *signum*) first appears in the Christian epoch.[1] To be precise, it emerges as a reflection of Augustine's, one which can be seen to put in motion the specifically modern approach. Before Augustine, going back to the Greeks, a sign (Greek *semeion*) was a physical phenomenon, an external marker, like the track of an animal in the snow, or an elevated temperature as symptom of a fever—something known generally as a "natural" sign. This is in fact very much the way Jesus uses the word in the gospel, referring to natural phenomena that predict the weather (but then, of course, "signs of the times," which suggests already cultural phenomena too [Luke 12:54–56]).

Augustine was the first to apply the term in a systematic way both to these phenomena *and* to words, broadening the concept, therefore, to include the linguistic "sign." The general concept resulting led to the abiding question, What is the philosophical status of an entity that straddles both the conceptual-cultural and concrete-natural spheres? For the moment, however, what is of interest is the reason for Augustine's intervention bringing about the broadening of the term. He did this because he wanted to describe a particular class of signs—those revealed from and about Christ—and these necessarily included the words of scriptural revelation along with the sacraments (baptism, Eucharist, etc.). It is the materiality of these signs which leads him to establish a commonality between natural signs and words. As Deely comments, Augustine's thought is mobilized by

---

1. Deely, *Four Ages*, 214–24.

"his special interest in the words of scripture and the sacraments of Christian life, for both of these signs *directly involve the senses*."[2] Prompted by the apparatus of Christian revelation Augustine leaps in one bound across the traditional and generally unthought Greek distinction of natural signs and ideas/words.[3] So is born the science of signs, an inquiry which would literally take ages to mature but which was founded in a materiality of the traces of God in the world. Augustine had absolutely no interest in elaborating a doctrine of signs, after having first established the field, but his acute sensibility to Christian scripture as a privileged factum of truth led him to recognize a semiotic perspective. Already for this "doctor of the church" scripture was a system of transformative signs.

Deely's work is singularly apt to the purposes of the present book. Not only does it trace the subject of semiotics from the earliest days into the present "postmodern" era, it describes key points of arrival in the writings of the American philosopher and semiotician Charles Peirce and those of the Italian author and semiotician Umberto Eco. Together with Saussure these figures represent the champions of semiotics, the paladins of its contemporary importance. Collectively they produced a theoretical development which underscores today's relevance of semiotics and provides a sufficient theoretical base for the overall argument of the present study. Our reflections on Girard and Derrida in the previous chapter brought us into the maelstrom of deconstructive analysis of language. Deely does not consider Girard and he treats Derrida to some degree dismissively. His own work lacks the anthropological shock of Girard and the metaphysical allergy of Derrida, but he is fully attuned to the way our system of signs constructs our world for us—yet all the while connecting us to a "real world."

The particular dynamic of his own reflection is the way it sketches this understanding through the medieval scholastics up to (for Deely) a landmark thinker at the end of the Latin age, then onward to the postmodern era. Presenting this journey in a more imaginative figure we could say that Deely is following a grand "Silk Road" to semiotic discovery, a fabled path, known at first only to hardened adventurers, then little by little to the whole world.

2. Deely, *Four Ages*, 223, my italics.

3. It was Umberto Eco and his collaborators who first pointed this out. "One must realize that Greek semiotics, from the corpus Hippocratum up to the Stoics, made a clearcut distinction between a theory of verbal language (onomata) and a theory of signs (semeia)." And a little later: "With Augustine, there begins to take shape this '*doctrina*' or 'science' of signum, wherein both symptoms and the words of language . . . all become species [of a single genus]." Quoted by Deely, *Four Ages*, 216–17, italics original. Plato's *Cratylus* broaches the topic of language, but under the topic of names (*onomata*), which are always a reflection of ideas. To focus on words as signs quickly demands a practice—and even a worldview—of interpretation. For Eco, see below.

The route includes a number of curious byways, subsidiary or minor trails, and also comprises quite a major deviation—even a drastic turning back, if we are to believe the author—in the second half of its story. As suggested, Deely is concerned throughout with a postmodern defense of realism, judged primarily through the lens of the medieval or Latin conceptual scheme which assumed the real world as a natural part of their thought. The modern era broke this congenital bond (of thought and the real) and Deely sees semiotic postmodernism as part of a long return to this relation. We can see then why he does not approve much of Derrida's brand of postmodernism which seems, in some measure at least, to snap that bond even more sharply than the modern era. As we go ahead, however, we will underline the signal importance of paying attention to "the text" of our truth claims and why this is so crucial to a transformative semiotics. An ultimate realism is not excluded by différance and the trace—on the contrary! We remember that the so-called realism of the Middle Ages included the Crusades and offered no spiritual defense against the devastating wars of the Reformation.

It is not our task to rehearse in detail Deely's long historical-philosophical argument, but we need to give enough of it to grasp his particular combination of semiosis and realism. Moreover, its conceptual journey unfolds the final and most fundamental interest of his study, which is the suggestion of some inner progression of meaning, some engine of intellectual change—one which is hinged particularly around the biblically impacted world of the Middle Ages. As we go forward, we cannot help recognizing how semiotics steadily distinguishes itself as a philosophical theme, but even as it does a deeper, biblical pathway also breaks the surface, telling us that the change of signs mediated by the Bible guides the development of (cultural) understanding.

Deely traces the story of semiotics to what he sees as a crucial waypoint in a relatively unknown author named John Poinsot (1589–1644) at the end of the Latin age, that is, just before the beginning of philosophy in the national languages of Europe. He suggests that if Western thought had followed Poinsot, rather than Descartes and Locke, then we would not have had to endure the aporias and anomalies brought about by these thinkers. You get the strong impression that the third age of understanding, the "Modern" period, subsequent to the Greek and the Latin, was a deviation we could well have done without; but that does not really matter to the overall thesis either in Deely or in the present book. Deely lays out the historical map to a semiotic understanding of human existence. In doing so he provides a transformative template, one that can easily be referred to an underlying biblical dynamic. The history that gets us from A to Z is necessarily a generative pathway, illustrating a slow, painful, but real development of human understanding. Deely describes the transitions from one stage to another, without giving a mechanism by which the changes occur, but basically begging one into being.

Clearly the shift from the ancient world to what he names the Latin age involved a critical turn to Christianity, but he does not seek to examine the current of movement for itself. (Indeed, as so often, we are shown the continuing presence of Greek thought in the Christian era.) So, what we do get from Deely is simply a picture of the slow coming to clarity of the science of semiotics. Nevertheless, if we remember the broad biblical character of the Latin age, and at this contemporary stage of the journey also introducing Girard, and likely Derrida too, we are given material and intellectual evidence of the subterranean impact of the biblical tradition in Western culture. There then emerges a strong probability that it is in fact the reconfiguring influence of the Christian and biblical tradition that has continued to knit together anew the Western cultural world. We are led, therefore, to suspect that the mainspring of Delly's millennial change must be the changing pattern of meaning via the biblical text. In which case—to alter the image again—Deely's book acts as a broad map of territory with a main watershed and the course of a gathering river. The book you're now reading might be said to offer the deep hydraulics which produced the watershed in the first place. *Four Ages of Understanding* is an argument for semiotics as the essential and best channel of thought for postmodernism, with tributary streams in the Middle Ages. *Theology Beyond Metaphysics* tells us that it is the Hebrew and Christian Scriptures which create the underlying springs, both changing actual meaning and, in parallel, prompting semiotics as a crucial discipline for attention. In every case we are navigating across a revolutionary terrain.

Thomas Aquinas and Metaphysics

Deely's account of Thomas Aquinas is a good place to begin. Even as it takes its framing from Greek metaphysics, especially Aristotle, Thomistic thought is an intellectual landmark in the way it makes "being" part of the overall biblical message of a creative and redemptive God.[4] Deely lays this out as

---

4. It is very difficult to get a consistent protocol for writing the word "being" in technical philosophical terms. It has any number of nuances, shifting from a mundane everyday language use to specialized philosophical meaning. The problem becomes even more difficult when the thought of Martin Heidegger is introduced. I tend to move back and forward between a normal text, quotation marks and italicization: quotation marks highlight a general philosophical intent, and italics give a dynamic sense close to Heidegger's. Heidegger's favored German word is *Sein* which is the infinitive, "to be."

a core element of the Latin age, endorsing the metaphysical realism of the claim. He does not see a tension between this and his semiotic approach, but according to the discussion we have pursued—of the violent sources of metaphysics—there is clearly a problem. However, by developing an understanding of Thomistic thought, as we follow Deely's road, we will see the claim of theological semiotics in fact strengthened. We will gain an intensified awareness of the contingency and provisionality of the metaphysical language we use, in contrast to the living quality of a relationship it perhaps attempts to convey. Thomism offers a definitional name for God out of the philosophical repertoire at his disposal. This may in fact have the effect of impeding that relation rather than enhancing it. On the other hand, and paradoxically, we can still find a semiotic value in its use.

Esse in Thomistic Latin means the act of being, or existence itself. In the thought of Aquinas existence is the most fundamental category of reality, but nothing we actually experience in existence possesses the act of being, or existence *in and of itself*. Things appear and disappear, in a constant universal flux. Our experience therefore—according to Aquinas—demands logically the existence of *a* being which possesses *being in and of itself*, in order to undergird all this transient existence. "What was original with Aquinas was the singling out of existence as such, the act of being . . . as *itself* an effect to be accounted for *as* effect . . . As the one effect without which there are no other effects to consider, existence then appears as the one effect proper to the creative activity of God."[5] God is the being whose quality of being differs from any other being, meaning that God possesses being in and of himself.

As such God is the source of existence for all other beings who do not possess that quality. This is the thought of God as *ipsum esse subsistens* (self-subsistent existence, pure act, the reality whose existence is existence itself). It is given by Thomas Aquinas as the first and most proper name for God. Thus, there is brought into "God" not only a fundamental concept of first cause (derived already from Aristotle's earlier Unmoved Mover), but *as existence itself* God *is* the fundamental existence of *everything* else.

This is a powerful notion of God *as* being, but where did it come from? As just suggested the concept of "First Mover" already presents the idea of an ultimate mobilizing agency in relation to all things, but this agency in

---

Often the translation of *Sein* is a capitalized "Being," but I avoid that as it expresses a formal and essentialized noun, losing the verbal character of the German. The matter is further complicated when Heidegger uses *Seiende*, which is the participle, meaning what we normally term "beings" in the plural. In the singular neuter use it is rendered here as "be-ing."

5. Deely, *Four Ages*, 292–93.

Aristotle works on an order of reality always already in place (Aristotle's eternity of the world), and in itself the First Mover remains remote and indifferent to all but its own self-contemplation. Aquinas's concept of a dynamic source of existence owed a considerable debt to the Persian Islamic philosopher and polymath Avicenna (*Ibn Sīnā*). Avicenna's *Book of Healing* became available in Europe in partial Latin translation some fifty years after its composition (c. 1020 CE). It covers areas of logic, natural science, math and metaphysics, and Aquinas read and appropriated much of the metaphysics. Avicenna taught that the primary subject of metaphysics is being as being, because there is nothing more universal. Even God is not the subject of metaphysics as such because "God" is not universal enough.[6] However, as God *does* exist, being in God is one and simple and proper to God as such. Aquinas took up these metaphysical notions and, concentrating on the *esse* of God, made it, as mentioned, God's most proper name. He refers to the text of Exodus where God declares himself as "I am who I am (3:14), and takes this as warrant for the philosophical name.

> [T]he name *thing* (*res*) is applied to a thing from its quiddity [its "whatness"], according to *Avicenna*, while the name *who is* or *being* (*esse*) is applied from the act itself of existing (*ab ipso actu essendi*). Now since it is true that in every single created thing *its essence differs from its existence*, that thing is *properly denominated* from its quiddity and not from the act of existing; for example, the human from humanity. But in God *his existence itself is his own quiddity*. Therefore, the name that is taken from existence (*esse*) *properly* names him and is his proper name, as the proper name of the human is what is taken from his quiddity.[7]

Thus, God is named from his being *as* being, and this is the grounds for the "science" of theology. With the tools of a metaphysics of existence it becomes possible rationally to examine and explain much of the material of faith. God, for Aquinas, does not fall under a common or universal feature of being. God is outside all things as their principle and cause. Nevertheless, as God imparts existence to everything else it is possible to understand God, up to a certain point at least, by the "analogy of being." If we can reason back from the existence of things to the necessary existence of God there must clearly be some continuity in the very identity of being, from things to God, and God to things. Thus, the feature of being becomes

---

6. Houser, "Avicenna and Aquinas."

7. Thomas Aquinas, *In 1 Sententiis*, D. 8, Q.1, Art.1c; 195, quoted in Houser, "Avicenna and Aquinas," 8.

an overarching theme, metaphysical in function and fact, by which theology is framed and conditioned.

There is of course the Bible and church tradition, but these fall inevitably within the scheme of metaphysics. They do not operate separately from it. "Theology for Aquinas was the use of human reason in the service of the mysteries of faith, and the mysteries of faith all go back to God. Scripture and tradition are materials for theologians to use, because they convey the mysteries to us; but it is up to the theologian to give these materials a rationalized form, using indeed the autonomously valid intellectual tools of logic and philosophical reason."[8] In simpler terms, the "science" of theology found its object in the light of revelation, while examining it with the tools of philosophical reason.

So it is that a unique combination of metaphysics and scripture creates a distinctive Christian medieval thought-world. God as *ipsum esse subsistens* is the same God who called Abraham, who spoke from the burning bush, and who in the gospels, where his identity becomes triune, is proclaimed to the nations. It is not hard to sense a weird, unearthly, oppressive weight to the thought of this God, a constitution of pure being plus narrated historical intentionality. A truly massive concept! Its effect is to put metaphysics on a kind of permanent and inflated life support in the culture and world of the church.

But we remember the origins of metaphysics: it is the frame of totality which takes its existence from the shock and raptness of the primate mind seared by original violence. As a discipline metaphysics always seeks back to the most total or universal concept, and so carries within itself the original frame of totality created out of the birthing event of violence-become-peace. The effect of this seems repugnant in both aesthetic and revelatory terms. "Being" as a name for God seems to expand to the level of the infinite a human experience of "being" which is always defective and prone to loss. We fill it in to the level of perfection and completion, but we can only do so by means of the same defective material we know as humans, and so create something bloated, uncanny, monstrous—a hypertrophy of defective being. The metaphysician might reply that we have not carried out the *via negativa* with sufficient rigor—denying of the subject "God" all possible defect or imperfection, to the point we arrive at true transcendence. Nevertheless—and here is surely the whole point—this mental process can only be achieved by an accompanying exclusionary or sacrificial gesture which necessarily repeats the founding violence of humanity—once again invoking the founding construct. Meanwhile the semiotics of the Bible text continues to express something utterly

---

8. Deely, *Four Ages*, 258.

different, something alive, transformative, truly other to what we know out of our violent beginnings. It reaches out to a cohesive relationship with a God fully alive, compassionate and nonviolent.

Creation, Violence and Heidegger

We can see the question exemplified in connection to the creative role of the figure understood as God. The first chapter of Genesis is by no means a neutral account of creative power. It is to be understood rather as a conscious rereading of violent origins, a semio-ontological gesture of resolute boldness and compassion. It deliberately and fearlessly shifts the semiotics so that the text *remakes the world away from violence and by means of peace*. The bloody battles and sacrificial deaths by which the earth and heavens are first constructed are too well known in world mythology to need rehearsing. The Bible itself contains strains of violent beginnings, and their robust presence throughout the text (cf. Ps 74:14; Job 26:12; 41:1; Isa 27:1) gives testimony of how necessarily "modern" the Genesis 1 account would be. In terms of composition it would have to come in a dramatically changed cultural-spiritual setting—probably the circumstances of exile, or afterward, when Israel had learned their relation with the Lord could survive and thrive even when they had lost national instruments of violence. Genesis 1 gives us a new semiotics of beginning, one where God creates by the effortless generosity of a pure word, one conspicuously without conflict. The repeated antiphon "God saw that it was good" is not an abstract philosophical comment: it relentlessly affirms that the created space is not an enemy, nor does it contain enemies, but rather it can be trusted as a suitable space for life and its triumph. The repetition of "good" is a linguistic (possibly liturgical) echo-effect, reinforcing the semiotic validity of the nonviolent creation. Far from being a "literal" claim about a "seven-day creation" (and the authoritarian worldview that seeks to go with it), it is a much more dynamic rereading of the whole anthropological condition, effectively beginning the world again out of nonviolence. It is a revision at root, *in radice*, of the human story, and it is *that* which is revelatory and constructive of the real. In many ways Genesis 1 sets the scene for the whole semio-ontological program of the Bible.

Another key aspect of Genesis 1 is the tradition that describes it as a creation *ex nihilo*, out of nothing. Augustine already saw this as Catholic doctrine and he read the seven-days account of creation in Genesis in harmony with this viewpoint.[9] An important motivation for his writing here

---

9. Augustine, *Confessions* XII, 8; Augustine, *On Genesis: A Refutation of the Manichees* I.6 (Hill, 45).

was his opposition to the Manichees, including their dualist cosmogony. For Augustine, Genesis gave no grounds for a second, evil (violent) source of creation. All the same there seems to have arisen an intense debate in the thirteenth century about the possibility of an eternal world versus *creatio ex nihilo*. Aquinas himself asserted that there was no logical contradiction in the idea of an eternal world and basically accepted the beginning of the world *ex nihilo* on faith—that is, from the scriptures.[10] In which case we may conclude Genesis 1 acts as a source code for a great deal of subsequent reflection, its radical consequences unfolding over the centuries. In the reference just given Aquinas actually says "out of nothing" does not mean a priority of "nothing" as a kind of "something" from which the world arises.[11] But the very fact of having to make the argument indicates that such an idea can be gotten from the phrase. The possibility puts us in abrupt proximity to another seminal thinker of the twentieth century, one who had a profound impact on many of the thinkers we have mentioned in the previous chapter. To bring him into the discussion gives us a major new link-road on which to pursue our journey, one that Deely will soon access himself. To think of "being" also as a kind of "nothing" is, I think, to investigate ontology in terms of originary violence, rather than the pure abstractions of metaphysics; to do so brings us, paradoxically but as a matter of fact, closer to the transformative dynamic of biblical revelation.

Martin Heidegger was a philosopher who produced a thought of "being" of exceptional vigor and consistency, but one which had nothing to do with God. His work stands as an epoch-making horizon in Western thought, one which influenced the whole century after him. He gave us a concept of "being" as primordial experience or event, prior to any thought or need of the biblical Creator. Setting this in contrast to Aquinas's thought brings us quickly to the possibility of radical problems with the latter. Heidegger thus becomes essential in our discussion, exactly because his analysis returns philosophy to a direct sense of what constitutes existence, without the element of formal theology. With Heidegger's philosophy we are in a parallel place to Girard's primary scene where "the god" is simply an aspect of human existence, or of "being," in intense crisis. The name given to Heidegger's philosophy is "ontology," and the name which he applied to the traditional thought of "being" subordinate to God (in other words, Thomist thought) is "onto-theology." There is thus a distinctive parting of the ways at the philosophical level between the medieval universe and the one described for us by Heidegger in the early part of the twentieth century. Introducing

---

10. Aquinas, *De aeternitate mundi*.
11. Aquinas, *De aeternitate mundi*, paras. 13, 14.

Heidegger in our discussion brings in new threads of argument, but it also allows us to tie these and others together, and possibly achieve a new synthesis. As just suggested, what is of crucial interest is the way his thought can be understood to twin Girard's anthropology, without the presence or role of a metaphysical superstructure. We shall return to this parallel more than once below. But first we note Deely's own high regard for Heidegger, although it is given for another reason.

Deely is working his way to the sign or *signum* as a fundamental locus of philosophy, and to do that he has to find his way across the major topographical barrier of modern idealist thinking, sometimes summed up under the heading "epistemology." We shall get back to this too, but for the moment we can say that for Deely, Heidegger, along with Charles Sanders Peirce, represents the critical break with the modern rationalist age, entering instead into the postmodern age. "[T]he combined works of these two men ignorant of one another—Charles Peirce in America and Martin Heidegger in Germany—more than any others, effected the overthrow of the epistemological paradigm which defined modernity and began that new epoch of philosophical thought and history which we designate, for want of a better name, 'postmodern.'"[12]

Heidegger becomes a turning-point figure and does so because he reconnects human being directly and immediately with *being*, without the metaphysical or onto-theological detour. In fact, Heidegger is appreciated by Deely as a herald of realism, alongside Peirce. But Heidegger's realism is of a very particular kind and as we begin to understand it, we will grasp the connection with the previous themes. *Creatio ex nihilo* pointed us not only toward existence and the act of being, it showed us, as a backdrop, an implicit scene of "nothing," the meaning of which was clearly debated in medieval times. I have not encountered anywhere a sustained reflection on this point, but we know in the language of Heidegger "no-thing" plays a constitutive role for his thought of *being*, so we may wonder how much of it was influenced—even unconsciously—by the traditional discussions of Genesis 1.

Heidegger's presentation of "no-thing" is related to the existential mood of dread, something that is itself revelatory of *being*. "Nothing," therefore, takes on the sense of a shadow or underbelly of being. "In the clear night of dread's no-thing, the original openness of be-ing as such arises for the first time in such a way that it is a [kind of] being and not nothing."[13] As always with Heidegger we should beware of building up too much of a naturalistic picture. He prefers to speak in abstract, if not abstruse, terms; for example,

---

12. Deely, *Four Ages*, 342.
13. Heidegger, *Pathmarks*, 90; translation from Groth, "What Is Metaphysics?"

"the essential belongingness of the *not* to being as such."[14] At the same time, and necessarily, this not/nothing cannot be separated from the being for whom *being* is an issue, human existence which he names in the German as "Dasein." For human existence "Nothing" acts as something in itself, it "nihilates," and not as one occurrence among many, but something that happens in "the clear night" of originary experience. Therefore, it is not truly nothing. Continuing from the quotation at the beginning of this paragraph, he says, "The essence of the originally nihilating no-thing is found in this: it brings Dasein for the first time before beings as such." Thus, nothing is both a primordial element in human awareness and of being as such. In the context of the experience of nothing "beings" come before Dasein.

It may seem that we are going off on something of a tangent, and an obscure one at that. But if we continue to follow these lines through there is a promise of arriving at the scene of human meaning with much greater clarity and urgency, one underlying the emergence of human signs. It is possible to decode Heidegger in terms of Girard and find in his writing anthropological phenomena marked by violent origins, although presented in ontological terms. At the same time a Thomistic thought of "God"—a metaphysical source of existence as product of a logical argument—might well evolve into something much more human and meaningful. To gain all these points with maximum effect we need first to circle back once more in the direction of Aquinas and the Bible.

The characteristic claim of the Angelic Doctor's thought is that it sets itself out not as philosophy but as the science of theology whose formal subject or matter is divine revelation. It simply uses philosophy to explain itself, and in the process to show that theology is not contrary to reason. The problem is that in that process reason (specifically metaphysics) acquires a conceptual excess over the language of revelation, so that all the suppleness and shock of the scripture, and in particular the story and person of Jesus, get buried under the mass landscape of Aristotelian logic. We recall once again that the most exceptional thing about Genesis 1 from a literary and textual point of view is the astonishing lack of violence in creation. Compared to the *gigantomachies* of Babylonian and Greek mythologies, the biblical creation account is arresting for its serenity, peace and universal goodness. As already underlined, there are no enemies, and all is life by God's word. If we go on to the overall story-frame of the whole book of Genesis we are obliged to recognize that the creation account in the first chapter provides a proleptic theological critique of violence, in literary parallel to the story of Joseph at the end. Joseph is a man sent by God to save and bless both the exodus

14. Heidegger, *Contributions to Philosophy*, 222, para. 160; cf. 80, para. 47.

enemy, Egypt, and his own rivalrous, murderous brothers. If we admit this is the case from a literary and semiotic point of view, then *creatio ex nihilo* should be read much more radically as *creatio extra* or *sine violentia*: creation outside, *without* or *otherwise* than violence. And the Heideggerean revisioning of "nothing" may be thought as effectively the restoration of this violence at the heart of creation-as-*being*.

In which case, Genesis's changed codes at the foundation of the cosmos are neither a literary accident nor some purely metaphysical statement of effortless monotheistic power. They are a deliberate reconstruction of anthropological identity, carried through by means of a theology without violence. And if we insist on monotheistic power as indeed a sense of Genesis 1 then underlying that, and providing its most radical source, is divine and human nonviolence. In contrast, Heidegger's no-thing, revealed in dread, is real to our actual violent existence. Its twentieth-century ontology, composed in the aftermath of the First World War and the desperate circumstances of twenties and thirties Germany, gives a much more actual sense of *being* than Thomas's *esse*. But then, conversely, Genesis 1 offers a radical new *beginning* to *being*, out of and away from violence, a biblical re-creation which is always the plan and purpose of God.

Genesis is never a flat literal description of creation, a banal report of sovereign potency. A semiotic reading gives us instead a truly *prophetic* description of creation, one that is true to the deep original purpose of God but that will be fulfilled only in the seventh (or eighth) day of God's final sabbath blessing. Actual prehistoric death (including the dinosaurs!) is elided in the account, not because original creation was without death, but for the sake of an amazing transformative revelation of *future* creational peace and life.

So, from a semiotic and anthropological perspective, things are much more revelatory and redemptive than either a literal reading or strict Thomistic philosophy would make them. Thomistic thought includes the logical necessity of God as first cause of everything. God here reinforces a hierarchical order of origin, authority, and, necessarily, violence. In contrast, as biblical semiotics the "God" of Genesis plunges into the ongoing struggle of a semi-independent creation, providing in the midst of history a language and culture of human and cosmic transformation.

Here is the point where our argument stands up on a formally theological level. It begins to say that the biblical message—specifically the message of the gospel—is much better served by a claim to a change in the roots of human meaning than a formal structure of metaphysical ideas. However—and we must at once admit this—a question may immediately be leveled on the lines of the following. What is the use of a redemptive semiotic argument if from a metaphysical angle we cannot know or say what "God" is? To talk redemptively via a pure linguistic gesture—a kind of poetry—might offer a brief moment of consolation, but it cannot constitute a case for human meaning as such. Moreover, just to turn to semiotics, rather than metaphysics, does not get rid of metaphysics. The writers of Genesis 1 certainly employed a metaphysical concept to denote the creator of the world, albeit in a nonviolent framework.

And that in itself must be the answer!

The signifier "god," with all its metaphysical baggage, is part of the legacy of human culture, and more specifically of biblical culture. It has an assured place within the received array of human signals, and it remains a general possibility of truth. The term also carries a wide set of signifieds attached to it, and they retain huge anthropological relevance, especially in terms of the violent configuration of existence humans have inherited. Why indeed do people use "the divine name" again and again as an epithet for personal shock, horror, anger, outrage? Its totalized and totalizing sense concentrates the response and voice of the speaker with unparalleled force. For someone to use God's name in this way is semiotically to unleash the primitive crisis of violence: at the very least to reinforce a point, if not deliberately to aim intense mimetic doubling at an individual or situation. For that very reason it is of profound importance that this signifier is instead used within a transformative set of signs to communicate a new existence of nonviolence. Positively stated, it is necessarily life-giving to allow an essential language of nonviolence progressively to infiltrate and change the signifier "god" together with all its metaphysical baggage. This then becomes the role of Christian theology—to shape in discourse the transformative nonviolence of Jesus, his Father/Mother and the Spirit that comes from them. If, as a result, the human receptor of language finds herself holistically aware of a loving figure who speaks the universe into life and goodness, is she not then closer in truth to the message of Genesis 1—rather than fitting out petrified forms of Greek thought with biblical trappings? Theology is a matter of translation rather than orthodoxy; trans-semiosis rather than dogma.

In any and every case the message of the gospel is traditionally and continually capable of flooding our souls with a new sense of being, one arising within the world and changing the world from within. We will need to return to this in a little more detail, in the final chapter when we give a semiotic reading to a key writing of the New Testament, the Gospel of John. There we will perhaps gain a better sense of how trans-semiosis might work. In the meanwhile, the metaphysics accompanying the gospel can be compared to the items we purchase from a thrift store: knowing full well the clothes are secondhand and (almost) worn out we still make use of them. They can never possess that mystic quality a garment carries when it comes straight from the maker, but neither do we want that. Rather, we wear them because, as Paul says, the whole point is genuinely new clothes are on their way, and the present ones, in all their shabbiness, can perhaps point in that direction!

Ens ut primum cognitum

The journey Deely leads us on continues to throw up powerful vistas helping reinforce the perspective of the present book while mapping its way in the overall context of Western thought. So, let's continue!

If we remain within the Thomistic world around a few more bends in the road we will take in another vital feature, one that will help confirm the Girardian and Heideggerean insights we have begun to develop. It is a concept Deely gleaned from Aquinas, something called *ens ut primum cognitum*—being-as-first-known. It means a primary relationship of the human mind to its world, something which Deely will quickly associate with Heidegger's analysis of human existence in relation to *being*. Being-as-first-known arises apart from the general environment of material things which Deely says is proper also to the animals: "the common material out of which each species of animal constructs its species-specific objective world."[15] *Ens ut primum cognitum* is species-specific to human beings. Yet neither is it any form of metaphysics, any concept of *esse* as such. Rather, it is the primordial horizon proper to human beings in which—according to Aquinas—everything we can learn from experience, including God, is contained confusedly. It is a world which does not submit directly to our understanding but to which we are peculiarly, linguistically and intellectually linked. This is definitely a scholastic conception in as much as built into it is the *esse* of God, in a preconceptual, confused way. In the scholastic world it represents a transcendental condition of awareness, including the ultimate possibility of a thought of God. But the confusion—something Deely describes, in the words of the psychologist William James, as "blooming buzzing confusion"[16]—does not sit easily with a thought of God. In the context of the Girardian primary scene the confusion may easily be understood as generated by violence; it is not simply the lack of focus of an immature eye. The experience necessarily awaits the coming of the primordial sacred to bring cognitive order to an intolerable situation. Moreover, Deely explicitly invokes Heidegger in his explanation, a reference which does not fit with a theistic viewpoint. "With

15. Deely, *Four Ages*, 341–42.
16. Deely, *Four Ages*, 355.

94 THEOLOGY BEYOND METAPHYSICS

Heidegger . . . philosophy for the first time in its long history was forced to begin systematically to thematize, directly and clearly, the profound problem of *ens ut primum cognitum*."[17] Introducing Heidegger once more into this conversation brings us again to his breakthrough ontology and, with that also, the immediate intellectual context in which both Girard and Derrida worked. We sketched just above aspects of Heidegger's thought. It is valuable now to pause a little longer in order to situate ourselves properly in regard to the references Deely is making. Doing so will continue to show how Heidegger's thought at the beginning of the twentieth century fundamentally shaped the terms of debate and can be seen in Deely even to condition the Thomistic ontology he presents. In turn it will strengthen a convergence of Heidegger and Girard I think impossible to avoid.

For Heidegger being is revealed to human existence where the latter is known, as we have mentioned, under the name "Dasein." The German word means literally "*there*-being" (or, more fully and technically, *being-in-the-world*), the place where the event of being is revealed. So, we have the famous statement, "[Dasein is] that entity which in its Being has this very Being as an issue."[18] Encounter with *being* is the very character and nature of Dasein. It is the root structure of human existence as such. In his seminal work *Being and Time*, Heidegger describes this structure with an intensity and verve which is both the mirror and the inverse of Aquinas's. Instead of the massive presence of God as *ipsum esse, existence itself*, there is the impersonal constant of *being*. At the same time—as so many commentators have remarked—many of the dynamics of Christian theology and spirituality seem to be carried over into relationship with *being*. It is an instance of what we have already seen named by Derrida as a "nondogmatic doublet" of religion,[19] and it is the quasi-religious vibrancy yet, at the same time, pagan indifference of the relationship that give Heidegger's work its urgent atheistic character.

The reason why Deely celebrates Heidegger is because of the immediacy of *being* to Dasein—such that it is directly disclosed in human existence. It provides a signal victory over what is known as Cartesian dualism, the teaching of a rigid separation between "inside" and "out," mind and body. This is the division that Deely sees as the major defect of modern thought, a highly regrettable interruption in the emergence of semiotics. We will continue to unpack his complaint below, but for the moment we can see how it is overcome in Heidegger's analysis of human existence and why,

---

17. Deely, *Four Ages*, 342.
18. Heidegger, *Being and Time*, 68, para. 42.
19. See 78, note 21 above.

incidentally, the German philosopher offers such a conclusive break with modern thought. Heidegger's understanding of language is not separate from the manifestation of *being*, such that you would have to construct a secondary bridge between a "thing" and its concept. Speech belongs to a primary reflection of *being* and is not part of a further moment or order. For Deely this is hugely significant, *returning the sign to the direct experience of being*. He then sees the *primum cognitum* as the situation where that happens, the primordial setting which gives the sign its ontological validity. He quotes at length a Thomist scholar who refers to semiotics in connection to the *primum cognitum* and also within an explicitly Heideggerean frame. The result is to place us at quite a striking philosophical juncture—a place where semiotics and ontology share common ground. The thinker Deely quotes is Vincent Guagliardo, who tells us that being-as-first-known "provides an alternative to the approach of either idealism or empiricism, both of which trivialized the question of being."[20]

What he means is that idealism separates us from the world, while empiricism makes our connection to it too naïve and simplistic. Guagliardo overcomes both by introducing semiotics (and thereby anthropology) into the root meaning of Da-sein—the semiotic connected to the ontological. Doing this he also signals a certain open-endedness and possibility of transformation in human existence, rather than its determination by fate. In effect this would be the point where the biblical narrative reinserts itself into Heidegger's atheistic relationship with *being*. If we repeat Deely's full quote from Guagliardo speaking of being-as-first-known, we will see how these elements are present.

> In this context being is not reducible to the human intellect. But neither is it known without the human intellect, so that being is not simply reducible to sensible things either. Being, then, has a peculiar semiotic quality: knowable only to an intelligent being (thus excluding animals) as the properly human way of knowing but not referring (at least in its primary instance or meaning) to the human knower but to otherness. In this primal phenomenon—as Heidegger saw—being "negatives" [nihilates], i.e., expresses an elemental "not," which allows the semiotic chain of meaning to develop beyond any mere "here" or "now," "this" or "that" of the things of experience, as well as to develop beyond the knower in his/her state of actual knowing, opening up the realm of further possibility, further semiosis. All this is to say that "being" is foundational to both the things known and the human knower who knows, to any

20. Guagliardo, "Being and Anthroposemiotics," 51; quoted in Deely, *Four Ages*, 348.

determinate object or interpreting subject. If this be the case, then being serves as the condition without which there would be no anthroposemiotics.[21]

This is really quite an extraordinary statement and in it we reach a major interface of the various strands of argument in this chapter. The description appears very little different from what we have said in previous chapters about the Girardian scene of human meaning, albeit within specifically philosophical parameters. But the moment "semiotic" is introduced, together with its constitutive function within "being," then a window is pushed open toward the primary human scene: that is why Guagliardo speaks of "anthroposemiotics." The writer is dealing with the most primitive factors conditioning specifically human meaning, and "primitive" spills across mutually between a basic philosophical structure and a scene of prehistory. Heidegger's writings have a lot of this spillover quality, although he would be insistent to deny any anthropological reference. But it is always a deconstructive insight to find a cross-effect between departmentally separate zones; and from an evolutionary perspective it makes perfect sense that a core phenomenological structure would repeat prehistoric origins, and vice versa. We can be confident, therefore, of an anthropological decoding of Guagliardo's description of the *primum cognitum*, along with its Heideggerean backdrop.

Being is not known without the human intellect, but neither is it reducible to the intellect. In other words, the opening to "being" is something specifically human, something only a human can access—while, at the same time, it is not to be simply identified with the human mind. The introduction of semiotics marks the dramatic humanity of the situation, the emergence of language or symbol as the scene of *to on*, of "what is." It is in fact the startling breakthrough to semio-ontology: "Being . . . has a peculiar semiotic quality." We are led, therefore, to a further, vital level in our inquiries, where "being" and "sign" are bound together in an indissoluble nexus.

What then is "being" in this light? It is other than the sensible world; indeed it refers to "otherness" as such. At the Girardian level, we could then say that "being" is the dawn of the human world out of the primitive crisis of undifferentiated fighting hominids (prehumans not enclosed within the safe world of animal hierarchy and instinct). This would account for its confusion and its terrifying character. Heidegger's "dread" and its connection to "nothing" easily fit at this point. The dawn of the human world moves rapidly to violence and murder, and neither can these elements be separated from

---

21. Guagliardo, "Being and Anthroposemiotics," 51; quoted in Deely, *Four Ages*, 348–49.

the primitive confusion, emptiness and dread. Altogether, these phenomena belong intrinsically to Girard's "first non-instinctual attention." The content of this attention is the uniquely human, vertiginous grasp of *being*.

At the same time the insight of semiotics contemporaneous with being reflects the Girardian understanding that signs and language are the most immediate concrete product of the crisis and its resolution. Signs, therefore, constitute the most primitive formal realization of "being," capturing and enshrining the new awareness in a word, a gesture, a symbol. There is no *being* without its accompanying sign, because the first significant event—the original murder—contains within itself the concentrating force that makes of the environment—the animal *Umwelt*, as Deely likes to call it—a sudden shocking "other" which necessarily at the same time contains its own electrifying signal of meaning. The founding murder that "informs" the hominid about her world is already the matrix of the sign itself. Everything stands forth in a psychotic separation from the biological norm that obtained previously. It is an altered state stretching out the tissue of sensation into a specifically human "consciousness," one both of horror and its mythologized religious resolution. Girard calls this "the sacred," and its huge psychic weight in the particular group of traumatized-and-scarred-over hominids constitutes the first ground of metaphysics. Signification is born simultaneously with being, and it is entirely logical that actual signs are born out of the event: cries, gestures, and, later, the sacrificial repetition that makes the god once more present. The moment a sign is used suggesting the totality and height of the experience, taking its power reflexively, at a second stage, from the power of the event, then we are in the realm of metaphysics.

As already noted and Guagliardo points out, both *being* and the sign refer in themselves to otherness. The "reality" discovered by the first humans is, so to speak, shot full of holes. The world itself is the "other," rendered present in a sign, yet strange, infinite, congenitally open itself, by virtue of the mysterious, "nihilating" event of the sacred. The tenuous, threatening frame of the victim opens "being" to what is other, because the reality of the event is occluded at the same time as it is affirmed. So, a sign has a given name and identity, but this itself has an emptiness, an otherness, and so requires another sign, and thus sets up an infinite chain of signification both forward and backward. Meaning and signs move forward, prompted by the "elemental not," toward more and more signs to fill the ever-incomplete semioverse. At the same time, they move backward, perchance to recover the abandoned origins, in the depths of human storymaking. As Derrida said, "deferral" (*différance*) is an essential part of meaning.

Once again, therefore, the world is born "ex nihilo" which, in this case—in contrast to Genesis—is *ex violentia*, out of the negation contained in violence. In such an analysis "being" is always a honeycomb land, always demanding more and more signs in which to fulfill its truth hollowed out by the birth trauma of violence. Could this be one of the reasons that Heidegger invented his idiosyncratic language (especially in *Contributions to Philosophy*, which has been accused of willful obscurity and near parody)? A lexicon and syntax that are barely intelligible but pregnant with meaning allow for a kind of boundless semiotics which like a mist fills up all available space.

We have to delay a full response, to this and related issues, to the penultimate chapter, but right now we might anticipate by reaffirming that Heidegger's view of *being* is indeed an authentic revelation of primitive ontology. It arises in stark contrast to the theistic ontology of Aquinas, which itself is a combination of Aristotelian metaphysics and Christian faith. We can reiterate the idea that Greek philosophy is in fact given an unwarranted new lease of life by this strange, unnatural liaison.[22] In the meantime the Christian gospel actually represents a full-blown *new* revelation, a *new* logos of what is, one *realized* semiotically. The Crucified and Risen Messiah is the ultimate other, that which is yet to come, under circumstances and under guises we are yet fully to know, but always in every case as the victim returned to itself, and to us, in love. We come, therefore, full circle and find that *being* cannot possibly be the true basis for the actual existence *of God*, certainly the biblical God. How could the experience of violent mimetic crisis leading to sacrifice give any authentic sense of the God who said, "For as the heavens are higher than the earth, so are my ways higher than your ways and my thoughts than your thoughts" (Isa 55:9)? Onto-theology is indeed a disastrous starting place for theology.

Instead, the starting place for theology is in the semiotic universe, the *semioverse*. Given that signs exist—that is, after they erupt into (*as*) human existence and their version of *being* is before us—then there arrives on the scene of history, apparently from outside its compass, an event with sufficient force to reverse the vector of flight of human sign-making. The deferral of signs that continually skates across the surface of the surrogate victim—in mythology, metaphysics, drama—this movement is given a generatively new, alternative and subversive power. The deep constitution of our sign-making is no longer an ever-oscillating flight toward and *away* from the victim, but becomes instead a life-giving stream of giving and grace *from* the victim. The *ens ut primum cognitum* is remade from within (semio-ontology), by an event which mimics its root construction from

---

22. Gilson, *God and Philosophy*. Obviously, Gilson does not think it unnatural.

the body of the victim but turns inside out its core dynamic. The victim is no longer the passive victim of collective violence, but rather a massively proactive agency of forgiveness and love. So rather than, as before, "being" being formed out of violence and dread, there is a new *ens primum cognitum* in which configuring violence is transformed by and as love.

Its essential character is nonviolent relation and at once the phenomenon of "being" becomes something utterly different, no longer uncanny and dangerous, but urgent with reconciliation and peace. The root constitution of the world is remade, because there is a sign system which holds the ontological space of signs but exactly as its metamorphosis. It's as if a cell should begin its life as cancerous, as always *the same*, self-replicating and *other-negating*, and then be changed by genetic recoding to be ordered *to the other*, to be *other-serving*. Or, in semiotic terms, we begin with a set of signs which construct the other as danger and hatred but then, by an apocalyptic reversal, we are given the significance of the other as reconciliation and peace. The Apostle Paul tell us that the time will come when "prophecies . . . tongues . . . knowledge . . . will come to an end" (1 Cor 13:8), meaning that by means of this relational movement the other will ultimately be encountered entirely as love. At that point the semiotic must disappear and something without words, without signs, take its place. But until that moment it is the work of transformative signs to carry us there.

Here then is the work of theology. We must not be misled to think that by abandoning metaphysics we abandon the power of thought and its ability to reach truth. What is being offered is of much more consequence: it reflects the power of the postmodern situation in which the sign has emerged as the final locus of meaning, and its relationship to being as both genetic and revisable. This makes truth of immensely more interest and import than anything simply speculative. The *existence of God* is not an arid piece of scholastic metaphysics—one deeply compromised from its birth as onto-theology—but the vitality of love erupting in the heart as an impossible primary phenomenon. The heart here is a metonym for the semiotic self, the whole body-self which picks up information on multiple levels and in multiple ways. If we take the semiotic thesis of the Bible at full value, especially the gospels—and, in particular, the nonviolent cross—then it is possible to suggest that there is a set of signals at work in the Bible which emanates from a source otherwise than science or metaphysics and yet, at a primordial, semiotic level, is generatively meaningful. It reaches its true receptor in the whole body-self which at some point discovers its message as fully transformative. It is the emergence of being as love, as nonviolent relation. In which case we have arrived at a place where semiotics takes on its full value as first philosophy for the sake of theology. Or, more accurately, theology itself has altered philosophy, to the point where it has promoted semiotics as first philosophy. In any case, we have arrived at the authentic beginning or *arche* of theology for the sake of new human existence. It is a discovery, not a logical proposition, an encounter, not a deduction—although there is very much evidence for it.

7

Mountain of the Modern

The Way of Ideas

AN EPIC VISION LIKE Deely's sets out to scale all the high peaks of Western thought, so it can claim to have mastered the whole range. One lofty crest he gets to the top of and surveys from its vaulted summit is the mount of modernity. The ascent of this peak is via the twin philosophical routes known as empiricism and rationalism, and Deely associates them both with a final, triumphant path-to-the-top of "idea" or "ideas." It is again beyond our task to represent the whole of his argument, but it's important to provide some general impression given that this material provides Deely's final passage to the necessary breakthrough of semiotics. Many of the names and viewpoints will be broadly familiar to readers here: after all, most of us still have one foot very much in the "modern." What we perhaps don't appreciate is some of difficulties involved in this way of thinking.

It was René Descartes (1596–1650) who gave birth to the thought of "clear and distinct ideas" as the source and guarantor of truth, beginning with the first idea, that of the *thinking self*—perhaps the best-known single formulation of philosophy: the "cogito ergo sum" (*I think, so I must be*). Descartes also considered "God" to be a self-authenticating idea, and in an even purer sense than the "cogito." The idea of a perfect being cannot be derived from an imperfect mind, thus there must be an actual "God" at the source of the idea that represents such a being. This idea/being is implied, by way of contrast, in my very thought of myself as an imperfect being.

In presenting these ideas Descartes deliberately and systematically forswore any appeal to the massive edifice of scholastic Aristotelian philosophy which had dominated medieval thought. In tandem with all the prominent ecclesiastical thinkers of the period, especially Aquinas, Aristotle constituted the universally acknowledged "authority." Descartes's brutal break with the past, and the method of his break, was astonishing and astonishingly successful. In place of the piled-high and convoluted skeins of argument that represented scholastic thinking he offered a single, sweeping blade cutting through the lot and, as it seemed, to the heart of the matter. Standing just behind and giving confidence to his knife's sweep was Galileo (1564–1642) and his new vision of the heavens, which had done so much to discredit Aristotelian cosmology. Galileo worked by direct observation and experiment, discovering through his telescope the mountains of the moon, the phases of Venus, the moons of Jupiter, all discrediting the perfect luminous spheres of Aristotle's heavens. Descartes published his famous *Discours de la méthode* (*Discourse on Method*), containing his argument of the "cogito," in 1637, just four years after Galileo had been condemned by the Inquisition. In it, Descartes gave as one of his rules of thought "never to accept anything as true that I did not plainly know to be such . . . and to include nothing more in my judgments than what presented itself to my mind so clearly and so distinctly that I had no occasion to call it in doubt."[1] The individual mind and its vision are thus the final and authoritative court of appeal for truth. The atmosphere in which Descartes presented his thought was one of a bright new immediacy of intelligible truth. The dawn of rationalism had arrived.

However, although there seemed a natural affinity between the scientific rigor of Galileo and the thought of Descartes, the experimental method suggested an entirely different basis for truth from ideas, that is, the physical facts plainly made known to the senses. A near contemporary of Descartes, John Locke, reacted forcefully against the all-conquering Frenchman and set out what he saw as the foundation of what can be known to be found only in empirical sensation—not the self-reflections of the mind. According to Locke, the content of human understanding is either the ideas we get straight from sensation or those we derive by reflecting on the mind's own working with the materials of sensation. But immediately, if at a hidden level, there is a tremendous difficulty, and it is at this point that Deely's overall semiotic argument comes rushing to relevance. If sensation is the basis for what we know, but sensation is itself only known in the internal perceptions of the thinking self, then by what guide or meter do we have any notion of what actually *produced* the sensation? Of what actually *is* the case? This is an objection that both Descartes and David Hume understood, and the latter thought insuperable. Hume points out, plainly and bluntly, that "the mind has never anything present to it but the perceptions, and cannot possibly reach any experience of their connection with objects. The supposition of such a connection is,

1. Descartes, *Discourse on Method*, 11.

therefore, without any foundation in reasoning."[2] In a puff of rational smoke the external world disappears!

A good illustration of this overall problem could be the movie *The Matrix*. The film's eponymous theme is a computer-generated "real world" which is in fact just streaming computer code connected to millions of sedated humans incubated for the electric energy they produce while they're kept happy with the "information" ported into their heads. The iconic picture of ribbons of green digits on a black screen shows the viewer the final "real" composition of that world, a vast array of flickering combinations of code. This could be a worthy symbol or logo for the empiricist world, one which provides a visual illustration of the philosophical necessity it is reduced to: the objective reality behind sensation is simply a conceptual or perceptual creation, something for which some mind (the "Architect" of the movie, or, philosophically, the human brain itself) first wrote the code.

Meanwhile, the supposed objects are just not there. The dilemma moved Immanuel Kant (1724–1804) to create his very special *Critique of Pure Reason* in order to support the scientific discoveries which were burgeoning all around him. If we are unsure of the connection to the "real world," then how can we justify all the claims of science to tell us, precisely, about such a world? Kant said it was Hume's skepticism which awoke him from his "dogmatic slumber," meaning that you can no longer take it for granted that there is a real world out there, or at least what it looks like. He thus created a philosophy of reason or understanding which built a true world for us through *a priori* "concepts" while the "thing-in-itself," although existent, was unknowable. Thus, the connections of time and space, of number, causality, etc., are "transcendentally" real because our mind makes them so in respect of how things appear. How they actually are we don't know, but we can be secure that external things are really there because without them the understanding would have nothing to work on. According to his classic aphorism, "Perception without conception is blind; conception without perception is empty." Thus, objective reality remains a necessary but totally opaque "limit case" behind and beyond our perception, which is only able to see because of the mind's conceptual apparatus.

We realize, therefore, that Kant's solution is simply another (and heightened) form of the empiricist paradox: sensation connects us to things, but only the mind tells us anything about them. This, for Deely, is "the way of ideas," the last leg to the top of the rationalist mountain shrouded in the impenetrable mists of the mind. He will continue from there to make his descent

---

2. Hume, *Enquiry Concerning Human Understanding*, sec. 12, pt. 1, para. 12; quoted in Deely, *Four Ages*, 532.

in order to get to another peak where he can find a truly clear perspective on the whole panorama. This next summit is the viewpoint of semiotics, the thought of the sign as ontologically related to what is signified.

Giambattista Vico

But before we follow him along this other, perhaps more postmodern road, it is worth repeating a quote he makes from another thinker moving in that same eighteenth-century modern milieu. It is from Giambattista Vico (1668–1744) and it sums up nicely the overall turn that philosophy was taking. But right at the moment Deely introduces Vico there appears a vital gap in Deely's own response. Somehow, he fails to mention the quite profound contribution that Vico himself made to semiotics. In fact, the silence at this point is quite deafening. It alerts us to a serious flaw in Deely's general uptake of the question, one that has been barely noticeable up to this point, until he is dealing indeed with the modern period. Let us repeat the quote from Vico and then we will be able to make a sketch of what is missing and find a clear reflection of what is at stake.

> In the night of thick darkness enveloping the earliest antiquity, so remote from ourselves, there shines the eternal and never failing light of a truth beyond all question: that the world of civil society has certainly been made by men, and that its principles are therefore to be found within the modifications of our own human mind. Whoever reflects on this cannot but marvel that the philosophers should have bent all their energies to the study of the world of nature, which, since God made it, He alone knows; and that they should have neglected the study of the world of nations, or civil world, which, since men had made it, men could come to know. This aberration was a consequence of that infirmity of the human mind by which, immersed and buried in the body, it naturally inclines to take notice of bodily things, and finds the effort to attend to itself too laborious; just as the bodily eye sees all objects outside itself but needs a mirror to see itself.[3]

This passage is given by Deely as illustration of the Kantian shift toward the human subject—Vico is seen as endorsing critical or transcendental philosophy because he is focused on the eye, using a mirror to see it, rather than on the objects which the eye sees. There can be no doubt that this is an essential shift of the modern age, the self-reflection of the

3. Vico, *New Science*, para. 331.

human subject. But Deely refers only to Kantian philosophy of reason and understanding, and completely ignores Vico's vital concern which is human society and the signs that go with it. Vico is a fervent critic of Descartes and the pure philosophy of ideas. While not excluding the ideas of rationality he sees an entirely different generation of truth also at work, something a good deal more mythic and opaque. Primitive human beings were "poets," meaning that they created a broad world of signs, including language, customs, and law. As he says, there is "the never failing light of a truth beyond all question: that the world of civil society has . . . been made by men." This is Vico's principle, to be placed on a par and opposite to Descartes's "cogito." It says *verum esse ipsum factum*, "truth is precisely what is [or has been] made." At once we are in a much denser, darker world than Descartes's ideas of pure reason. We are in the world of human culture and its multifarious expressions beginning to be uncovered across the globe by European exploration and colonization.

It's strikingly obvious that Vico's fundamental insight is the same as Girard's—the world of human beings is made by human beings. So, it also seems strange that Girard never employed Vico in his argument. Vico's dynamic sequence to human societies also sits close to Girard; he posits a three-age scheme of cultural stages: ages of gods, heroes and men. He goes on to distinguish these by the type of signs that were used in each stage. In the first, human signs were concrete and physical, using glyphs on stones and walls, tokens and gestures. The next gave rise to metaphor and metonym, actual languages and the imaginative realities they made possible. Finally, the age of men gives birth to reason and rationally organized societies.[4]

How significant that Vico marks his human changes by changes in the sign system, by semiotics! It is probably Vico's greatest contribution to the science, the suggestion that our signs change as we do, or vice versa. He also points out that our humanity has been guided by what he calls "imaginative universals," encompassing both the earlier stages. These are signs belonging to the storytelling and metaphoric levels of human "poetry" or "truth-making."[5] The whole picture that emerges is how our traditional sign system is not about rational analysis of the world but about imaginative manufacture of the world, and this fits very closely with Girard's sense of original myth and mythology. At the same time, Vico also sets the Bible outside his general frame of human culture, seeing it as independent from the three stages elsewhere.[6] Certainly he did this to avoid unwelcome atten-

---

4. Trabant, *Vico's New Science*, 25–26.
5. Verene, *Vico's Science of Imagination*, 65–95.
6. Trabant, *Vico's New Science*, 24.

tions from the church. But it has the collateral effect of placing the Bible in a different category from the cultures of the nations. Vico points out that the Hebrews lacked the altar of divination—that is, sacrifice as a semiotic device in which the meaning of the world can be read.[7] This would clearly fit with the Girardian understanding of the Bible as fostering a nonsacrificial (nonviolent) meaning of human life. It follows naturally within the Vician scheme that the Hebrew tradition must therefore have its own semiosis, or built-in sign-making with which to make the world.

A theory of the development of signs, of imaginative universals and mythic, metaphoric qualities fills a space abandoned and disregarded by Cartesian rationalism. The full detail of Vico's arguments does not matter as much as his profound insight that the tools of human knowledge, including signs, have been birthed and developed over the age-long journey of human societies. In claiming his insights he makes his own pathway of inquiry parallel and equal to Descartes's solitary musing—forswearing all previous knowledge and setting out to gather the information that only presents itself to him directly from the traditions of the nations.[8] He underlines with this gesture a totally new field of reflection and knowledge; a *new science* is born. For Deely not to recognize this *other* intellectual pathway hints that he keeps close his own form of rationalism, albeit the scholastic type. The violent, chaotic origins of humanity intuited in Vico's ages of "gods and heroes" does not fit well with the ordered, hierarchical world aspired to by the Middle Ages and any of its subsequent admirers. But a theory of signs has to ask Vico's questions—where do our signs come from?—don't they themselves have a history?—rather than simply concentrating on the present-tense, synchronic function of our sign system. We have strengthened these questions enormously along the way by presenting the thought of Girard and, in tandem, a Girardian reading of Heidegger. We are in a good position, therefore, to understand the *signum significans*, what Girard would call the ur-sign, the original sign that gave birth to human meaning as such, and to all the other signs after it. However, from the Cartesian and Humean position it is the status of all the other signs after it, and their connection to the "real world," that remains the true question—the question of epistemology. Deely now looks in this direction too, but as he does he brings us directly to a late-medieval thought which he believes has the capacity to resolve the issue.

It is the content of this latter thought which is perhaps the greatest and most enduring result of Deely's opus. The status of *relation* as a fundamental

---

7. Kunze, *Thought and Place*, 49.
8. Trabant, *Vico's New Science*, 7.

feature of semiotics allows us to answer both levels of the question. The ursign birthed in an original relation of violence, and then all the subsequent signs, all carry in themselves practical and real relations to the world. But these relations must themselves be open to revision, because signs are not metaphysics. When the sign is a relation and the relation is a sign there is always the possibility of new semiosis, of new meaning.

Reality and Relation

Deely is a thoroughgoing Latinist. What this means is not just that he liberally sprinkles Latin phrases throughout his discussions—above all from his revered Aquinas, the medieval saint's Latin like "miles of the clearest water"[9]—but that he believes the Latin age reached an intellectual clarity which has been unjustly disparaged by its overweening successors. Deely's claim is that there is a crucial epistemological sophistication to Latin thought, and that it arrived at its full development in a semiotic discovery and thus an opening through into the postmodern. In consequence the whole Modern period is an unfortunate deviation from a philosophical opportunity that very few of the moderns even knew existed. However, as we have noted, Deely himself deviates away from the turn to the human subject so characteristic of the Modern period and central also to Girardian anthropology. The self-investigation of Vico's "bodily eye" is essential to any final account of our sign systems and what they may or may not achieve in the business of truth. Nevertheless, Deely's long trek to postmodern semiotics is by no means wasted. By making a bridge between the Latin mind and semiotics he is able to introduce a core concept which will prove invaluable, *especially* when we consider the role of the human subject in making its truth. If the fundamental character of the sign is *relation*, then the mode in which and by which human subjects establish their semiotic relation to the world will have a profound effect on the nature of the world they perceive.

Latin thought was realist in spirit and concept. It knew nothing of the modern division of the mind and the world. Rather, a fundamental tenet was that truth and being were convertible, that is, *what is* is coextensive with the rational and the knowable.[10] However, the final achievement of this thought, according to Deely, was to see ultimately that the convertibility of truth and being was always mediated—in *signs*. So it is that Deely's concept of postmodernism is one where semiotics comes to a long overdue, triumphant prominence *and* its results connect us to the real world. Thus, the

9. Deely, *Four Ages*, 663n149.
10. Deely, *Four Ages*, 569.

Kantian critical separation from actual things is overcome through the work of the sign. In a long complex sentence Deely guides us to the conclusion; I include it all for the sake of its summative character.

> If indeed experience begins with sensations, as empiricists claim . . . ; and if the formation of sensations as perceptions requires, as all agree, the formation of images by the mind on the basis of which the sensible qualities are further presented *as* this or that; and if the understanding of what is perceived also requires the elaboration by the mind of ideas or concepts in order for what is objectively perceived to be understood in this rather than that manner . . . ; and if, in Peirce's formula, as Aquinas . . . and others of the Latin milieu had argued, "all thought is in signs," meaning that all concepts—all images and all ideas—are related to their objects as signs to significates, and every thought must be interpreted in another thought; then indeed the whole of experience, the being proper to it, from its primitive origins in sensation to its elaboration in perception and further development in understanding, all experience from its lowliest origins in sense to its highest attainments in theoretical understanding, is a continuous network, tissue, or web of sign relations.[11]

The web of connection runs from beginning to end, and this is Deely's objective, to restore the tissue of connectivity between the mind and the world, *via* the work of the sign. To establish the matter Deely proposes a concept which he believes the Latin age had been working toward across the course of its long centuries. The point of arrival comes in the thought of the seventeenth-century Portuguese thinker John Poinsot (1589–1644), the one who, according to Deely, reaches the greatest degree of clarification of the meaning of *signum* in the Latin tradition. The concept proposed is not easy in its technical sense, depending on a distinction between relations in the material world and relations of a purely conceptual character and yet brought together under the heading of relation as such. It sounds like a typical scholastic idea, worked out over a thousand distinctions and providing a purely abstract solution. But because we are dealing with relation to the world and the fact that the sign makes that possible there is reality to this particular thought, one of exceptional value and vigor.

As Deely insists, the Latins had a tremendous sense of relationship running through all things; indeed, "everything has to be explained in terms of something besides itself."[12] On the one hand, they derived from Aristotle the

---

11. Deely, *Four Ages*, 534, italics original.
12. Deely, *Four Ages*, 423.

thought of "substance" as a stand-alone reality, the rock on which all thought was built. On the other, substance itself had to be explained in terms of categories or "accidents," of conditions and qualities that located it in being. One of these categories was itself "relation," which Aristotle defined as a feature whose essential condition of existence is "being toward another." It is, of course, a secondary feature to substance, but under pressure of the question of sign it forces its way to the fore; and this is the real story, as the newspaper people say. The concept proposed is "ontological relation" (*relatio secundum esse*), a character of being as such, or, rather, being-as-relation.

To try to understand the concept let's play a thought game.

Imagine all the physical relations of the world as a near-infinite mesh or lattice in a two-dimensional plane or surface. This itself is a highly simplified diagram with each crossing point, node or "substance" shown connected only to four other points, but representing features like time, space, quality, quantity, all the relative matters that help explain what, where, how, why something is what it is. Now, let us introduce a third-dimension, by placing another version of the same lattice in a vertical connection to each point in the horizontal mesh, so that each node or point is now connected to a vertical scheme. This time its neighbors in the mesh might be the same or very different, for they can also move around and change frequently. This other, vertical mesh, then, is the set of signifying or semiotic relations possible across the field of existence in the real world, repeating the real world but as signs. Each vertical set of neighbors to the horizontal node or "substance" is a sign or set of signs by which it is communicating and communicated to everything around. Once we see this, we see that there really is an infinite field of relations possible. Relationality or pure relation becomes a mind-boggling phenomenon, connecting the world infinitely, both on the material and perceptual level. This is ontological relation. If you think about ontological relation, it does not define itself by a "what," but *relation as such*. Indeed, the very "substance" of the node or point can change according to the relations around it. Thus, relation becomes a way of being, or being-as-relation. *Relation begins to supersede "things" as real.*

There follows here a representative statement from Poinsot, given in a bare-bones fashion. It may sound a little like scholastic gobbledygook, but it is given like this to keep it to essentials. It serves as the final conclusion of the process of Latin thought, bringing us to the pivotal notion. The essential point is that what signs in nature (tracks in the snow) and signs in the mind (concepts) have in common is the ontological feature and character of relation.

> We speak here of ontological relation . . . because we are discussing the sign in general, as it includes equally the natural and the social sign . . . And for this reason, the rationale *common* to signs cannot be one which pertains exclusively to the order of physical being, not even that of a physical relation as such. By the same reasoning, the common rationale of all signs could indeed be that of ontological relation as such . . . according to the point made by St. Thomas in the *Summa theologiae*, I, q. 28, art. 1. . . to wit, that only in the case of these things which exist toward another is found some mind-independent relation and some mind-dependent relation . . . which . . . is called a relation according to the way it has being (an ontological relation) because it is purely a relation and does not import anything absolute.[13]

The basic takeaway, then, is that both natural signs and conceptual signs depend on relation as such. It is an "ontological relation" because its being and sole nature is to be toward another. Deely underlines that the sign itself is not a thing, an object we name a sign. "[O]bjects are called signs not because of anything intrinsic to what they are but because of something sustained by and yet *over and above them* . . . [T]he sign is constituted in its being a sign . . . by an invisible relation."[14] In which manner, we have arrived at the end term of scholastic thought on signs, a doctrine of a world in relation, including both the "external world" and the mind.

It does not take much to realize we are in a distinctly non-Kantian universe—one, in contrast, where the "thing-in-itself" is bound to the perceiver by a relation through a sign or a sign that is a relation. It also suggests to us that the character of the relation can change while still being a relation. This perhaps is the most distinctive (if not startling) feature of this level of relation—because it is relation as such (not according to any specific modality) it must be able in some degree to change in significance while not letting go of core connection. This thought will remain with us as we gain more traction in the contemporary developments in semiotics.

Meanwhile, we can summarize: relation for the Latins so runs through all things and constitutes all things that they give it a status in its own right and for its own sake, one that covers both physical relation and relation in

---

13. Poinsot, *Tractatus de Signis*, Book 1, Question 1, 117/28; quoted by Deely, *Four Ages*, 473–74.

14. Deely, *Augustine and Poinsot*, 68–69. As Deely also comments, "[T]he sign has no existence in itself, but only in what other things become. It is the lattice, not the objective terms, of experience" (*Human Use of Signs*, 21). He is also led to posit some sense in which signs are operative outside of the purview of cognitive or sensate beings, as a feature of the universe itself. He calls this "physiosemiosis"; see Deely, *Impact on Philosophy of Semiotics*, 8–9.

thought. Indeed, it is ultimately the shared status of both these areas under the heading of *sign* that forces the idea of ontological relation, relation-in-itself. In this case the whole world becomes a complex of multilevel relations in which each level potentially connects to or repeats another. A relation can, therefore, be discovered to be a relation in more than one sense, bringing other levels of reality into relation with the first level of relation. For example, smoke is a sign of fire, because it has/is a relation to fire and its human sign-function repeats/mimics that relation in its own right. (Ultimately, this is a theory of *mind-in-relation* or *mind-as-relation*—a relation that depends on the relationality of everything else.[15]) The problem, however, is that this might sound like a world in which everything possible is true and there is no actual falsehood; and for obvious reasons this has to be denied. It is related to what Deely calls "the possibility of being mistaken," and we will return to it shortly.[16] For the moment we are in the presence of a complex physical and mental universe where the sign is in ontological relation (relation as such) with the signified.

---

15. Dramatically, and yet consistently enough, Poinsot traces his thought about relation to Aquinas's doctrine of the Trinity in the *Summa theologiae*. The Persons of the Trinity are able to subsist as purely relative beings because of the mode of being *of relation*. In other words, the ontology of relation in the Trinity can be taken as a pattern of relation in all things. Even so, the intensely relational doctrine of the Trinity, evolved over a millennium of Christian formulation, acts as a matrix of semiotic thought. As the three Persons are in communion, so are all things. Deely, *Four Ages*, 462–63.

16. Deely, *Four Ages*, 636.

8
Postmodernity: Semiotic Triumph

Charles Sanders Peirce

THE ONTOLOGICAL INTEGRITY OF the semiosphere—where signs belong to the real—is Deely's core intuition, but for us what is of interest here is not so much integrity as transformation, not so much epistemology as eschatology. To get to a full theoretical level which can underpin this interest, it will be important to pursue Deely's "Silk Road" to its term, gathering as much warrant as possible, telling us that, indeed, transformation has to be the ultimate meaning of semiotics. Where, then, does Deely's road end? If we relate the metaphor to its geographical inspiration, then it comes to an end not in the capitals of Europe, nor (going the other way) in the Far East, in a city in China, but, rather, it finds its destination across the oceans, in—of all places—the New World, America! Bertrand Russell said of Charles Sanders Peirce, "Beyond doubt . . . he was one of the most original minds of the later nineteenth century, and certainly the greatest American thinker ever."[1] It is Peirce's semiotics that are the storied point of arrival of Deely's long pilgrimage.

It is correct to say "storied" in connection to Peirce, both following the "Silk Road" theme and because individually he really was an amazing figure, someone who never allowed convention or established opinion to determine his style of thought and the places it should lead him. For most of his life he worked as a scientist, employed intermittently by the U.S. Coastal Survey and Harvard Observatory. From 1879 to 1884 he was a nontenured professor in logic at Johns Hopkins University, the only academic post he ever occupied. The sole full-length book he authored and saw published in his lifetime was a monograph on the applications of spectrographic

---

1. Russell, *Wisdom of the West*, 276.

methods to astronomy (1878). Nevertheless, he wrote voluminously for scientific and scholarly journals, and his published work today (anthologies, collected papers, etc.) runs to 12,000 pages, while his unpublished manuscripts total 100,000 pages. Peirce made several striking discoveries in the fields of mathematics, symbolic logic and statistics; he foresaw that logical operations could be performed by electrical switches, thus anticipating digital computers. Yet, at the same time, he read the Latin scholastics, especially Duns Scotus, and in quite a strong sense he could be understood as a medieval realist. (Hence some of Deely's enthusiasm.) In philosophical terms he was self-taught. During his freshman year at Harvard he began reading a little of Kant's *Critique of Pure Reason* every day in the original German. After three years he finished his reading and concluded the whole enterprise was voided by the work's "puerile logic." He never changed his opinion of the *Critique* for the rest of his life.[2] After that he dedicated himself to study and research in logic—a subject which for him was a branch of a general theory of signs, semiotics, or, as he called it, "semeiotic."[3]

An immediately salient feature of Peircian semiotics is its triadic structure. In fact, the presence of triads in his thinking is so embedded and multiple it amounts to a semiotics-approaching-a-metaphysics. There are many thinkers who use a triadic structure, including Vico, as we have seen, Hegel, Comte, and James George Frazer, to mention a few. The attraction to a threefold goes back at least as far as Joachim of Fiore (c. 1135–1202) and his three ages—of the Old Testament, New Testament, and Holy Spirit. The imprint of the Christian Holy Trinity is explicit at this level, and there must be considered once again the effect of biblical language and signs on culture and meaning in general. For Peirce, however, triadic relationships belong to language or semiotics itself, as we shall see. There can be no effective sign unless it refers us forward to a further element which makes the dyadic structure (sign and object) intelligible. The third is not a mere addition; it belongs structurally in the overall sign, and the effect of meaning would not take place without it. There is something triadic in our actual process of thinking, and for Peirce—as a realist—this eventually seems to suggest something triadic in the overall structure of the universe. In other words, the "third" suggests inevitably an "other" which is the source of human meaning, an excess which exercises in each case its living effect on everything and determines its nature. The following gives us a sense of Peirce's view here and at the same time the complex and vivid tenor of his mind and thought.

---

2. See Burch, "Charles Sanders Peirce," sec. 1, "Brief Biography."
3. For Peirce's life, see Brent, *Charles Sanders Peirce*.

[T]he problem of how genuine triadic relationships first arose in the world is a better, because more definite, formulation of the problem of how life first came about; and no explanation has ever been offered except that of pure chance, which we must suspect to be no explanation, owing to the suspicion that pure chance may itself be a vital phenomenon. In that case, life in the physiological sense would be due to life in the metaphysical sense. Of course, the fact that a given individual has been persuaded of the truth of a proposition is the very slenderest possible argument for its truth; nevertheless, the fact that I, a person of the strongest possible physicistic prejudices, should, as the result of forty years of questionings, have been brought to the deep conviction that there is some essentially and irreducibly other element in the universe than pure dynamism may have sufficient interest to excuse my devoting a single sentence to its expression. For you may be sure that I had reasons that withstood severe, not to say hostile criticism; and if I live to do it, I shall embody them in a volume.[4]

He didn't, but this brief suggestion will stand as a better formulation than what we might imagine he would have proposed if he did write that volume. For what Peirce is mooting here, I think, is not something like Aristotelian philosophy—a metaphysical scheme of efficient and final causality. Rather, he is talking as a scientist-semiotician, and the hint he has received about the universe he has gotten from the very structure of meaning as he has researched it. If life is logic or meaning—he might say—then perhaps meaning is also life: perhaps the open-ended and yet continually motivated research of science tokens, whether it likes it or not, this "irreducibly other element." And the "other" it is summoned by and to (Derrida's specter?) is a necessary and wonderful part of all experienced and signified life. From the discussion of the present study we know that in the first instance meaning looks back to the primary scene for its ability to make reality in a sign. But the deliberate obliqueness of Peirce's words suggests he is struggling beyond this, shying away from any dynamic of violence that might impose itself. Is he not already under the impact of a peculiarly semiotic, nonmetaphysical thought of the "other element in the universe"?

The best-known and most powerful triadic formulation Peirce gave in relation to the sign is the *sign/object/interpretant*. Here the "sign" corresponds roughly to Saussure's signifier and the "interpretant" to Saussure's signified. Peirce accepts a more re-presentational role in the sign (i.e., it is not as arbitrary as in Saussure, but effectively connected to the object); however, that role

---

4. Peirce, *Collected Papers*, 6.322; quoted in Deely, *Four Ages*, 630.

is swiftly swallowed up by the mercurial, commutable function of the interpretant. Here is the uniquely dynamic and open-ended character of Peirce's semiotics. "A Sign is anything which is related to a Second thing, its Object, in respect to a Quality, in such a way as to bring a Third thing, its Interpretant, into relation to the same Object, and that in such a way as to bring a Fourth into relation to that Object in the same form, *ad infinitum*."[5]

One interpretant begs into existence another, and so on endlessly. Immediately we are led to suspect that the interpretant must depend on relation. The connection of the sign to the object would be one of lockstep identity if it were not in fact an open-ended relation. The fact that it is a relation means that the meaning of the sign can grow or change, and thus there is always an interpretant needed. Peirce's triadic structure is the first semiotics to explicitly build in the dynamic of relation. As such it is a huge leap forward. Moreover, in the light of the interpretant representation is not strictly representation. It is itself much more like relation, one which Peirce believes leads forward progressively.

> The meaning of a representation can be nothing but a representation. In fact, it is nothing but the representation itself conceived as stripped of irrelevant clothing. But this clothing never can be completely stripped off [rendering a Cartesian idea]; it is only changed for something more diaphanous. So there is an infinite regression here. Finally, the interpretant is nothing but another representation to which the torch of truth is handed along; and as representation, it has its interpretant again. Lo, another infinite series.[6]

There can be no such thing, therefore, as a final statement. Even if the next interpretant in the sequence is not given in the words of the present speaker it happens in the actual world. The stream of semiosis can result in actions, in changes of emotional state, in revolutions. Meanwhile, the physical universe itself also carries on a kind of conversation through signs, placing human communication in a much wider and coherent framework. This is where Peirce's semiotics continues the scholastic understanding of signs as phenomena common to the physical world and to specifically human communication. There is no rigid Cartesian division between mind and world. He speaks in fact as if the universe is having a giant conversation with itself.

---

5. Peirce, *Collected Papers*, 2.92; quoted in Deely, *Four Ages*, 635.
6. Peirce, *Collected Papers*, 1.339.

> The action of a sign generally takes place between two parties, the *utterer* and the *interpreter*. They need not be persons; for a chameleon and many kinds of insects and even plants make their living by uttering signs, and lying signs, at that. Who is the utterer of signs of the weather . . . ? However, every sign certainly conveys something of the general nature of thought, if not from a mind, yet from some repository of ideas, of significant forms, and if not to a person, yet to something capable of somehow "catching on" . . . that is, of receiving not merely a physical, nor even merely a psychical dose of energy, but a significant meaning. In that modified, and as yet very misty, sense, then, we may continue to use the italicized words [*utterer* and *interpreter*].[7]

But what then of *truth*? If everything is a sign, then clearly, as he suggests, there can be false, misleading signs. And human beings, preeminently, may be misinformed by their signs. In all this fizzing mass of communication, how do we sift the true from the false, truth from illusion? Peirce remains adamant that we are in contact with a real world (we are *not* in the Matrix). But *at the same time* that real world is always given in a sign (and so to some degree we *are* in the Matrix!). The universe is the semioverse, just as the semioverse is the universe.

> [W]e have *direct experience of things in themselves*. Nothing can be more completely false than that we can experience only our own ideas . . . Our knowledge of things in themselves is entirely *relative*, it is true; but all experience and all knowledge is of that which is, independently of being represented . . . At the same time, no proposition can relate, or even thoroughly pretend to relate, to any object otherwise than as that object is represented.[8]

There is an apparent contradiction here—that we have knowledge of things in themselves, and yet it is always also a *re*-presentation. But it only appears a contradiction because we do not grasp the medieval scholastic understanding of the sign, which Peirce inherited. This is Deely's understanding of Peirce's position. What is critical is the "ontological relation," the nature of the relation between the sign and the referent according to "the way relation has being." Relation maintains the reality of the link between sign and referent even as it allows that link to be relayed/represented in (possibly) changing ways. The sign comprises a relation, whose term in some sense is

---

7. Robin, *Annotated Catalogue*, MS 318, ISP nos. 205–6; quoted in Deely, *Four Ages*, 629.

8. Peirce, *Collected Papers*, 6.95.

always the real, but which itself, *as relation*, also constitutes the real. Peirce embraced this dynamic notion of reality, hence the vital role of the triad as always containing both the object and the interpretant.

But again, how does this help in the quest for truth? For the question remains, what is *really* real? Or, if, as Peirce says, our knowledge of things is entirely "relative," then where does this leave the human creature facing the "not so real"? What about systems of oppression, destructive relationships, religious or ideological schemes claiming our loyalty, and/ or the lonely search for personal truth? As a human problem it is acute. It's the question classically expressed by Augustine in the *Confessions*: "I have become a question to myself!" At this point Peirce offers us a sense of process or evolution as the only ultimate judge or arbiter of the true, the only final determinant of the real. And it is an evolution that can only be experienced collectively, in a human community as such. For a man and woman to come to a decision about the real it has to happen in relation to a totality of human experience and its value.

> The real . . . is that which, sooner or later, information and reasoning would finally result in, and which is therefore independent of the vagaries of me and you. Thus, the very origin of the conception of reality shows that this conception essentially involves the notion of a COMMUNITY, without definite limits, and capable of a definitive increase of knowledge. And so those two series of cognition—the real and the unreal—consist of those which, at a time sufficiently future, the community will always continue to reaffirm; and of those which, under the same conditions, will ever after be denied.[9]

It seems at this point we have arrived at something approaching an adequate conceptual scheme for the semiotic shift, that is, for change in human meaning in its formal structure and character, and we have Peirce to thank for it. If signs blink on and off like a trillion stars we can only hope to sift through them, align them, organize them, as a human community numbered ourselves in the billions, and in multiple generations. However, if the human community is itself a panoply of signs, if every person, indeed every thought, is a sign, then there arises one core exigency. Human self and its identity must first and foremost become a question to itself, so that there can be a primary set of questions guiding all the others. The primary signs to be investigated are in fact ourselves—only then do we have any chance of correctly responding to all the other signs, of knowing them accurately, authentically, and not distorting them prejudicially and

9. Peirce, *Collected Papers*, 5.311; capitals in original.

destructively—beginning with hostile confusion between human signs ever seeking to impose themselves on one other. The Girardian revelation of original, mimetic violence must intervene at a determinative level before we can truly assess and evaluate the universe of signs around us.

The nature of this case is enormously different from how we might view the matter if we were dealing with the human subject as pure Cartesian cogito. How could you possibly trust a metaphysics as egotistic and godlike as that to reveal and spread the possibility of truth? What chance would this self of pure ideas have of bringing to harmony the chaos of similar Olympian egos spread throughout the world, all in mimetic competition with each other? A rationalist Cartesian worldview would have to throw its figurative hands in the air and despair: the world of self-enclosed thinkers is irredeemable. In contrast, an anthropology of sign-using creatures impacted collectively by a transforming semiosis—one that possesses its own dynamic and is able to multiply its signs progressively—is much more credible. Such a source has the ability to switch off and on the panoply of signs until there is found, ultimately, a full signification of peace, the living possibility of a semioverse of love. Both the logic of transformative semiotics and the evidence of its concrete existence make this understanding of the human condition absolutely preferable to modern rationalism. Moreover, Peirce himself seems to have envisioned something of this nature.

Thirdness and Evolution

As mentioned, Peirce has multiple examples of triadic structure in his thinking. One of the most startling and revolutionary is his proposal for a new set of "categories," the classic philosophical scheme, going back to Aristotle, presenting the "transcendental" divisions or forms by which anything at all can be known and identified. The audacious simplification which reduces ten categories (Aristotle), or twelve (Kant), to three, witnesses both to the transformation that semiotics brings to philosophy and to the theme of transformation itself in Peirce's understanding of the world. For it fits with how we have just described the concept of "the real" in Peirce, the thought of a growing, maturing semiotic universe. In the same vein, it can be seen to repeat fundamentally the line of analysis we have threaded between Girard and Heidegger via the *primum cognitum*. The coherence of the overall reflection strongly reinforces the argument of semiotic transformation at the core of the present book.

Peirce's categories are named, with disarming simplicity, *firstness, secondness, thirdness*. They provide a logical scheme for the way in which we construct meaningful predicates. Essentially, Peirce is saying (as so often) that all thought resolves into a triple operation as it embraces the universe around us. *Firstness* "precedes all synthesis and all differentiation; it has no unity and no parts. It cannot be articulately thought: assert it, and it has already lost its characteristic innocence; for assertion always implies a denial of something else. Stop to think of it, and it has flown! What the world was to Adam on the day he opened his eyes to it, before he had drawn any distinctions, or had become conscious of his own existence—that is first . . ."[10] It's not hard to recognize here the confusion of *ens ut primum cognitum*, which is, in turn, something stretching into the next category. *Secondness* is the stage and function that awakens the mind from its dream, introducing actual individual things, structures and relationships. It is itself the object of the sign and brings us immediately and indivisibly to *thirdness*, the interpretant, and the sorting out of relations into a semiotic whole. All these things happen with a near simultaneity.

Deely provides a penetrating commentary, while introducing a compelling image: our collective understanding is a living tissue or web which "catches" our reality from the natural wildness of a surrounding world.

> Peirce's categorial scheme is neither a scheme designed to express exclusively what is there in the objective world prior to the scheme and independently of it, as Aristotle's was, nor is it a scheme designed to express exclusively necessary aspects of the mind's own working in developing discursively the content of experience, as Kant's was. Peirce's scheme is designed to express the mixture and interweave of mind-dependent and mind-independent relations which constitute human experience in its totality as a network of sign relations, a semiotic web . . . This web is a living tissue of relations. It not only ties together nature and culture, but it does so in a community of understanding, a "community of inquirers." As the spider depends on its web to catch its food, so the understanding sustains and nourishes itself from what its web of relations catches of reality and transforms into culture.[11]

The simultaneity of the whole process can be seen to dovetail neatly with Girard's claim of the organic birth of culture from primary crises, while returning us once more to the Heideggerean-Girardian nexus. The "firstness" of mimetic violence results organically in the surrogate victim, primordial order, and the first differentiating sign followed by progressive

---

10. Peirce, *Essential Peirce*, 1:248.
11. Deely, *Four Ages*, 662.

semiosis. The big difference, of course, is the presumed innocence of "firstness" as Peirce describes it. For our part, we have seen the *primum cognitum* as easily implicated in Heidegger's dread and its Girardian explanation in violence. At this point, however, this is not the concern: the *outcome* of culture becomes the thing of greatest interest. For Peirce is not finished. His thought of human community capable of progressive increase in knowledge brings him to a powerful concept of human evolution, one which implies a need for transformation out of firstness and secondness. He presents the thought in yet another, dramatic triad. He posits two modes of evolution, one by chance (which he calls "tychasm") and the other by mechanical necessity ("anacasm"). He then adds a third, something he calls "agapastic development" or evolutionary love. The clunkiness of the phrase belies the beauty it tokens. This third brings us even more clearly to the theme of semiotic transformation, to the concept of a deep change in human identity brought about by generative signals of love.

> The agapastic development of thought is the adoption of certain mental tendencies, not altogether heedlessly, as in tychasm, nor quite blindly by the mere force of circumstances or of logic, as in anancasm, but by an immediate attraction for the idea itself, whose nature is divined before the mind possesses it, by the power of sympathy, that is, by virtue of the continuity of mind; and this mental tendency may be of three varieties, as follows. First, it may affect a whole people or community in its collective personality, and be thence communicated to such individuals as are in powerfully sympathetic connection with the collective people, although they may be intellectually incapable of attaining the idea by their private understandings or even perhaps of consciously apprehending it. Second, it may affect a private person directly, yet so that he is only enabled to apprehend the idea, or to appreciate its attractiveness, by virtue of his sympathy with his neighbors, under the influence of a striking experience or development of thought. The conversion of St. Paul may be taken as an example of what is meant. Third, it may affect an individual, independently of his human affections, by virtue of an attraction it exercises upon his mind, even before he has comprehended it. This is the phenomenon which has been well called the divination of genius; for it is due to the continuity between the man's mind and the Most High.[12]

---

12. Peirce, "Evolutionary Love," 191.

The first example of how it affects people may describe the broad Christian movement itself, including its "virtual" realization in the world.[13] Individuals are influenced by the collective body even if they do not consciously "get" the central idea. The chosen example for the second variety is the classic of Christian conversion, Paul on the road to Damascus. The iconic value of this instance should not be lost on us: Peirce provides a direct example of how the biblical tradition helps crystallize his thinking. As he describes it, there is "a striking experience or development of thought" which brings the individual into a dramatic effect of sympathy with the body. We know that Paul "fell hard," meaning that his personal change came with the sudden, powerful collapse of his previous form of life. It seems this has to be a formal semiotic effect, something that happens to the whole body-self of meaning, at its multiple levels, rather than a pure progression of ideas. The third instance is even more highly individual, concerned not with collective affections, but a direct, mysterious connection of the mind with "the Most High." This is the realm of prophetic inspiration, and perhaps Peirce has in mind the figure of Christ himself. But even in this case there is an "attraction" exercised in the mind, parallel to the attraction and sympathy in the first two cases. Thus, it is clear that we are dealing with a transformative effect, one that necessarily—in the sweep of Peirce's philosophy—works at the level of signs and interpretants. People are persuaded by love at the level of deepest semiosis whereby their root understanding of reality is preconsciously reordered and transformed. Here, in one, is the triumph of semiotics: as a philosophy of human meaning it has reached the point of describing how a process of semiosis brings humanity to a new way of being human, one of love. Signs work before reflective thought, and they are capable of penetrating even the most obtuse and indifferent minds, bringing them to a new reality. Semiotics is as natural to the gospel as Aristotle is not!

Nineteenth-century optimism led Peirce drastically to underestimate the role of violence in the generation of human meaning and, in consequence, to fail to see how revolutionary must be its transformation into love. It would take the horrors of the twentieth century and the infusion of Heideggerean dread to alert the turn to the subject to the subject's congenital dysfunction. Peirce's innocent firstness is shot through from the beginning with mimesis, hatred and murder, and this indeed might be an apt exegesis of what he, in one place, calls "brute secondness," perhaps recognizing a certain violence in the emergence of mind from its dream.[14] At all events,

13. Bartlett, *Virtually Christian*.

14. Deely, *Four Ages*, 660–61. It is very possible that Peirce was more alert to history's potential disasters than I have suggested. The *Monist* article cited definitely displays hints in this direction.

by use of the scheme we are able to see that human meaning is earthly and evolutionary, not metaphysical. It breaks from the scene of firstness into secondness, conditioned always from within, and from there its effects move outward through a world of signs and culture, law and governance, toward the constant possibility of semiotic change, that is, a possible revolutionary thirdness. If then there should be a sign emerging in human culture able to repeat the primary earthquake within firstness, not as terror, but rather as surrender, self-giving and peace, then little by little, as sure as the sun rises and day follows night, the primary core of human semiosis is changed. This in turn explains the "attraction" and "sympathy" of agapastic evolution. It works in the elemental nucleus of our human meaning, changing it to the peace it has always desired but has always falsely achieved in and through the abandoned victim. A singular atom-splitting radiation reconfigures the elemental particles of culture, voluntarily signaling the abandonment of violence, bringing into being a new creation.[15]

True or False, or Journey of Love?

Deely draws a rigid distinction between the semiotics of Saussure and those of Peirce, insisting on a different name for the former—semiology. The reason is Saussure more or less ignores natural signs ("tracks in the snow") to concentrate on linguistics and words. This leads to a restriction of the science of signs to spoken language and results, according to Deely, in another round of Kant's problem of the "real world." In Deely's book, Saussure and all those he has influenced end up embracing a form of nominalism. In contrast, Peirce's semiotics hang on to the real despite affirming that all things are in some way *also* signs.

We could perhaps describe Deely's thought in the following picture. A dog who has caught the track of a rabbit is responding to a sign of "rabbit." The dog does not think "this is a sign of a rabbit" because it does not use language or abstract conceptualization. Nevertheless, the dog has received a

---

15. "Thirdness" is in formal contradiction to Girard's Clausewitzian "duel" as the binary code to history's unfolding, something we find in *Battling to the End*, Girard's final published work. Here the "third" would seem to reduce to some kind of universal conflagration bringing history to a violent conclusion. It's a thought which discounts a more profound Peircian "third" at work (of which Girard's earlier work could be seen as an historical verification). There is always the risk of great suffering and setbacks to human existence, but to narrow historical possibilities to a duel-plus-mutual-destruction seems semiotically reductive and actually a form of Cartesian rationalism (because comprised only of isolated selves in rivalry). It actually depends on what "third" as interpretant is chosen.

genuine sign of a rabbit because that is the way the dog world, and the world in general, works. Now, here on the printed page we also access the sign "rabbit" but in a very different form. We do so in a story about a dog and a rabbit, using words and sentences. The rabbit is not just up the trail, ready to be caught, but in our heads, in our imaginations. All the same, Deely believes there is a continuity and even identity between the two types of sign—the real life one and the one in our heads. And that is because all signs belong to "ontological relation," a relation that stands in its own right and truly and informatively connects one thing with another (or one level of relations with another). The sign is not the relation as such, but it certainly comes into being because of it, and expresses it in various ways. The existence of the triadic interpretant as essential to the sign ensures that there is always some sort of "story" to be told about the object, and thus there are a million different formations of the sign. Accordingly, the sign of the rabbit on the page is both discontinuous from and continuous with the rabbit on the track, because of the ontological relation and the interpretant that realizes it. And even with the rabbit on the track there is still a degree of discontinuity and the dog too must have an interpretant—whether it is chasing the rabbit for its own sake, or for a human master; whether the rabbit's scent on the trail is weak or strong; the dog's degree of hunger and motivation, etc.

So, once again, the problem that arises directly is that a sign, any sign, can be false. Even the dog on the trail of a rabbit could be old and confused. We know that dogs dream, so they could be chasing figments of rabbits in their dreams. What is the character of the relation here? It is when you get to human signs, especially those made by words, that the problem explodes out of any control. Human beings have always made stuff up! In fact, they do so as a matter of evolutionary necessity, if Girard is to be credited. A myth is a fraudulent sign that is necessarily true in its own way. The belief that the sun went around the earth, every day repeating a circuit of enclosed flat space, served humanity very well in knowing what time of day it was, which directions were east and west, and generally that there was a stable cosmic order which could be relied on. So, what happens to the "ontological relation" of the sign when it is in fact a lie? The model of science is, as we have seen, a major force in prompting both Cartesian "pure ideas" and the empiricism that sought to rely on sensation as the source of truth. Its general success tells us again and again how our previous signs have not properly grasped the nature of reality, of the way things "really are." We are continually astonished at the *DNA* of things, after having seen them in terms of magic, or some form of primitive science. It seems small wonder that the way of ideas then is preferred to signs—the sense of a pure, unmediated, intellectual grasp of truth as revealed by scientific method.

But, of course, "DNA" is a sign itself, and at multiple levels: an acronym, a set of words, a metaphor, and—then at the physical level—itself a code (a set of signs) for the transmission of life, which are themselves liable to mutation. The whole thing is shot through with semiosis. So, we have to conclude that at the general level, signs may be, and most often are, *both*: fraudulent and truth-bearing! Even the use of mathematics to create a fully accurate description of things is always open to revision: Newtonian physics, while true at a certain level, needs to be revised by Einsteinian relativity.

If we then return once more to the myths or stories we tell ourselves about who *we* are, about the meaning of our lives, it is unarguable that at this level our signs are filled with falsehood. The Nazi swastika and the story of Aryan supremacy are universally agreed to be false signs about human meaning. So how can we confidently posit an authentic "relation" for any sign related to human meaning? The answer has to be linked to Peirce's growth in human meaning, by which the human community slowly and progressively sifts through the options presented to it and, little by little, begins to affirm and confirm a particular set of signs. Thus, in relation to the story we tell ourselves about ourselves, the "turn to the subject" is inescapable, and it is something which Deely has sidestepped in his enthusiasm for an authentic "postmodernity" of semiotic realism. There can be no presumption of realism when the object of inquiry is the inquirer herself. Humanity is far too invested to be trusted. If now postmodernism has dropped the metaphysics of objectivity in the human story, if it insists with Derrida that it is the "other" (not the same) which is to be awaited, expected, is this not the sign of a breakthrough?

A defensive assertion of philosophical realism in conjunction with overwhelming scientific and technological success negates the deep (un)reality of human identity. "Natural signs" are generally more trustworthy because the exercise of actual life depends on them and getting them responsively right—the dog chasing the rabbit, the DNA passing on the genes, and the electron-microscope verification of the DNA double helix by scientists—is a general condition of successful everyday life. Certainly, a correct reading of the color yellow is essential to recognize a variety of nature's dangers signals, from the golden dart frog to the yellow jacket, and then, afterward, the color is read consistently on yellow road warnings and hazard suits. But the human coding of yellow is, as we have seen at the beginning of the book, a much broader and flexible sign possibility, integrated into a huge range of semiotic chains.

And, unlike examples of color, etc., absolutely no stricture of nature applies to the stories we tell ourselves about who we are. Indeed, to underline the point again, telling a false story might actually be useful if not necessary to a group's survival. Plato's "noble lie" is the ancient iteration of this thought. However (and this is the point where the orchestra music manifestly changes), we have also arrived at the place where a trail of reflection—from Lévi-Strauss and other thinkers, through anthropologists like Girard, and philosophers like Derrida and Heidegger, while always looping back through the Bible—has led us to the exposure of the least noble lie of all: the false guilt of the scapegoat. And on this there is no going back. Everywhere the victim is victorious. A real evolution has taken place, and it is as inescapable as Galileo's moons.

Behind it is a profound break from violence, a semio-ontological clearing that allows us to see the victim as victim, not as enemy. It has to be a register of signals based in compassion and forgiveness which brought this about. And so, where before there was a semio-ontological relation to violence and its mythic narratives, there is now a relation to love. Our journey in company with Deely has led us to a place of trans-semiosis in which we are currently consumed like the ancient Hebrews following Moses in the wilderness. We need to note one more thinker and his technical description of how human signs can change, before we conclude our journey (shamelessly mixing metaphors) along the high peaks of Western thought looking out toward a semiotic land of promise.

The Eco of Semiosis

Umberto Eco's work in the latter half of the twentieth century provides us with the most developed set of tools yet for the technical understanding of signs, and especially their potential for dynamic change. As well as his academic books Eco wrote novels, including his first and wildly popular, the medieval detective novel *The Name of the Rose*. The book was a sensation, selling more than fifty million copies worldwide (one of the bestselling books ever). Its plot turned on the question of a lost manuscript from Aristotle on comedy, and its likely disruptive effect should it be found. The setting is the medieval church and its looming Inquisition, and, in physical terms, a grimly isolated monastery in northern Italy. Eco produced a compelling parable of both the power of texts and of an ultimate vanity in seeking to establish grand narratives. The book's title refers to a twelfth-century poem by Bernard of Cluny which says something along the lines of "only the name of the primal rose remains, we possess bare names..."[16] The echoes of nominalism place Eco squarely in the "non-realist" camp of the medieval tradition and the "way of ideas" from Descartes forward.

16. See https://en.wikipedia.org/wiki/The_Name_of_the_Rose.

However, the fact that multiple murders within the monastery walls provide the mainspring of interest tells us that what's ultimately at stake in the novel is the spilling of blood. The willingness to shed blood on the part of the monks, and the Inquisition, tells us that somehow truth has often been founded by blood, and *this* is the pivotal semiotic question of the twentieth and twenty-first centuries.

Eco's theoretical approach is no longer the question of the basic structure of the sign (binary or triadic). Nor, as suggested, does it dwell on Deely's Latin worldview and its quest for ontological relationship. Instead, it seeks a comprehensive technical account of how semiotics actually work in ordinary human discourse. It thus develops a much finer-grained description of communication. One of the key innovations is to move the accent from "sign" to "sign-function," putting the focus on the overall semiotic activity that produces the sign rather than a supposed metaphysical entity (the sign) in itself. A sign-function occurs when elements of expression and content enter into correlation according to rules provided by codes. Codes are effectively the schemes of relevant meaning given by connected interpretants.[17] They are the heuristic set of conditional meanings that apply in any statement. Thus a "plane" is either a carpentry tool or a flying machine depending on the overall code being used ("carpentry" or "flying").

Obviously, each of these codes can itself be seen as related to (or comprising) a multitude of markers or signs. Together this multitude makes up what Eco terms a "sememe," that is, the full "encyclopedia" of semantic and syntactic elements, together with context and circumstance, which determine the meaning of an expression.[18] The code is not the sememe as such, but the conventional rules which generate the sememe and thus the sign-function. Who decides what the rules are or what is relevant for the sememe? There is no answer to those questions. Eco posits instead "unlimited semiosis." As he says, the category of the interpretant "shows us how signification (as well as communication), by means of continual shiftings which refer a sign back to another sign or string of signs, circumscribes cultural units in an asymptotic fashion, without ever allowing one to touch them directly, though making them accessible to other units. Thus, a cultural unit never obliges one to replace it by means of something which is not a semiotic entity, and never asks to be explained by some Platonic, psychic or objectal entity. *Semiosis explains itself by itself.*"[19]

---

17. Eco, *Theory of Semiotics*, 71.
18. Eco, *Theory of Semiotics*, 72, 105.
19. Eco, *Theory of Semiotics*, 71, italics original.

Eco is pointing to the reality of language as self-authenticating. It offers a constantly shifting bank of metrics providing the meaning of a given statement, one which we can certainly get near to in analysis, but which we can never completely lay out on the laboratory bench, so to speak. Because, in order to do so, we have to make use of another set of signs, which in turn needs to be examined and explained in a string of signs, and so on indefinitely. We are not far distant here from our "neural studio" proposed in our opening essay, but with a development. What we are given is a picture of two converging lines of meaning (neural pathways?) which never quite touch, and in which the first line is already itself a reading of the human world of signs, and that line is at once interpretable by a second, and the second by a third, and so on *ad infinitum*. What results is an extraordinarily dynamic, fluid system of human meaning which may appear chaotic, but through its constant interplay with factual physical reality and cultural experience renders on an ongoing "reality check" through and of itself. The point is that it works in practice, without ever allowing itself to be reduced to "objectal" status.

One of the striking consequences of Eco's approach is what he calls "the possibility of lying . . . [as] the *proprium* of semiosis."[20] This means that the defining characteristic of semiotics or human sign-making is its capacity to deceive, to dissemble. Or, put the other way around, anything that can be used to tell a lie is the subject matter of a theory of codes, of semiotics. Many of us remember as children the astonishing realization that it was possible to dissemble, and that the possibility was somehow built in to the very fact of language. It is a species of the forbidden fruit, of the simultaneous knowledge of good and evil. In Girardian terms, of course, this makes perfect sense, as the first or ur-symbol is necessarily a misrecognition or lie about the victim, a code for the crisis of rivalry and violence, which is always also a cover-up. However, the biblical account of names of the animals given *before* the crisis of the tree and its fruit does suggest an impetus toward the truth despite the congenital myth-making of language. Language itself is not held guilty. And this is because, just as unlimited semiosis means the possibility of falsehood, by the same token it also means the possibility somehow of a better language, a better story, of what might be held to an asymptotic standard of truth. Thus, Eco's *proprium* of lying implies necessarily its opposite, the semiotic *proprium* of truth. If the signs we have can lie and we are able to state that, then there must be other signs that don't, beginning exactly with that first clause. This is the place, therefore, where a semiotics of transformation would find its authentic and necessary ground.

---

20. Eco, *Theory of Semiotics*, 59.

Underpinning this we find that Eco's sense of fluid semiosis allows him to enter an account of invention and aesthetics that provides for the possibility of semiotic novelty. "We may define as invention a mode of production whereby the producer of the sign-function chooses a new material continuum not yet segmented for that purpose and proposes a new way of organizing (of giving form to) it in order *to map* within it the formal pertinent element of a content-type."[21] What Eco is talking about here is creating a space for a meaning within a given aesthetic continuum such as music, graphics, architecture, verse, etc. He then adds, "The main problem arises when trying to determine how it is possible to map onto an expression continuum the properties of something which (because of its cultural oddity or formal complexity) is *not yet culturally known*."[22] This is exactly the question the present work is dealing with, and the fact that Eco formulates it demonstrates that the science of semiotics is structurally open to the question of new cultural meaning. In which case we have arrived formally at the place of transformative signs, and their invention and entry into the continua of human meaning.

He gives two types of invention at this level. One he calls "moderate" and refers to a percept that the artist has "of nature" and then maps physically onto a continuum. The examples would be classical paintings such as Gainsborough's *Mr. and Mrs. Andrews*, something which perfectly captures a new cultural theme while mapping it onto an established medium. In this way a new cultural content is brought into being, one which the addressee or viewer is able to reconstitute by making her way back from the surface of the painting to the artist's percept. What the artist has seen becomes visible to all. But there is also the case of "radical inventions," meaning situations in which the artist more or less makes up the percept on the canvass surface itself, bypassing the perceptual model. The example he gives is the work of Impressionists which was not at first recognized or understood by the viewers. (The same could be said of very many instances of expressionist or modern art.) "In such cases what takes place is a radical code-making, a violent proposal of new conventions."[23] By these means humans are able to see the world in new forms derived directly from the art itself. In regard to the aesthetic use of language, similar effects can be brought about by what Eco calls "code violation," including deliberate ambiguity, making the object strange or uncanny, forcing the reader to give repeated attention to the text

---

21. Eco, *Theory of Semiotics*, 245, italics original.
22. Eco, *Theory of Semiotics*, 249, italics original.
23. Eco, *Theory of Semiotics*, 254.

to try to decode it. "[T]he entire operation, even though focused on codes, frequently produces a new type of *awareness about the world*."[24]

Eco thus provides the theoretical grounds for transformative semiotics. He shows how semiotic codes contain in themselves the potential for new signification, for new signs, and with them a new meaning of the world. To apply these insights biblically demonstrates the possibility of transformation of human meaning via the various strangeness and challenges of the biblical text. There also has to be a feedback loop between certain "secular" texts providing new codes (hermeneutics) for the understanding of the biblical text itself. The Girardian reading is certainly a case in point, one which releases in turn an extremely powerful realization of new code-making by the Bible tradition. Theology is not about an impression of colors in some painting by Renoir, although it could be about the vibrant relationships depicted in his paintings. Theology deals with core human relationships, and if it is true that the strangeness of the biblical text has changed our semiotic codes it has done so at the most basic level of relationship. At root it is the theological relation itself that is at stake. What is being argued is that a divine relation has effected an intervention *at the most original level of code-making*. If there is a God and this God cares for the world, then it is by changing the actual root dynamic of our human codes that God intends to save us. Legal and transactional models of divine intervention simply reinforce established codes founded in violence. Transformation of human meaning is infinitely more painstaking and unquantifiable. Yet it is by the same measure richer, nonviolent and miraculous. We remember that *humanity does not live by bread alone, but by every word from the mouth of God* (Matt 4:4). The metaphysical externalism by which we have understood "God," "heaven," "salvation," "body," "soul," etc., cannot be

---

24. Eco, *Theory of Semiotics*, 261, italics original. It is worth making mention again of the reflection of Charles Taylor. Taylor's particular argument is with the Lockean version of language, which sees its function as strictly descriptive of a given "enframing" reality. Taylor understands language as also "constitutive," allowing human beings a wide range of creative "topographies" of self in their everyday language use. This parallels Peirce's interpretants and Eco's code use and invention. Taylor says that linguistic constitution can provide "a new way of describing, or a new model for understanding, our human condition and the alternatives it opens for us; and through this we come to see and perhaps embrace a new human possibility. We may come to this existential insight through meeting, or hearing about, some paradigmatic figure (the Buddha, St. Francis), or by reading a book about ethics or the meaning of life or (more often) through reading a novel or seeing a film . . . In all these cases, the impact can be described as regestalting of our world and its possibilities, which opens a new (to us) way of being." The only reason Taylor cannot automatically bring the Bible into his series of reframing examples is the relentlessly legal, metaphysical, or—alternately—purely historical-critical, interpretations to which it has been submitted. See Taylor, *Language Animal*, ch. 1, and pp. 41 and 46.

simply dispensed with, but little by little an internal density of meaning and relation can displace it, and there is nothing more internal to human beings than the language by which they speak and know themselves. In language and its codes there is power to change the face of the earth, and in ways beyond recognition, transforming the human space from anger and conflict to wholeness and peace. It is not by accident that in the Bible's first chapter God speaks the world into life, and does so wholly without violence.

We have arrived at the full underpinning of transformative semiotics. Indeed, from the way our whole discussion has gone semiotics cannot be other than transformative. Once again, therefore, this is why the field provides a preferable basis for theology than metaphysics. What follows now is a development of the argument of Peircian "realism" broached above, seeking a more conclusive statement about the relation of love as an answer to the question of the real. It aims at a theological semiotics reaching beyond the frame of primordial ontology, producing human meaning beyond the grim calculus of being.

9
Ontology: What's *Really* Going On?

Real or Alternative Facts

Just as all roads lead to Rome, all thought leads to ultimate questions. What is the final nature of things?

This book takes "signs" as its leading idea, its gold standard of reflection and understanding. But as metaphysicians sometimes like to tell us, to base thought in semiotics is to grasp a tiger by the tail. By this they imply that semiotics can only render uncontrollable chains of signifiers without anchor in the ultimate and real. As we have followed the story of semiotics, in the Girardian and postmodern scene, and then tracking back through the history of Western thought, concern for the real and the ultimate has been an inescapable underlying thread. If we grasp the snarling chain of signifiers, where does it lead us? Round to the tiger's mouth of systemic uncertainty, and, implied perhaps, a doom of endless human violence? Or is there the possibility of something else, something both transformative and real?

As an idea "signs" is delightfully diaphanous. You are meant to see through it, to "something else." As Peirce pointed out, however, the see-through character is never exchanged for an absolute term, only for something "more diaphanous." "The interpretant is nothing but another representation to which the torch of truth is handed along; and as representation, it has its interpretant again. Lo, another infinite series."[1]

So, is it veil upon veil upon veil, a hopelessly gossamer truth? A bridal unveiling where the bride's face never finally appears? Existence cannot be such a tease, surely? Or, is there something about signs which of itself leads us forward on the inexorable search for truth, and so cannot help promising we will "get there" eventually?

---

1. Peirce, *Collected Papers*, 1:339.

Here, I think, is the point of the "ontological relation," the concept to which we have come in our journey indicating some connection in our signs to the way things are in an ultimate sense. But it is also evident, as I have suggested, that "ontological relation" can change—thus it is the relation itself which is real, not necessarily what it is suggesting about the nature of reality! This may appear as an intolerable confusion, or at least a considerable defect in theory: our semiotic relations may be per se false and misleading. At the same time, it may be one great advantage of a semiotic philosophy, allowing a thinker to keep open the thought of human destiny and not see it set in some preordained fabric of the cosmos. Hence, the thought of semio-ontology. Returning again to *The Matrix*, when Morpheus asks Neo, "Do you believe in fate?" Neo answers no. Neo is not being asked about a rational truth; he is asked about his belief. And as a powerful piece of semiotics, *The Matrix* obviously sides with the possibility of affecting, if not changing, the working signs by which we live.

But the question then becomes even more urgent: what is there in the "ontological relation" which connects effectively with the way things are so that it is able *both* to "falsely" construct our world and yet, at a subsequent (or simultaneous) moment, "truly" render the meaning of human existence? We could be reminded of the notorious "alternative facts" of U.S. politics in the second decade of the present century. Do "ontological relations" support these, simply allowing us to choose which version of reality we are inclined toward?

Clearly scientific thought cries out against this. Water boils at one hundred degrees centigrade at sea level, and one hundred degrees is the temperature of boiling water at sea level. Change any part of this and the predictable, organized modern world falls apart; and the normal response to such a world would indeed be a very exasperated "It makes absolutely no sense!" However, the frustrated and frustrating debate over global warming—where, according to the NASA website, 97 percent of actively publishing climate scientists agree that anthropogenic climate change is real[2]—tells us that even scientific data can be politically questioned, so that the ontological truth of climate change (i.e., *what* exactly is it?) can itself seem to mutate from group to group, individual to individual.

This seems to be a particularly acute problem of our contemporary world, where a great deal is at stake in the assessment of facts about the actual earth. Normally, however, and for the vast majority of people, there do exist accepted postulates of a real world—for example, the sun circuits the observer on earth once ever twenty-four hours, regardless of which bit is actually

2. See Conway, "Global Warming Consensus."

doing the moving—and without these solid postulates ordinary, day-to-day life would be impossible. In all these cases, signs are by no means negotiable, their relations are not alterable at will; they appear fixed in the fabric of the cosmos. Sustained experience and observation—and, within that, the strict application of scientific, experimental method—provide, therefore, a privileged criterion of realism, one that many people claim to be the standard for all claims to truth. In such conditions "ontological relation" would not appear to be free but to belong strictly to the ontological half of the term: the relation is exactly determined by the "way things are."[3]

However, human story goes well beyond "science," hence the actual debate over climate change. And, in parallel, the immense popularity of the storytelling of movies, with wildly impossible tales of magic, superheroes, zombies, horrific aliens, galactic demigods, etc., shows a positive human appetite for narrative, whatever its rootedness in reality. Human beings consume stories, alongside scientific realism, as if their lives depended on it. And, indeed, they do. Part of human "reality" is the overall story we tell about ourselves and the universe, and it appears very much that it is precisely in this area that "ontological relations" attain their most proper value as "a way of relating": one that somehow belongs within the freedom of the human being while still configuring the truth of being as such.

---

3. We have to set alongside a claim to fixed rules of the cosmos the developments of quantum mechanics, which tell us that at a certain level of reality there are only probabilities, and the act of measurement itself determines their outcome. This understanding, developed among physicists in the early decades of the twentieth century, must itself be part of contemporary human assessment of the world, reinforcing its "storytelling" nature. But scientific inquiry will always be concerned with overall stable laws determining physical reality. As Einstein famously put it, "God does not play dice with the universe." Furthermore, the accurate comprehension of small particle uncertainty takes a level of math which the great majority are incapable of, including the present writer. So, "for everyday purposes" we will continue to make traditional assumptions about the reliable, constant nature of the cosmos. All the same, it cannot escape attention that significant forms of "relation" have been introduced into the deepest levels of physical research. When we hear about "quantum entanglement"—electrons that have been generated together, or interacted in a certain way, maintaining a form of physical identity even at huge distance—we are confronted with a level of connection we do not properly understand. It strongly suggests "ontological relation" operating in ways that are more radical than may previously have been thought. If we then consider the role of human beings, with their unique mass of neurological connection forming reflective awareness, it becomes possible to think of human relation able to reach out through time and space, linking to unseen but real shifts in the material order—including the possibility of resurrection itself. Moreover, learned "entanglements" of this kind are perhaps still in their infancy. See the burgeoning literature in this area; for example, Rosenblum and Kuttner, *Quantum Enigma*.

Philosophy and the Icon

Philosophy has always sought to overcome the conundrum of such relations, prying out a definitive answer to what lies behind all the stories, the myths, the narratives of the gods. The Greeks set out looking for the ultimate stuff of the universe, prior to gods or men, ending up inquiring about Aristotle's *on hē on*, about *being as being*. A final answer to the question would presumably tell us the final character of the ontological relation, demonstrating the necessary place of human being and all its sign-relationships in the midst of a given and ineluctable universe. We've already had cause above to examine the work of Martin Heidegger, and there can be little doubt that the twentieth-century German philosopher provided the outstanding contemporary account of the character of *being* and human existence within it. Probing his thinking one more time can help us situate our problem more precisely in terms of philosophy, and within a particular framework which, more than any other, fits the issues at hand. We will track Heidegger's thought through the work of another philosopher, the French phenomenologist Jean-Luc Marion. Marion looked to develop a reflection that escapes Heidegger's powerful critique regarding theology. He does so by using concepts both responsive to Heidegger and not totally distant from our thematic of "signs."[4] His startling insights offer us a way to think existence without a rigid tether to being.

Heidegger's work is a mountain range looming above a city on a plain. It frames the twentieth century and maintains its effect powerfully in the twenty-first. It offered the world a definitive shift in understanding of "being," from one theme among others—that is, a general or common concept for "things," a simple term among many possible other disciplines. Instead, the thought of *being* took on a determining anteriority which was able to undercut or preempt the thought even of a divine reality, that is, "God." Heidegger accomplished this by establishing what he called "ontological difference." *Being* cannot be thought of as *a* being, as one more instance of all the individual beings of the world, just much bigger. *Being* has to be in itself a condition of possibility that can only be thought in difference from the range of individual beings it makes possible.[5] As Marion says, "Being never finds itself thought as such, but always and only as the unthought of being [das Seiendes] and its condition of possibility."[6] *Being* is what we *don't*

---

4. Marion, *God Without Being*.

5. "[W]e think of Being rigorously only when we think of it in its difference with beings, and of beings in their difference with Being." Heidegger, *Identity and Difference*, 62.

6. Marion, *God Without Being*, 34. We remember that *Seinde* is another word Heidegger used for *being*, the present participle of the verb to be, *Sein*, meaning generally what crops up, or "individual beings."

think about when we think of the being of a table or a horse, but we have to presume the former in order to do the latter.

As commented, the thought of "God" is profoundly affected by this understanding: God as "Supreme Being" and yet the source of all being is still *a* being and thus does not escape the anteriority of *being*. To think of *a* being as the source of *all* being is what Heidegger calls onto-theology. It is simultaneously the character of metaphysics, producing a scheme of thought rendering ultimate realities effectively in the same class as individual tables and chairs. It makes the highest being just the supreme instance of an item like a table or chair in thought. In the process it also creates the very scheme of lower and higher. "Because it makes be-ing [*Seiende*] as be-ing an idea, metaphysics in itself is in fact two-in-one: the truth of be-ing in the most general sense and in the highest sense. In its essence it is ontology . . . and theology."[7] And because metaphysics does this—creating an idea of being and the divinity of theology at the same time—it has the decisive effect of a forgetting of *being*, of *the* orginary unthought condition. It therefore amounts to a profound misrecognition of the nature of reality.

This reflection has tremendous consequence. It strongly suggests that the metaphysical tradition (its onto-theology), to which theology has been wedded for something like nineteen hundred years, is in fact a defective form for the communication of the Christian message. It mistakes metaphysics for anteriority and therefore sells the gospel short. Jean-Luc Marion is persuaded of this truth and puts the essence of his response this way:

> If, to begin with, "God is love," then God loves before being, He only is as He embodies himself—in order to love more closely that which and those who, themselves, have first to be. This radical reversal of the relations between Being and loving, between the name revealed by the Old Testament (Exodus, 3:14) and the name revealed, more profoundly though not inconsistently, by the New (First Letter of John, 4:8), presupposes taking a stand that is at once theological and philosophical.[8]

Marion then pursues "love before being" by means of a phenomenological distinction he draws between what he calls "the idol" and "the icon." He

---

7. Heidegger, "What Is Metaphysics?," 26. Here Groth translates *Seinde* as "be-ing," to accent its verbal quality.

8. Marion, *God Without Being*, xxii. In his reading of Exodus 3:14 as referring to *being* Marion is following the scholastic exegetical tradition we have already noted. In the next and final chapter, we will see how the Old Testament name already possesses undertones and overtones of the relation of love, tones carried over into the Gospel of John. Marion himself understands that the biblical names are not in fact inconsistent, and his basic point remains.

doesn't mine the Christian philosophical tradition as Deely does, isolating a semiotic strand that offers a possible way forward, but dives directly into a revelatory phenomenology allowing him to present a mode of relation which escapes the priority of *being*. As we shall see shortly, this is by no means alien to a semiotic approach, but it is also salient how Marion's work may easily conform to a Girardian perspective. If we also seek to merge—as we did in the historical chapter—Heidegger's ontological perspective with some of Girard's anthropology, then perhaps we can determine the space where a radically different mode of relation can arise. If ontological relation is primarily *relation*, then anything that brings a truly new possibility of *relation* into the world must disturb the given order of being, even its very priority. We may say in fact that love, in every sense, *relativizes* being.

Marion distinguishes between the idol and the icon on the basis that both are examples of a *signum*, a sign. "One thus would have to interrogate the *signa* concerning their mode of signaling, suspecting that the idol and the icon are distinguishable only inasmuch as they signal in different ways, that is, inasmuch as each makes use of its visibility in its own way. The diversity of these ways for signaling and becoming *signa* no doubt, however, decides everything between the idol and the icon."[9] He at once concedes, therefore, that "sign" is a more basic concept and there is the possibility of signaling "in different ways" and this makes all the difference. We must suspect that it is relation that makes the difference, specifically the mode of relation based in violence or nonviolence. This will be the deciding perceptual alternative creating the radically different signs. We are in the realm, therefore, of a dramatically new, transformative semiotics, even as Marion proceeds in the discipline of phenomenology, that is, on the basis of the "visible."

He tells us that "the idol depends on the gaze that it satisfies, since if the gaze did not desire to satisfy itself in the idol, the idol would have no dignity for it." And a little later, "The gaze alone makes the idol, as the ultimate function of the gazeable."[10] It is the human *relatio* that makes the idol, but it happens in an obscured and obscuring way. The gaze, as Marion identifies it, travels out to the idol and comes to rest there, basking in its brilliance. The idol is in fact a mirror which does not show itself as such. The idol simply reflects back the energy of the human gaze while entrapping vision in its deceptive material presence; yet this is still only the case because the gaze has somehow chosen this to happen. Marion underlines this falsified and falsifying closed circuit of the gaze and the idol—everything depending on the gaze but seeming to find final meaning in the idol. He does not unpack the

9. Marion, *God Without Being*, 9.
10. Marion, *God Without Being*, 10.

violence of this, only the falsification. But in something as heavily freighted as "the idol" violence is impossible to avoid. The mirror of the idol, he says, serves to fix the gaze "as mortally immobile as coagulated blood."[11] The idol, by thus dazzling the gaze (as coagulated blood), serves to bring the gaze to a halt, not letting it travel beyond the material element. In Girardian terms this would be the stabilization of the universe fixed in place by the violent moment of sacrifice and the non-instinctual attention it brings.

The idol has a falsifying relation with the visible because it traps the gaze and does not allow it to go beyond. In contrast the icon opens a relation with the invisible. The icon "attempts to render visible the invisible as such, hence to allow that the visible not cease to refer to an other than itself, without, however, that other ever being reproduced in the visible."[12] The invisible here is a metonym for whatever cannot be grasped, controlled or possessed in the gaze. "The icon summons the gaze to surpass itself by never freezing on a visible, since the visible only presents itself here in view of the invisible."[13] Marion of course is dependent here on the Christian artistic tradition of "icon," while making explicit reference to scripture and patristic texts. Neither does he fail to refer to Conciliar definitions that resolved the controversial issue of icons for the Eastern churches when devotional use of the paintings was accused of idolatry. "He who venerates the icon venerates in it the hypostasis of the one who is inscribed in it."[14] *Hypostasis* here is a technical term and a wondrous one at that. It is the crucial term used at the Council of Chalcedon (451) for the divine selfhood of Christ, neither substance nor nature, but the unfathomable identity of the Son of God now the selfsame identity of Jesus of Nazareth. The word was rendered *persona* in Latin, translated as "person" in English, providing one of the essential pathways for the contemporary, almost boundless prestige of that word. Thus, the one who venerates the icon is in personal communion with the person of Christ.

> The icon opens in a face, where man's sight envisages nothing, but goes back infinitely from the visible to the invisible by the grace of the visible itself: instead of the invisible mirror, which sent the human gaze back to itself alone ... the icon opens in a face that gazes at our gazes in order to summon them to its depth.[15]

11. Marion, *God Without Being*, 13.
12. Marion, *God Without Being*, 18.
13. Marion, *God Without Being*, 18.
14. Council of Nicaea II (787): Denzinger, *Enchiridion Symbolorum*, 302; quoted in Marion, *God Without Being*, 18.
15. Marion, *God Without Being*, 19.

At this point, it is impossible not to recognize that Marion's pathway has brought us to relation and relationship, and of the most profoundly human kind. Whereas the idol sends the human gaze "to itself alone," that is, unrelating in the fixity of an idolatrous universe, the icon opens "in a face," into a bottomless abyss of relationship which is itself the definition of the invisible. As Marion continues to point out, the icon is the perfect inversion of the idol: where the latter belongs to the human gaze returning purely to itself, the former belongs to the gaze of the other inviting the human to endless giving relationship.

Marion's reflections take us, therefore, in an evident circle from *signa* (signs) of idol and icon, through to relation, where relation is the final meaning of the icon. Relation (to the other) becomes for Marion a meaning higher than being—"higher" because *for the other* and, as we shall see, free of idolatry associated with Heidegger's *being*. We are talking about "relation" here in its most paradigmatic sense. Because it is a relation with a transcendent meaning (to and for the "other," or what Marion would call the "invisible") it creates a potential feedback to all human experience. Marion's description joins with the core vector of this book to tell us that the icon offers itself as a new primary scene, propagating its own meaning in every direction through the world. Thus relation—in the sense of relationship as such—becomes a radically new way of understanding all existence.

As we just suggested, hypostasis is confirmed in its meaning as the fount of relation by its Latin translation as *persona*. We can anticipate a little the next chapter, understanding that the character of this hypostasis/person is the endless self-giving of God revealed in Jesus. So, it is that the "invisible" of the icon is the bottomless pouring out of the self, experienced in Christ. It is not an immaterial "spiritual" world (an original and perfect version of this one freed from the limitations of matter), but this world released into the endlessness of love. "In the idol, the gaze of man is frozen in its mirror; in the icon, the gaze of man is lost in the invisible gaze that visibly envisages him."[16]

We may then have every confidence at this point to say that from a Christian perspective the final nature of the universe is relation rather being, *hupostasis* rather than *on hē on*. The triumph of the sign is related tightly to this perspective: a sign "only" makes a relation, it does not re-present a thing: it insists on the question of relation, not on the presence of *things*. The impact of Christian *hupostasis* has led step by step to the emergence of semiotics as premier philosophy, highlighting more and more over the centuries the way human signs, including words, do not convey pure thoughts and ideas, so much as possible relations with and in the world.

---

16. Marion, *God Without Being*, 19.

Idol and Icon, Ontology and Hypostasis

At this juncture we should pause to assess again the crucial term we have made so much use of in respect of signs—*ontological relation*. In light of the above, it might now appear a somewhat ambiguous formula. How can something "ontological" provide the pathway for the emergence of the sign when *being* is placed in contrast to *hupostasis* and we are claiming that it is the latter which is the real catalyst of semiotics? But we may stress that in the "ontological relation" it is always the relation that is real. Yes, it has to play its part within "being," while, as Marion indicates and we shall clarify in a moment, *being* has the effect of masking relation. Nevertheless, the sign (*signum*) remains a real relation, "relation-in-itself," and this is the fundamental claim.

Now, from a certain scientific perspective there are "natural laws" governing all physical objects. And as we have had cause to mention more than once, the goal of science is to understand and make use of these laws. But the view of "ontological relation" is more fluid and alive than a cosmic court with an implacable set of laws determining cause and effect. If we say that the fox follows the scent of the rabbit it is because the fox has a relation with the physical signals of the rabbit. If we say that a pothole in the road caused the front wheel to fall off it is because the shock of the impact has a relation with the broken axle rod. If we say the MRI has shown the infant will die it is because of the relation between the growth of the inoperable tumor and the onset of fatal pressure. If we say that the plague in Thebes was the fault of Oedipus who married his mother and killed his father, it is because for humans there is a relation between the resolution of a crisis and the finding of a scapegoat. These are multiple relations, given and interpreted by multiple signs. But we may see that *none* of these signs are determinative, and while it is impossible to arrive at the relation outside of the sign, it is *also* possible that the sign *can change* and so also the relation.

Thus, Oedipus was found innocent because the plague's actual virus was discovered—or, was it in fact the other way around? That the science of viruses became possible when the mythic thinking of blameworthy scapegoats decreased? In the case of potholes, a car's sonic and radar sensors and their signs may learn always to avoid them. Taking the sick child on pilgrimage to a place of healing may sometimes be followed by the complete disappearance of the tumor. And a fox may be selected and taught to eat kibbles and play with rabbits. So, it is that "ontological relation" may be considered always under the pressure of true "hypostatic relation" and our given universe to be an unfathomable mix of the two, as it seeks its own final liberation from violence. "Ontological relation" is a stage on the way, itself already a loosening of metaphysics (as via Deely's "four ages of understanding");

and this is always because of the in-breaking of *hupostasis* prompting the discovery of the word (of scripture) as sign and thus progressively the human world as a tissue of relations. Once the radically new relation (the icon) of *hupostasis* came into the world it became possible to think of everything from a semiotic and thus transformative viewpoint.

Emerging into a universe where the fixity of the idolatrous gaze is displaced by the freedom of a world invited only by the gaze of love, then it is much more likely that instead of metaphysical essences the human mind will see just signs of relations—signs which are themselves dynamic modes of relation. The possibility of transformative sign-relations in turn progressively impacts the actual conditions of existence. This is obviously true in practical terms of the moral and legal consequences of our worldview and their stories, but at a deeper level there is a living congruence between our semiotics and the kind of meaningful world we inhabit. Little by little, the actual world we see and experience changes its tone, its quality and meaning.[17] This flows from *hupostasis* as revelatory source of meaning. The self-pouring-out of God encourages a universe of possible relations and invites them into its own *hupostasis*. A sign in its deepest sense is a mode of communication (relation) which holds open this transformative possibility.

Turning back to Heidegger we can see that this formidable philosopher capitalized on Christian *hupostasis* to formulate his indelible account of human existence—of "Dasein"—in *Being and Time*. Dasein/human existence is the hero of this book, not because it sets out to be any kind of humanism (the error he accused Sartre's existentialism of[18]) but because ontology/being would simply not happen without the role of the human. Marion says this formally, referring to the "turn" or shift in Heidegger's thought away from what is disclosed in human existence to a discourse more about being as such.

> In fact, one should not forget, in reading the texts subsequent to the "turn," the (in fact *definitive*) accomplishment of earlier texts having to do with the analytic of Dasein and the fundamental essence of phenomenology. To say Being/Sein quite

---

17. Looking for palpable examples of such shifts in "seeing" we can turn to cinema as a complex technical medium (a *Gesamtkunstwerk*) able to communicate, at least to some degree, radical semiotic change. It would exceed the project of this book to analyze films in detail, but we can cite, among many possible others, Alfonso Cuarón's *Gravity* (2013), Guillermo del Toro's *Shape of Water* (2017), Denis Villeneuve's *Arrival* (2016) and his *Blade Runner 2049* (2017).

18. Heidegger, "Letter on Humanism," in *Basic Writings*, 213–66.

simply would not be possible if man were not able to attain his dignity of Dasein . . .[19]

In other words, Heidegger's first establishment of the philosophy of *being* depended on the primary role and content of the human in relation to the theme. Marion does not use the word "relation" but Heidegger's *Being and Time* is shot through with Dasein's relations—to objects, to other humans, to death, to time, to *being*. These are the phenomenological relations that make the disclosure of *being* possible in the first place. But Heidegger converts these relations into the priority of *being* by diminishing the human role. So Marion again: "The later isolated anteriority of *Sein* is secured concretely by Dasein over itself; phenomenologically, the anteriority of Being can be developed and justified only by the anteriority of the analytic of Dasein."[20] You could say, therefore, that far from being the hero, Dasein is the slave of *being*, the one whose existence provides the essential preconditions for the Master but who must then pretend and project the Master's anteriority.

Marion, therefore, successfully suggests an associated idolatry of Heidegger's *Sein*. Because Heidegger's ontology covertly but decisively has human existence aim at *being*, and then decide on "God" within that frame, then it is the human gaze which always settles the question. "The proposition 'God is a being' itself appears as an idol, because it only returns the aim that, in advance, decides that every possible 'God,' present or absent, in one way or another, has to be." But then, as he asks provocatively, "Is it self-evident that God should have to be?"[21] Rather, he implies, is it not the case of one (God) who gazes on us, with unfathomable love, from outside any possible constitution by the human gaze?

The emergence of such a possibility is the whole thought of the present book in its struggle to disclose a transforming sign and its corresponding relation. Girardian anthropology confirms that the "god" first appeared as the sacred freezing of humans' violent gaze, brought to a moment of absolute attention by the coagulating murder of the victim. From then on "being" (entities) crystallize around this fixed point, receiving the associated glow of the god/idol's dazzling fixity. Heidegger's philosophy successfully removes the luminance of metaphysics from being, and it is for this reason that it is an epochal achievement. In its covert way it is a Christian project

---

19. Marion, *God Without Being*, 42.
20. Marion, *God Without Being*, 42.
21. Marion, *God Without Being*, 44. Marion's goal is "to think God without any conditions, not even that of Being, hence, to think God without pretending to inscribe him or to describe him as a being" (*God Without Being*, 45).

and preparatory in fact to Marion's "God *without* being." Meanwhile, in the place of metaphysics, *being* for Heidegger is the primordial event of the world, coalescing into actual beings but always bearing the trace of an original violence. Girard points this out explicitly, as we shall see shortly. More subtly, Heidegger continues to say in his later writings that being also *withdraws*.[22] It can never give itself conclusively. Why? Heidegger states it as a matter of fact, but we may rightly infer that there will never be a consistent self-giving or wholeness to *being* because it belongs to the annihilating crisis prior to the world. Metaphysics serves to fix this in place, but once we remove its dazzling light we are faced with the chaotic flux from which being came. The resolution provided by the victim waits in the wings, always needing to be renewed, but it does not happen: only the crisis remains. Thus, through ontology the incandescent light of metaphysics collapses, leaving the still more dangerous phosphorescence of being. It is the displacement of conventional ordnance by nuclear physics.

Marion does not talk exactly in these terms, with their Girardian backstory, but the congenial fit of his reflections with a Girardian analysis permits we make the identifying leap. If the human gaze always decides in advance that all transcendence ("every possible 'god'") has "to be" is it not because this transcendence belongs essentially to original violence, to a founding construction of the world out of anger and blood?

However, if this should be so, what should we think of a "God without *being*" breaking into this hell of existence? Would not such a God be necessarily a "God *without violence*"? A God who is foreign to our false coalescences of being, coming to us from an unimagined and unimaginable otherwise? Would not such a God look very much like the exegesis of divine "glory" we give in the final chapter? And would not such a God work by, precisely, a *hypostasis*, an existence of unfathomable giving, a "stasis" which is in fact a movement, always flowing down, *hypo*, below—a spring, a fountain, a giving, always able to pour out more? And, finally, should such a God touch our human hearts would that not leave the sense of something, of some incommensurable truth to be signed/signified rather than caught in a falsifying realm of ideas achieved by the mirrored gaze? The gospel boldly signs (pro-claims) this claim, nothing more nor less.

In which case Heidegger's critique of onto-theology and theological metaphysics is reinforced rather than diminished. As we have seen, Heidegger's understanding already receives a dramatic underpinning by a Girardian reading. Once you think "ontological difference" from the Girardian

---

22. Heidegger, *Contributions to Philosophy*, with multiple references establishing a counter-revelatory movement, for example p. 88, "being [archaic spelling] itself is essentially determined as this self-withdrawing concealment."

point of view of original crisis, you understand at once that "god" belongs to something human beings do, rather than a God "from the outside" might be thought of doing. The next step is to see that the metaphysical tradition is nothing other than a dishonest understanding of where our concepts come from—by radical forgetting of their source in the murdered victim, and thereafter a transformation into "pure ideas." If we add Marion's analysis of the conceptual idol it further underlines Heidegger's seminal critique of metaphysics. "Conceptual idolatry does not remain a universally vague suspicion but inscribes itself in the global strategy of thought taken in its metaphysical figure."[23] After this, we may rightly suspect that such idolatry and metaphysics have infected the whole conceptual apparatus by which "God" has been grasped in the Christian tradition.

It remains painfully easy to fall into this mode of thought, but what we stand before today—and Marion's work underscores it—is an epochal shift from the "metaphysical figure" to a semiotics of nonviolent transcendence. By definition, such a transcendence cannot be taught inside a conceptual idolatry. It can only come somehow *despite* concepts. By deconstruction, community, song, gift of tongues, art, movies, silence, centering prayer, contemplation, conversation, storytelling, signs, sacraments, scripture, personal discovery. The work of the thinker and theologian is to use the language of the conceptual tradition in order to find freedom from it, and to point the believer, the near-believer and the nonbeliever in the direction of the irruptive relation that is the character of the true God. Marion himself focuses on the iconic event of the Eucharist, and while this is certainly a privileged sign of the *hupostasis* of pouring out, his single emphasis can seem somewhat pious and churchy. If the hypostatic relation has entered into the world—such that the ontological relation of signs becomes more and more central to human meaning—it tells us that it is impossible to control in advance where the in-breaking of God might show up.

Logos and Violence

A few exceptional, spellbinding pages in Girard's writing reveal him fully to recognize and declare the semiotic novum brought by the gospel. He goes a good bit further than Marion, because his point of departure is more basic—anthropological rather than phenomenological. If the origins of humanity itself are tied up with violence, and the signification resulting from it, then whatever reveals this, and at the same time offers an alternative, has to constitute an entirely new semiosis or fount of human meaning. Girard

---

23. Marion, *God Without Being*, 36.

strongly suggests this very pattern by repeating some pivotal conclusions that Heidegger himself came to regarding the Christian "Logos" or Word.

Girard echoes and affirms Heidegger's confident dismissal of the New Testament Logos from the general territory of Greek philosophical thought. But what amounts to a rude and violent expulsion in Heidegger becomes in Girard a badge of honor. By affirming this Heideggerean gesture Girard, implicitly yet vigorously, affirms the critique of onto-theology that we have described, requiring in turn something like the approach here. The only thing he lacks is a fully dynamic account of the Christian Logos/Word, but, as we shall see, it hovers just below the surface. A Word driven out shows itself as such and, absent retaliatory violence, becomes necessarily the *hupostasis* of forgiving and self-giving. By finishing our reflections with this argument, we conclude effectively with a Girardian endorsement of theological semiotics.

As we have noted earlier, the middle section of *Things Hidden since the Foundation of the World* is formed by Book II (second out of three). The book or division's title is "The Judaeo-Christian Scriptures" and it provides first a "Non-Sacrificial Reading" and then a survey of "The Sacrificial Reading and Historical Christianity." It is well known that Girard recanted on his rejection of the language of sacrifice, accepting, later on, a certain Christianized usage of the word.[24] But that does not mean he gave up on his analysis of the intellectual pathway of Western Christianity. Indeed, it would be impossible to do so without renouncing the dramatic breakthrough of his own thought. Heidegger makes a fervent distinction between the logos of the Greek philosopher Heraclitus and the logos of the Gospel of John. The divorce Heidegger effects flies 180 degrees contrary to classic Christian theology, from early patristic times on, which saw Greek thought, and Heraclitus in particular, as intellectual anticipations of the gospel.[25] Instead Heidegger says, "The proclamation of the cross is Christ himself: he is the logos of redemption, of eternal life . . . A whole world separates all this from Heraclitus."[26] The Heraclitean logos for Heidegger is a primordial gathering of *being*, which involves the creation of difference necessarily by and through violence. Girard completely agrees, endorsing and establishing the separating out of John's Logos on the basis of nonviolence. "Heidegger recognizes that the Greek Logos is inseparably linked

24. Girard, *One by Whom Scandal Comes*, 33–45.

25. For example, Justin Martyr: "Those who lived reasonably [*meta logou*, "with the word"] are Christians, even though they have been thought Atheists; as, among the Greeks, Socrates and Heraclitus, and men like them . . ." See *First Apology* 46 (*ANF*, 1:178).

26. Heidegger, *Introduction to Metaphysics*, 135.

with violence."[27] Meanwhile, "The Johannine Logos is foreign to any kind of violence."[28] It is a simple but cataclysmic separation, one that has never been clearly before recognized, let alone made systematic. Girard goes on to assert, instead, the systematic domination of the Greek Logos and its thought in Christian thought and history.

> Heidegger is absolutely right to state that there has never been any thought in the West but Greek thought, even when the labels were Christian. Christianity has no special existence in the domain of thought. Continuity with the Greek Logos has never been interrupted . . . Heidegger, like any true thinker, participates despite himself in the immense process of the revelation [of the authentic Logos].

A little earlier Girard noted, "The distinctiveness of the true Logos has never been noticed, since to miss it is exactly the same thing as being under the illusion of welcoming it, while participating in the process of its expulsion."[29]

It would be hard to offer a more stringent reading of Christian institutional and theological history in the face of the dramatic novum of the Johannine Logos, the *hupostasis* of self-giving love as we have characterized it. Girard is writing here in the first dawn of his full hypothesis. There are no shadowed, dusty corners, no mumbles of compromise. As such, we gain an unrivaled moment of clarity, one that cannot be forfeited for the sake of any specially-pled grand tradition. The historic moment of crisis the world stands at, in face of its own engorged violence, does not permit us to look away.

Girard insists on the figure of expulsion. The Logos of John is expelled by the sacrificial reading and by the ecclesiastical tradition of Greek thought. It would be an error at this point for Protestant readers to insist that because the Reformation rebelled against scholastic thought it was somehow then in possession of the primitive biblical Logos. The fact that the Reformation asserted itself by force of arms showed that it had by no means escaped from Christendom and its Greek (Roman) heritage. Moreover, the rationalism of "Justification Theory" demonstrates some of this tradition's particular

---

27. Girard et al., *Things Hidden*, 265. There are several passages in *An Introduction to Metaphysics* which emphatically endorse the role of violence in *being*, e.g., 131, 149–50. See especially 62: "*Polemos* and *logos* are the same," just after quoting Heraclitus's Fragment 53, *polemos pantōn men patēr esti: conflict/war is the father of all* . . . For original gathering within this context see 128–29.

28. Girard et al., *Things Hidden*, 271.

29. Girard et al., *Things Hidden*, 272; and above, 273.

indebtedness to forensic logical form, one of strict retribution and restitution.[30] There is nothing nonviolent about this. For Girard, the expulsion of the Logos acts as a hallmark of its genuineness—a violent system cannot tolerate a nonviolent truth: "The Johannine Logos is foreign to any kind of violence; it is therefore forever expelled."[31] However, there is a level of contradiction in this argument, one that is not resolved by Girard.

How is it possible for Girard (with Heidegger before him) to detect the Johannine Logos, independent of Greek thought, if that Logos had not in some way opened its own space of revelation even as it was being expelled? This is where we must perhaps return to Marion and his "iconic" vision, where "the icon opens in a face that gazes at our gazes in order to summon them to its depth." From a rationalist perspective this might be termed "mystical," but in terms of the thought here it is nothing less than the semiotic breakthrough of divine selfhood into a violent world—a selfhood capable of transforming human selfhood into the selfsame identity. Because the selfhood of God is nonviolent it comes to us as fathomless depths that pour themselves out even as they invite us into the same. Therefore, what looks like expulsion, as driving *away*, becomes—in "the corner of the eye" almost—a continuing pouring out and a giving, and one that is realized, understood, repeated in the self of the observer. It is the mimetic response of the aggressor to one who "turns the other cheek": despite his violence he cannot help being infected by the alternative humanity enacted before and, neurologically, within him. The same with the nonviolence of the expelled Logos: it floods back into the whole human system as summoning gaze, as grace.[32]

No one can be immune to this reflux of grace, because every human being has that corner of the eye where the truth of the self-giving Logos can be seen. It is grace which reveals the victim, for it is first the entering of nonviolence into the human system withdrawing the mirror of violence totally from the victim. If not, Girard's whole thesis of the revelation of the victim by virtue of the cross fails; his whole *anthropology* of the Bible fails; indeed, his whole protest at the founding murder fails. But, in fact, Girard intends no such thing. He adds at the end of the discussion we have been

30. Douglas Campbell has demonstrated the rational calculus of justification theory, questioning however a great deal of its supposed logic. Especially this: how does the ethical frame of carnal man collapse and be brought to despair (and so move to accept Christ as savior) through a logic conceived from within its own worldview? Campbell, *Deliverance of God*, 44–49.

31. Girard, *Things Hidden*, 271.

32. It is worth commenting that this counter-movement of an expelled Logos is the exact inverse of the Heideggerean withdrawal of *being* even as it shows itself: the divine Logos gives itself even as it is expelled, the other removes itself even as it is constituted as or reveals individual beings.

describing, "All the same, the Logos is still in the process of revealing itself; if it tolerates being concealed yet another time, this is to put off for just a while the fullness of its revelation."[33]

So, it is that the universe of things which ontology celebrates must become "all things new" by virtue of the "without being" of *hupostasis*. How can we know this will be so? Because, precisely, the sign of the Logos/Word has entered the world. The philosophical Logos has been understood as the organizing principle of beings. Girard indeed defines the traditional term as "the divine, rational and logical principle according to which the world is organized."[34] Heidegger treats the Heraclitean logos no differently—as principle of power—but he does so ontologically and concretely, understanding logos as a gathering or collection, the togetherness of all beings, including, as noted, necessary opposites. It is the Christian tradition which has put the accent on Logos as discourse, narrative or word, rather than any kind of violent power. What is being said here is a radicalization of that tradition, insisting on the word only and as such, as *sign*. Only a word, a "simple breath of air" carrying forgiveness can enter a body and heart without violence. If we did not have such a word of nonviolence, one that had entered the world, then there would be absolutely no hope of "all things new." But because there is such a word, one that dramatically, drastically, impossibly and continually counters the violence of the world, we know that things can be changed. For such a word or relation to enter the universe of violent things is already and fully an impossibility. Where did it come from? How did it get here? The questions remain, but once that word is here, and once we grasp its radical strangeness, we are brought to a realization of what is impossible. Things can change, because this sign, against all odds, *signifies* as much. It will continue to signify again and again, telling us over and over that such a new world is possible. Of course, it is feasible to remain outside of this signification, to choose to remain in violent ontology. But that can never stop the *meaning*, the *relation*, of a transformed universe asserting itself.

Therefore, to finish, a story . . .

I was in my first year of grad studies. The room was dark, lit by candles; drinks and snacks were on hand. The doctoral students were sharing their "stuff," their individual interests and arguments which were to form the core of their theses and get them their PhDs. The purpose was a kind of sorority and fraternity of candidates, with the possibility of fruitful dialogue and cross-fertilization. The candles flickered, people were cagey. It was apparent that even here there were "cool kids," the ones who thought

---

33. Girard et al., *Things Hidden*, 274.
34. Girard et al., *Things Hidden*, 263.

that they were destined for greatness by virtue of simply being who they were. And, after them . . . everyone else. The cool kids already had a kind of language in common, one with "PhD" in a footnote to each sentence. One of the non-cool group gave too much away about his thoughts, and the kind of language he spoke was clearly non-cool; there were barely suppressed sniggers. Somehow the topic of violence also came up. And this is where the whole thing hit me and left a lasting impression. There was an almost immediate consensus that nonviolent self-giving was impossible, that it was a myth invented basically to suppress and exploit women and minorities. This viewpoint, with the *cool* imprimatur, was beyond argument. I knew I did not agree. I understood the way ideology can be constructed to maintain oppressive order, but at the same time individuals may truly be free to serve, to not retaliate. But I did not feel confident of enough of my own language to put my case, nor did I wish to expose it to the consensus of *cool*. But the word was real inside me. And now, approximately twenty years later, I believe I have brought it to light.

My point is that this Word exists, while all else seems like violence, and more violence. Progressively, this Word stands forth as the most real thing there is. If the violence of being destroys human-beings then *being* itself is no more—there will be no one left for whom it remains a question. The ontological relation will itself disappear. In which case the *hupostasis* relation is the only thing that can save being, the only thing to give beings their being. "Behold I make all things new!"

And, therefore again, "Heaven and earth [i.e., *being*] shall pass away, but my words shall not pass away" (therein and thereby making all things new).

10

The Semiotic Gospel

John as Transformative Semiosis

EMERGING LIKE A SHIP at daybreak on an unknown shore, the Gospel of John stands in the New Testament as a sudden event of transcendence that somehow was always there. Or, at least, that, once there, was always also meant to be there. Its use of signs and symbols is at an exceptional level of skill and effect, making it a masterpiece of biblical semiosis. John's Gospel's operation of signs is very likely the peak example of their function in the whole biblical corpus. Pursuing a commentary in the light of all the foregoing, should make this Gospel the textbook case and flag-bearer for the overall theoretic argument.

The story of the community of John's Gospel is of vital interest: it provides key background to how this remarkable literature was put in place. The scholarship of Raymond Brown offered a persuasive hypothetical reconstruction of the stages by which the Johannine group evolved—to the point where it produces its singular written Gospel from around the year 90 CE.[1] The story of accretions and shifts in the makeup of the community may be disputed in one or other features but the basic outline has retained its coherence, and it is important here as it indicates how complexity of

---

1. Brown, *Community of the Beloved Disciple*. Also, Brown's *Gospel according to John*, considered the "gold standard" of modern scholarship. Brown's reconstructed stages are essentially: 1) disciples of John the Baptist, still in some way loyal to him; 2) Jews of anti-temple views who brought with them a group of Samaritan converts and therewith the makings of a "high Christology"; 3) Gentile converts with a more universal or cosmopolitan viewpoint. There are also distinctions among Jewish believers, including some who embraced faith in Jesus but wished to avoid breaking with the synagogue, and still others who balked at the radicalism of Jesus as complete replacement of Abraham and Moses.

origins and multiplicity of voices are still resolved in the text into a single, highly distinctive literary character.

The influence in the Gospel of a core figure named the Beloved Disciple is a cardinal element, giving a unique authority and voice to the material. If we add, then, the actual author (and probably a third figure, a final editor of the Gospel) we begin to get an idea of a succession of critical individuals in its composition.[2] The unique style of the Fourth Gospel has to depend on these inspired individuals who lent their spiritual and intellectual quality to the final product. The difference from the other three canonical gospels is so marked as to give these other writings, by contrast, a collective name—the Synoptics. The three other gospels were composed on a linear plan (a one-time-only progression from Galilee to Jerusalem) and it is almost universally agreed that Matthew and Luke depended on the basic outline provided by Mark. John, in contrast, has its own plan along with a supreme freedom in staging and related discourse. And yet it is one of the canonical gospels, in the same exclusive community and genre as the other three.

Examining the figure of the Beloved Disciple provides a starting point for our semiotic study of this Gospel. After all, such a powerful reference without clear identity is pretty obviously a "sign," or, as Peirce could say, an open-ended *interpretant*. The individual appears only in the final stages of the Gospel (13:23–25; 19:26–27; 20:2–10; 21:7, 20–24) but has a formidable role in terms of closeness to Jesus, power of faith, and testimony to the Gospel's record. Traditionally seen as John, the son of Zebedee, modern scholarship is much more likely to see him/her as a historical character who is not to be identified with one of the Twelve, maybe a representative figure, or simply a textual device; or, indeed, all these things at once. It is hard to argue with Brown's statement: "The thesis that he [the Beloved Disciple] is purely fictional or only an ideal figure is quite implausible. It would mean that the author of John 21:20–23 was deceived or deceptive, for he reports distress in the community over the Beloved Disciple's death."[3] The very fact, however, that the "fictional" character of the Beloved Disciple is proposed tells us that there is something about this figure in the text which evokes a

---

2. Brown, *Community of the Beloved Disciple*, 102. See also Schneiders, *Written That You May Believe*. Schneiders's work provides something of a touchstone for the study here, from the historical, feminist and literary perspectives she uses. She is responsive to "John's superbly effective and highly charged use of language" (27) and bases her close reading of the text on what she sees as "the most important literary-theological feature of John's Gospel" (36), which she identifies as "symbolism." This is a different theoretical model from "signs" and "semiotics"—and we shall come back again to the quite significant contrast—but it recognizes the pivotal role of meaning-making contained in human discourse.

3. Brown, *Community of the Beloved Disciple*, 31.

literary or semiotic sense. Is this not a role, a dramatic character, much more than a real, historical individual? But, then again, if the community is centered on this figure—see 21:24, "This is the disciple who is testifying to these things and has written them, and we know that his testimony is true"—how could it be simply that? I can think personally of three or four intentional communities with a distinctive spiritual life—and in all these cases there must invariably be a generative individual at their core: it is impossible to think of the community without this flesh-and-blood source.

So why the hiddenness of the figure? Why is his/her identity "so carefully obscured in the Gospel text that it has been impossible, despite centuries of painstaking exegetical work, to identify this figure conclusively?" Sandra Schneiders's point is well taken. She goes on, "It is hard to believe that if this figure is, in fact, the authority behind the Gospel the identity of this person was simply lost to memory . . . In other words, the anonymity of the Beloved Disciple seems to be a deliberate, carefully executed literary strategy."[4] Why?

The answer must come at various prismatic angles of the same basic issue. If the Johannine community that produced the Gospel valued intimacy of spirit and heart with Jesus (see, for example, where the disciple leans on Jesus's breast, John 13:23) over hierarchical legal commission then it was very unlikely that it could make the role exclusive, even if there was one crucial figure who fulfilled this identity. There are indeed numerous candidates who have been argued for the possible historical figure at the root of the role, through Lazarus, Nathaniel, the presbyter of Second and Third John, the unnamed disciple of John 1:35–40, Mary Magdalene, the author of the Gospel, etc.[5] Any or all of them have valid claims to the title. In which case a first part of an answer is that the Beloved Disciple is a representative figure, comprising many individuals.

Metaphysics versus Codes

Brown's description of the final stages of the Johannine community shows us how the Beloved Disciple model of authority fell off the cliff of popular metaphysical religiosity. He describes how round about the year 100 secessionists began to leave the Johannine community. The Epistles of John reflect an "intra-Johannine schism" where a group of believers so emphasized the divinity of Christ that the earthly reality of Jesus was at least forgotten about, if

---

4. Schneiders, *Written That You May Believe*, 244.

5. Charlesworth, *Beloved Disciple*, identifies no fewer than twenty-two candidates for the role in the history of commentary.

not simply negated. Everything instead operated at the level of the eternal and spiritual.[6] Those who held this opinion "went out" from the community and its authority (1 John 2:19). Those gathered around the "Beloved Disciple" had little defense against this proto-gnostic spirituality sweeping the communities and, in the end, according to Brown, they were forced to seek refuge in the ranks of Petrine Christianity establishing itself around the Mediterranean. Only in this way could they preserve the incarnational materialism of their gospel alongside its exalted divine notion of Jesus.[7]

I shall remark some more below on the critical tensions on display in this very early Christian struggle. For now, the issue is still the plurality of possible candidates for the generative relationship of Beloved Disciple. Within the plurality, women necessarily appear on the list, and that provides another angle on the carefully preserved anonymity of this constitutive role. The implication of women's leadership obviously provides a connection to the situation just described (of the fragile institutional nature of Johannine communities), invoking women's suspect status within overall male apostolic Christianity. It is at this point that Mary Magdalene is indicated as a candidate with one of the strongest sets of credentials for the original role.

In her discussion Sandra Schneiders explains the nexus:

> It was not until Irenaeus (c. 130–200) offered his defense of the apostolic [John, son of Zebedee] authorship of the Johannine Gospel and epistles late in the second century that the Fourth Gospel claimed its canonical place in the New Testament. There seems little doubt that part of the reason for the uncertainty of the early church about the Fourth Gospel derived from its popularity among the Gnostics, who were being labeled heretics during the second and third centuries.[8] And part of the reason for regarding the Gnostics as heretics seems to have been the very important apostolic roles and functions they assigned

---

6. Brown, *Community of the Beloved Disciple*, 109–20.

7. In return they brought "high Christology" to the rest of Christianity, a frame of understanding which made a crucial contribution to the christological discussion and councils of the third, fourth, and fifth centuries. See, for example, Origen, *Commentary on John* I.6. What I will go on to argue here is that the divine identity of Jesus, developed over the centuries in conceptual language of hypostasis, person and nature, emerges in John with a very different dynamic, one rooted in a dramatic change in semiosis. It is this change which makes John's Christology "stick its landing," not the metaphysical conceptualization of later Christianity. In John, Jesus proves himself God by abyssal love, not abstract doctrine.

8. Brown has a short account of the various heterodox writings in the early and middle second century making use of John; see his *Community of the Beloved Disciple*, 147–48.

to women, even as the early church was retrenching from the egalitarian discipleship of the earliest Jesus movement. Not only were women prominent leadership figures in the Gnostic literature, but among the women so portrayed Mary Magdalene was clearly the most important.[9]

Schneiders goes on pointedly to summarize the parallels between the situation in some of the Gnostic literature and that of the Fourth Gospel. "[I]f a composite picture of Mary Magdalene is constructed from this literature, she appears as Jesus' favorite and beloved disciple because she loves him more and better than the male disciples and is more perceptive of the deep meaning of his revelation and therefore is charged by Jesus to transmit and explain it, for which reason Simon Peter considers her a rival and tries unsuccessfully to get her demoted by Jesus. But Jesus defends her and her preeminence among the disciples as well as the superiority of her understanding of him and his message. It is difficult not to recognize the features of the Johannine Beloved Disciple in this Mary Magdalene of the apocryphal literature."[10]

As already remarked, the Gospel of John is thought to have been written before the end of the first century, so it would seem the intentional obscurity covering a possible Magdalene candidature for Beloved Disciple actually predates the early second-century conflict around Gnosticism. It might thus suggest a more original layer of experience, one before the Gnostic interpretations took off and employed the Magdalene tradition in their propaganda. In which case the author of the Fourth Gospel wants both to neutralize a possible personal rivalry (between Mary and Simon Peter) and, at the same time, signal the very real grounds of a tension. We have here, therefore, a possible history with extremely rich connotations in a semiotic reading of the scriptures. If a woman is indeed the founding figure of the "Beloved Disciple" we need at once to avoid any trite sexual connotation and see how an alternative source of the Jesus tradition—female rather than male—automatically grounds interpretation in a different semiotics, in signs which generate female meaning. Relationality, sensibility, touch, compassion, tenderness, mothering, nonviolent suffering—these are all notes that can arise in such an alternate feminine semiosis. And the very fact that the author of John had to go to such lengths both to obscure a possible female leadership of the community and, at the same time, signal its actual dynamic in the narrative shows us that this Gospel is indeed

---

9. Schneiders, *Written That You May Believe*, 244.
10. Schneiders, *Written That You May Believe*, 245.

a matter of semiotic intention and transformation.[11] The implied drama of female relationship to Jesus of itself releases a communication that is not a matter of metaphysical definition but rather of hypostatic relation. We are looking at a late first-century semiotic *tour de force*, followed by a slow, centuries-long permeation of meaning that is ultimately able to change the character of Christianity itself.

It may be that necessity became a compositional virtue in the writing of the Gospel. If the need to obscure the identity of the Beloved Disciple was a matter of first-century ecclesiastical politics, it would not have taken long for a brilliant writer like the author to understand the gift they were being given. They would have understood immediately the semiotic openness and transferability of the trope, "Beloved Disciple." Or, perhaps both things came simultaneously, telling the writer that to create an anonymous figure in the place of a named, historical person served both to make oblique what in direct terms would be dangerous and to provide in the obliqueness an endless source of reference and possibility. This simultaneity—of flesh-and-blood individuality and anonymous generality—is the conclusion which Schneiders comes to. For her "the Beloved Disciple is neither a pure literary symbol nor a single historical individual. The Beloved Disciple is a kind of textual paradigm who concretely embodies in the text the corporate authority of the Johannine school . . . The textual paradigm is derived from real disciples who realize it in diverse ways."[12] These disciples include Lazarus, Thomas, Mary Magdalene, Mary and Martha of Bethany, etc. A "textual paradigm" is another expression for a semiotic code, one which, in this case, includes the sememe of all the vibrant models of discipleship in the Fourth Gospel, female and male, together with all possible subsequent readers who mimetically identify as disciples in the drama of the text.

In this way "Beloved Disciple" is perhaps the premier biblical "sign" of John's Gospel, in the technical senses both of "something that stands for something else" plus the intensely transformative function it carries. It inserts the role and reality of "Beloved Disciple" into gospel discourse, the ongoing core language of Christianity, and over against the simultaneously emerging and legally self-confident role of hierarchical apostleship. Its semiotic

---

11. Schneiders shows how in the Fourth Gospel "we find women presented in an extraordinarily positive light in relation to Jesus and in relation to male members of the community" (*Written That You May Believe*, 95). She highlights four episodes between Jesus and women in which the women have exceptional roles as witnesses to the revelation of Jesus and leading representatives of the believing community (101–14), and she considers the Woman at the Well "the textual alter ego" of the Gospel author, if not the author herself (253).

12. Schneiders, *Written That You May Believe*, 246.

subtlety and triumph will surely alert us to the semiotic values pervading the whole Gospel. If the author could create such a fluent and successful sign, then we must be alert to the employment of semiosis throughout the text. If we turn now from this privileged sign to more general architectural features, we can carry this sensibility to their understanding.

Lines of Semiosis

A way of identifying large-scale function is to draw connecting lines, and lines have been drawn in John's Gospel in multiple ways: from grand lines of structure, through major symbolic themes, to rhetorical and verbal patterns and styles. The overall shape of the Gospel has been compared to a mandala, a figure of concentric rings. The center in this reading lies with the images of Jesus walking on water and the feeding of the multitude, amounting to a new event of the exodus for a new Israel.[13] Picturing the Gospel in this way tells us that it lends itself to a holistic, contemplative interpretation, in which the whole is greater than the sum of the parts, achieving a single integral meaning. In many individual instances the written text displays a circular motif in which words are repeated with slightly different modulations bringing a cumulative impact, dense with meaning. "The cyclical repetition in the Fourth Gospel is like a spiral staircase that takes the reader up higher, down deeper, passing again and again the same familiar points . . ."[14] Again a feature like this points to a semiotic effect in which the nonlinear use of signs alerts us not simply to a surface of meaning but to a topography of depth, height, and panorama. At the same time, it draws us to the signs themselves and how they are employed with art and artifice to achieve an end, one beyond the straightforward narrative progression. This, I believe, is a major reason why the supposed author of the Gospel, "John," has been traditionally titled "the theologian." It is not that the other three Gospels are non-theological—far from it. It is because the Fourth Gospel uses the word, the *logos*, deliberately and systemically in this highly conscious way. The words of the Gospel are intended ultimately to carry a sense of the divine, and that is why the Gospel is *theo-logical*—communicating "God" in word and narrative. Tracing some of the lines of the Gospel in a semiotic register shows us how their conscious, technical design is able to bring about this effect. The dizzying, oscillating

---

13. Barnhart, *Good Wine: Reading John from the Center*.

14. Schneiders, *Written That You May Believe*, 29; see the parade example of the opening words of the Gospel, "In the beginning was the Word, and the Word was with God, and the Word was God. He was in the beginning with God."

working of the text is able to transcend linear meaning and bring about a remarkable impact of generative new meaning.[15]

In chapter 8, verse 12 Jesus declares, "I am the light of the world." This is a famous gospel statement, represented frequently in art and literature, a kind of kerygma in a nutshell. The abrupt announcement tells us that the person of Jesus is the light by which the world is illumined. The immediately declared consequence is that "whoever follows me will never walk in darkness but will have the light of life." Thus, we are told that the light is indiscriminately the light of the world, yet it suggests a personal choice to "follow" in order that the individual will in fact possess "the light of life." "Light" is a universal human symbol, something holding intrinsic meaning for life. Without the sun there is no plant growth, no physical health, and the opposition to darkness evokes for everyone contrasts of fear and security, cold and warmth, death and life. The continuation of the verse at once makes this semiotic connection: Jesus is "the light *of life*." He is the light carrying all those natural and human associations for life. The passage also connects internally to other passages of the Gospel, creating a line of semiotic force. Notably we hear in the prologue the following:

> What has come into being in him was life, and the life was the light of all people. The light shines in the darkness, and the darkness did not overcome it. (1:4–5)

The contrast with darkness is here a headline to the Gospel and constructs thereby not simply a sign of the truth but a structural opposition to that sign, and on a universal human plane. Connecting this to the passage in chapter 8 is to see the light not as a neutral abstract symbol, but a dramatic engagement with the person of Jesus. The Gospel, in this way, creates a powerful tension around this person, and the tension pervades the stories about him. The semiosis also connects forward from chapter 8 to chapter 9, which is entirely taken up with the miracle of healing a man born blind. The chapter is among the most beautiful subplots of the Gospel, as it gives so much space and development of character to the man born blind, the subject of the healing. The man moves progressively from passive recipient of Jesus's miraculous intervention to a formidable witness to the truth and

---

15. Some of the following arguments could easily be applied in terms of rhetorical criticism (see, for example, Phyllis Trible's *Rhetorical Criticism*), but the background here is always the generative character of semiotics, from their beginning in violence to their transformation in revelatory nonviolence. Tracing semiotic connections allows us to spell out this transformation explicitly, rather than viewing it seeing it simply as a "rhetorical exercise." For a straightforward application of rhetorical criticism to the material, see, for example, Salier's *Rhetorical Impact of the Sēmeia in the Gospel of John*.

believer in Jesus, a model of a disciple and, thus, another flesh-and-blood candidate to fill the semiotic shoes of "Beloved Disciple." The healing by Jesus is explicitly named a "sign" Jesus performs (9:16), and here is evinced a major thread in the weaving of the text showing us that the author is working deliberately with semiotic coding.

At 2:11 and 4:54 the signs of Jesus are numbered (first and second), leading commentators to posit an original "signs gospel," on which the canonical gospel was based.[16] In these instances, the signs are miracles, events that show power over nature, and this is generally the content given to the Fourth Gospel sign (*sēmeion*). The numeration, however, disappears after that (although, as in the present case, there are indications that other Gospel miracles could be considered a continuation of the series). But "sign" in the Gospel carries the technical sense of "sign from God," a work vindicating the agent's status as coming from God and giving rise to faith in the observer (see 6:26-30). In which case, the signs of Jesus have themselves to be interpreted in order to believe that God is working through him. In the passage in chapter 6 just cited there is the evident irony of the crowd asking for a sign to warrant their belief, after they have just witnessed and participated in the miraculous feeding of the five thousand. Jesus goes on to identify *himself* as "the bread of life" (6:35), so clearly the miraculous "sign" does not work unless it belongs to a living relationship with the person of Jesus. The Gospel of John's "sign," therefore, has to be continuous with the whole communication of the gospel, mediating the depth of what this person means.[17] John's *semeion* belongs to the fabric of the whole text and the deliberate interruption in the sequence of signs after the first two suggests that, although the miracles have a function, their sign value is never their strict literal interruption of the natural order; they are not to be fastened on in that external way. John's technique takes the "miraculous" sign and then breaks the code of its "natural" evidentiality, leading us to something dramatically different and new.

Returning to the man born blind, his healing is considered something extraordinary because he had been born blind—his blindness did not result from accident or illness but could be considered bound to a founding order of things, that is, to God's will. This is why his parents are involved (9:2, 18-21)—as likely original culprits bringing doom on their son through their sin. But Jesus denies connection to anything like blame or karma (9:3), claiming instead that the reason for the man's blindness is proleptic, that is,

---

16. Most notably, Bultmann, *Gospel of John*.

17. Bultmann famously thought the words as also to be considered signs (*Gospel of John*, 452, 698).

to be found in future things. "He was born blind so that God's works might be revealed in him" (9:3b). God's work is to release creation from its bondage to violence, and this can only be done from within that condition by a transformative relationship, because violence is itself a fundamental mode of relationship. The man is questioned three times about what Jesus did to him, once by the general populace and twice by the Pharisees. Each time the man answers more stoutly than before, ending up by theologically quashing the Pharisees. The last thing he says is a mic drop: "Never since the world began has it been heard that anyone opened the eyes of a person born blind. If this man were not from God, he could do nothing" (9:32–33). This tells us that what is at issue is something to do with the constitution of the world itself and, therefore, Jesus is in the business not simply of repairing what is damaged but of resetting the very order of things. Hence, this "sign"—of the healing of the blind man—can only be meaningful in and through the progression of the man's own understanding or sight, given in the whole story, and reaching its conclusion in this climactic statement.

The actual healing is carried out by means of an elaborate theater which is of course semiotic. Schneiders makes use of the word "symbolic" to describe the actions and stage directions from Jesus, and she sees "symbolism" as a major category for understanding the Gospel. She asserts bluntly, "The Johannine *semeia* are, in contemporary terms, not signs but symbols." For her, "Unlike the sign, which merely points to or stands for an absent reality that is totally other than itself, the symbol *renders present* the transcendent because and in so far as it participates in what it re-presents."[18] As well perhaps as being semiotically naïve, this viewpoint makes uncritical use of a concept of transcendence and the ability of human beings to access it via an unexplained mechanism of symbolism. At stake is a default Christian mindset of otherworldliness, and the presumption of a soul that belongs there and so can communicate with it. It's as if symbols act independently of the human mind, with a sovereignty belonging to their privileged access to content. But why then do they need to be explained—especially in John (including by Schneiders)? Why, in fact, do they need a scheme of *interpretants*? From a Girardian perspective, symbolism belongs to the primitive sacred and is only slowly subject to critique via a reflective and analytic system of signs. These, then, are serious concerns in respect of a theoretic of symbolism, but they clearly do not disable use of the language of symbol in respect of John. I would say, in fact, that this language rides

---

18. Schneiders, *Written That You May Believe*, 66–67, italics original. Schneiders derives this position from Paul Ricoeur, citing his *Interpretation Theory*. This understanding of symbols and symbolism goes back at least to Paul Tillich; see *Dynamics of Faith*, 41–45.

on the coattails of semiotic transformation, for it is the latter which truly "renders present the transcendent." In truth they talk of ontological relation, of the essential relatedness of the human sign system always seeking out its meaning. Meanwhile, "symbolism" and "symbolic" can remain useful terms precisely because of this, implying a meaning in John of transformed relation by means of a revelatory drama of signs.

Semiotics refers to the live action and process of human meaning, how it produces its effect, and how this may be changed. In the present instance, Jesus makes mud with earth and saliva and smears it on the man's eyes. If we think of this as the Second Person of the Trinity making a dumbshow of the eternal truth of spiritual regeneration, then we skip over the concrete shift that the text creates in the reader. The manipulation of mud in a context of "since the world began" awakens the sign of the Lord God forming the first man from the soil or the ground (Hebrew *adamah*, Gen 2:7), while the spittle of Jesus forms a parallel to the breath of God breathed into his nostrils. Then Jesus sends the man to wash "in the pool of Siloam (which means Sent)," and the parenthetic interruption by the author gives an explicit signal to the reader that she is being enlisted in a semiotic process, the construction of meaning. The man in fact is being "baptized" in Jesus, the one *sent* from God (3:17; 5:36). All along, therefore, the multiple sign functions of the text draw the reader actively into a relation, and it is this relation which is crucial, not a putative otherworld which the reader has constructed for them by metaphysical imagination. The nature of the relation arises in the text (including roots in the Old Testament) and the question whether it is "valid," that is, representative of final ontological truth, can only be answered in terms of the relation itself. This principle will become progressively clearer as we continue to pursue the Gospel's complex sign functions.

The luminous statement "I am the light of the world" is repeated in the story of the man born blind (9:5). It is, obviously, made up of the complement "the light of the world" and the first person singular of the verb *to be*, "I am." This verbal form (*egō eimi*) is scattered again and again through the Gospel in relation to Jesus (4:26; 6:20, 35, 48, 51; 8:12, 18; 9:5; 10:11; 11:25; 13:19; etc.). The words have huge resonance from the Old Testament as in fact the unique name of Israel's God. At Exodus 3:14–15 there are three iterations of God's name in answer to Moses's urgent question. Moses is seeking a way by which to announce to the Hebrews this mysterious liberating God who has spoken to him (3:13). First of all God gives the elusive but imposing formula "I am who I am," and to conclude he answers with the tribal name *Yahweh*, often paraphrased in the versions as "the Lord," and itself connected etymologically with the verb "to be."[19] In the middle he gives the simple statement, "*I am* has sent . . . you." Thus is born the powerful self-naming of Israel's God, beyond particular local or tribal signifiers, and crystallized in the universal first-person relational address of the verb *to be*. The prophecy of Second Isaiah makes extensive use of this sense in its moving post-exile announcement of consolation. "Comfort, O comfort my people, says your God" is the first declaration of this prophecy (40:1), and in the tonality of these words the prophet repeats that the first person of God is intentionally and lovingly with the returnees. One way the prophet does this is by multiplied use of personal pronouns (first and third person). The translators of the Septuagint rendered them using the Greek for the divine name from Exodus 3:14, *I am* (e.g., 43:10; 46:4). A paradigm instance is Isaiah 43:25. The English renders the three pronouns of the Hebrew ("I, I am He"), but the Greek Septuagint begins directly, "I am," *egō eimi*. So, when the Gospel of John decides to lace its text so liberally with a clear verbal echo of the divine name in the Old Testament, there is inevitably a sense of the same divine relation in and through Jesus.

The most clamorous "I am" is at John 8:58: "Very truly, I tell you, before Abraham was, I am." It is not surprising that at these words Judean people take up stones to stone him. It's hard not to hear, not simply an echo of the divine name, but a metaphysical, eternal claim. But the sense of an eternal truth, or even divine essence, cannot blind us to the actual dynamic of the text. The statement cannot be divorced from all the signifiers and markers surrounding it, and it is in continuing to treat of these that we will come to the genuine impact of the words. We have to ask, What is the relation they mediate, and in what way does this function as the *egō eimi* of the authoritative text of the Old Testament? Answering these questions will allow us to understand the semiotic, and therewith the revelatory, function of the Gospel of John.

The story of the man born blind is drizzled in irony: the blind man considered to be a doomed sinner by the Pharisees is able to know and confess the truth (9:30–34); the man who all his life has been unable to read scripture gives a lesson in theology, while the Pharisees, who've spent years in study, claim to see but are blind (9:30–41); the Pharisees continue to ask for an account of the healing in order to catch the man out, but thereby incur the repeated testimony of Jesus's action (9:13–27). There are numerous other examples of irony in John's Gospel: notably the dialogue with Nicodemus (3:1–10), the mistaken condition of Lazarus (asleep not dead, 11:1–16), the poignant misrecognition of Jesus by Mary Magdalene on Easter morning (20:11–18). We need to ask, then, What is the function of this major

---

19. See Stalker, "Exodus," 179c.

stylistic feature? It could never be simply a literary device, given the way it works theologically. Irony is a semiotic effect, dependent on the inevitable ambivalence of words and sentences; in the Gospel it is made to serve a major communicative purpose. In Peircean terms we could say that the author consistently offers an alternative set of interpretants, allowing the reader to slip almost unconsciously and continually from one possible reading to another. The movement sets up a pervasive sense of instability or openness in meaning, encouraging the reader to "see" things differently. The overall effect is semiotically to collapse one world into another, suggesting that the effect is not a matter of a metaphysical order constructed out of rational or spiritual descriptions, but the active work of the text breaking us into a new fundamental relationship of truth. The signs have to carry their own power of truth, and there is no way round it. The authors of the Gospel know this intimately, and it is why they launch the whole text directly with "word," and in a transcendent sense and setting. Yes, the first verses of John lead easily to a "logos" theology, a discourse of the preexistence of the Word and its divine identity. But, in sympathy with the Gospel's overall communication, "word" is inevitably also a "sign" and refers to the way, through Jesus, this word makes all things over in (its) "beginning."[20] We shall return below to this meaning of the "beginning," but for the moment our argument continues with further major lines of force in the matrix of the text.

Irony is not far off paradox, and there is good reason also to highlight this element in the construction of the Gospel. The whole passion narrative—especially if we begin it with the Last Supper discourse from chapter 13—is shot through with paradox. The person of Jesus is subjected to the most barbaric of deaths by the might of the Roman Empire, with no attempt at defense, no hint of physical resistance. Yet all along this person seems to be in charge and even to reverse the situation in terms of real power. Pilate interrogates him, but ultimately the feeling is Jesus has interrogated Pilate (19:8–11). He is brought out for judgment, but the language could be read as Jesus sitting on the seat as judge (19:13). He is crucified but speaks as if he is on his deathbed surrounded by loving family and friends (19:25b–27). It is this sort of picture that has encouraged some readers to see the influence of a form of Gnosticism in the composition, figuring Jesus as not truly human, and more a god in an artificial suit of flesh.[21] But, although it's possible to see

20. See especially John 20:30–31, where the writer talks of "these [signs] written in order that you may believe" (*tauta de gegraptai hina pistuēte*), suggesting that it is the overall *writing* of Jesus's deeds and teaching that makes the effective gospel.

21. Bultmann's *Gospel of John* sees one of the layers of the Gospel to be a gnostic-inspired discourse source. Brown comments on Jesus's "somewhat relativized" humanity in John and describes the gnostic uptake of the Gospel in the early part of the second century (*Community of the Beloved Disciple*, 114–15, 147–49).

how this picture could attach itself to the text, the concreteness of the Gospel is plain. The blood and water coming out of Jesus's side are testimony to a real and brutal crucifixion (19:34–35). And the episode with Thomas (20:24–29) forcefully underlines the reality of Jesus's body, even after resurrection. From the semiotic point of view the gnostic John is a superficial and lazy misreading. What is really going on is much more urgent and dynamic.

Slippage and Glory

Rather than the metaphysical dualism of Gnosticism, what we have to understand is that the paradoxes of John belong to the semiotic slippage of the text. To grasp this understanding, we have to first think of the horrible shock of Jesus's death, its evident brutality, the terminal violence it was intended to convey, and succeeded always in doing. And yet, at the very same time, the violence was somehow overcome, transmuted into forgiveness and peace. Thus, the semiosis of crucifixion—its visceral shock—was translated into its absolute reversal, into gentleness, compassion, and a declension or slippage away from retaliation. It is this that lies at the heart of the supposed "dualism" of John's Gospel, that constructs two totally divergent meanings, and, in effect, brings about the divine identity of the Christ. The slippage is actually a deeper category than either irony or paradox, and it brings us again to the heart of the present book's argument. Because human meaning is constructed originally out of violence, its inversion and subversion in the nonviolence of the cross constructs at once a new fundamental relation and, therewith, a completely new possible universe. This is first and foremost, and essentially, a semiotic event, but because it has taken us roughly two thousand years to think semiotically the default response is always to see it in preconstructed terms of metaphysics. Yet the truth is that the volcanic shock of violence becomes the gentle inversion of love, which is, at the same time, a totally new meaning of humanity, divinity and the whole of creation.[22] Let me now try to illustrate and underline this by reference to the Gospel text.

---

22. "Slippage" suggests a degree of passivity in which the recipients of the sign experience a movement without being fully aware or fully choosing. It is not dissimilar to the mimetic event of the *skandalon* (cause of stumbling) where the rival can create an obstacle for someone, and at the neural level, without either of the parties needing to reflect consciously at all on what's happening. At the same time, because the slippage is to do with changing the roots of human meaning, it must, in all probability, be stretched over a span of time, the product, individually, of much prayerful reading and study, and, collectively, of long exposure to transformative gospel semiosis. What I am presenting here is a condensed and accelerated hermeneutic, but one that, in its turn, may abet and

At 12:27–33 there is a crucial passage which provides the parallel scene to the garden of Gethsemane in the Synoptics, but in Johannine terms.

> "Now my soul is troubled. And what should I say—'Father, save me from this hour'? No, it is for this reason that I have come to this hour. Father, glorify your name." Then a voice came from heaven, "I have glorified it, and I will glorify it again." The crowd standing there heard it and said that it was thunder. Others said, "An angel has spoken to him." Jesus answered, "This voice has come for your sake, not for mine. Now is the judgment of this world: now the ruler of this world will be driven out. And I, when I am lifted up from the earth, will draw all people to myself." He said this to indicate the kind of death he was to die.

The apparent gulf between the will of the Father and that of Jesus in the synoptic Gethsemane is almost entirely closed here. But this is not because Jesus is now the Logos of the Trinity and has left his humanity behind. It is because the author understands that the gentleness of the cross is the perfect representation of the Father, and thus there is no gap between Son and Father. The flow of meaning—as far as we are concerned—runs in the other direction, not from God to Jesus, but from Jesus to God. (As far as Jesus is concerned, it does indeed run from the Father to him: hence "glorify your name"!). Here, then, is the supreme event of paradox, of Jesus "lifted up" on the cross and glorified: it should be an event of disgrace and humiliation, but it is not; rather, it's one of judgment upon the world and its ruler, and a drawing of all humanity into Jesus's new frame of reality, a new kingdom of truth. The text goes beyond paradox. There is a dynamic here which demands another semiotic category, one we hardly have a name for, but which goes to the very root of the transformation carried through, by and in the Gospel.

The theme of glory referenced at the beginning of the passage is pivotal in its two-sidedness. It seems natural to associate the trope of glory with heavenly vistas, triumphant parades, blinding theophanies. But here the term is tied to the hour of suffering, to Jesus's imminent death. And the Father's own truth and presence is similarly tied. Just before, at 12:23–24, Jesus has said, "The hour has come for the Son of Man to be glorified. Very truly, I tell you, unless a grain of wheat falls into the earth and dies, it remains just a single grain; but if it dies, it bears much fruit." Not only do we hear that the event of glory is taking place "in the earth," but we know at

---

quicken the process. The point remains that the essential principle of transformation requires this is a passive undergoing to which a disciple lays herself or himself open. It is a school, of beloved discipleship. But because it is also a semiotic process it cannot help infecting universal semiosis, wherein—politically—people still have to give themselves, at some level of surrender and acceptance, to new meaning.

once that it is the event of Jesus's death. At the same time, we are led to understand, as the text continues to unfold, that the glory of the Son of Man by means of his death will be the same thing as the glory of the Father's name. This latter echoes the first petition of the Lord's Prayer, "Hallowed be your name," meaning it is the lead motif of Jesus's kingdom project: it is to this which he commits his followers before anything else—to manifest the Father's identity to and in the earth.

"Glory" is in effect, therefore, the evangelist's word for the slippage of violence into grace through the cross and, within that selfsame relation, the full historical revelation of God. It is the final semiotic category of John's Gospel, invented out of the cross and fulfilled conclusively in the text. Already in the prologue, at 1:14, we have heard, "And the Word became flesh and lived among us, and we have seen his glory, the glory as of a father's only Son, full of grace and truth." The semiotic categories of word and glory bear upon the human scene as capable of changing its entire meaning, and at the same time we hear that this meaning is as of a Father communicated in and through a Son.[23] Hence the glorification of the name.

At the other end of the Gospel, in the Last Supper discourse, just before his passion, there is a final, dense commentary on glory. Jesus prays to the Father. He says, "Father, the hour has come; glorify your son so that the son may glorify you . . . I glorified you on earth by finishing the work that you gave me to do. So now, Father, glorify me in your presence with the glory that I had in your presence before the world existed" (17:1–5). Literally the Greek says, "And now glorify me, you Father, with yourself, with the glory that I had with You before the world existed."[24] The language of presence rather than personal pronoun has the classic effect of metaphysical entities present to each other, rather than relation as such. Jesus's glory here should in fact be read as the selfhood of the Father brought close and made public by and through the cross. The adverbial clause "before the world began" seems to

23. For a full account we would have to include here the revelation of the Holy Spirit. At John 7:39 we hear the Holy Spirit had not yet come "because Jesus was not yet glorified." The pneumatological aspect of the semiotic shift is not simply the revelation-as-truth of the nonviolence of God, but the semiotic slippage that brought this about amounting to an active indwelling of the nonviolent Holy Spirit. The transformation of violence into gentleness, which is itself the glory of God, becomes in the individual who has undergone this firsthand experience of the relational personhood of God. What from the side of human meaning is semiotic transformation is from the side of divinity the indwelling of the Holy Spirit. This is what the Eastern Orthodox tradition calls *theosis*, the divinization of the human. It does not take place in some separate spiritual part of the human, the "soul," but in the uniquely human part of being human which is the neurological formation of meaning. The Holy Spirit confirms the essential divine relationality of Christian truth within the organic human self.

24. See https://biblehub.com/interlinear/john/17-5.htm.

justify an eternal presence before time, but this is again Johannine slippage. The eternal sense is possible, but the author does not say "creation of the world" and we are therefore entitled also to read "before the violent construct of the world," very much in the Girardian sense of "the foundation of the world." The "before" here that John is talking of is something that the coming of Jesus initiates in every way, both semiotically and in the experienced flow of time, deriving its truth from the primordial relation of the cross. It is an absolute beginning to be read first in the semiotic sense, the new beginning of meaning; but once this beginning occurs then it is known necessarily as always already there, since it is an absolute relation. Transformed meaning becomes simultaneous with the cosmos on all sides, including its physical beginning. It re-founds the world according to itself.

We already mentioned the use of "beginning" in this absolute sense in the prologue, and if we look at the signifier in the rest of the Gospel the conclusion is reinforced. At 15:2 Jesus addresses his disciples as "you [who] have been with me from the beginning." In the weave of the text this signifier cannot be separated from the first line in the prologue, "In the beginning was the Word," and vice versa, The Greek word, *archē*, echoes back and forth, referring to the absolute beginning, in all cases, that the relation brought by Jesus, demonstrated in and by the cross, makes. The beginning of Jesus's ministry—which begins the journey to the cross—is in terms of semiosis the same as the beginning of all things. There is in fact an alternative, negative beginning mentioned. Speaking to the Pharisees who wish to kill him, Jesus says their father "was a murderer from the beginning" (8:44). There is also, therefore, a beginning to the world (from the *diabolos*, the adversary) which Jesus now preempts with his own beginning. The "beginning of the signs" at Cana (2:11) is another instance of this semiotic beginning, this time related explicitly to signs. The beginning of Jesus's signs is the beginning of a new human meaning, both in a historical objective sense and, again, in the absolute sense of preemptive relation.

At this point it is useful to refer once more to the repeated use of "I am" in the Gospel and its invoking of the divine name. This association of Jesus with a revelatory name for God could easily be judged egregious, if not flat-out blasphemous (as we have seen in the reaction of some Judeans). How can such an extraordinary claim actually work in the text of the Gospel outside of some gnostic interpretation? How can it stand up? It is only because of the text's semiotic slippage from violence to peace that something like 8:58 can hold its ground, can actually work. The factual power of semiotic slippage is the only possible engine of the Gospel meaning, plunging the reader into an endless depth of giving love, and therewith the revealed identity of the divine. Because it is embedded in transformative codes, as it has to be, it is all too easy to misrecognize in terms of metaphysics. Those who "went out" from the Johannine community at the end of the first century took the codes and ran with them into heavenly otherworlds, and this is a perennial danger. Nevertheless, the semiosis of the text continues its abyssal work, pulling us deeper and deeper into the one-sided reciprocity of love and its revelation in Jesus. Lately the truth of this has come to explicit attention, beginning with Girard. We are living in the aftermath of the gospel text, a semiotic age, despite the Greek detour.

The morphing of violence to love communicated itself to a distraught Mary Magdalene in the roots of her being on the first Easter morning, and from there on the semiotic motor of the Gospel was running. Despite the fact that the slippage was prepared for in very significant ways in Old Testament writings—like the Suffering Servant in Second Isaiah, or "one like a Son of Man" in Daniel—it was the actual traumatic events of Christ's death and resurrection that precipitated it in the form of a historical moment and movement. Only by such a factual revolution could the first sketch outline of the Trinity take shape in the minds of the first Christians. The "I am" of Jesus is testimony to this new beginning in meaning.

Glory of the Icon

The Gospel of John is an astonishing work of subtlety and simplicity. These literary qualities would surely be impossible to explain were it not for the testimony of the Beloved Disciple standing behind the text. It is the semiotic explosion in the heart and mind of this primary figure—whether single or multiple, unique or successive—which gives unity and power to the writing of the text. Nothing else makes sense of the immense conviction, passion and purity of the writing. But the Gospel obviously is not intended simply to record the insights of a religious exception; it wishes to pass on precisely the same revolution in meaning that the Beloved Disciple incarnated. It wishes the reader to embrace the condition of the Beloved Disciple and to that end the writing continually models the necessary shift in core ontological relation. One way perhaps to look at this process of modeling is to compare it to the use of icons in the Eastern Orthodox tradition, something now increasingly appreciated in Western Christianity. The lines of signification we have traced—through light, glory, beginning, I am, and irony and paradox—these can be compared to some of the characteristics of icons. The shapes, colors, forms and lines of an icon are all intended to bring the viewer into communion with its subject. The techniques of iconography seek to move the eye beyond the surface into a non-graphic depth, one which is more "spiritual" than it is pictorial. Circular motion, the gaze of the face, exaggerated physical form (of the body, hands, etc.), and minimal relation in space to other figures—all these things help to bring this about. It is possible then to compare these effects to John's text, seeing its mysterious, mesmeric lines supporting a gaze into something "beyond the text." We have already referred to the theme of the icon in the work of Jean-Luc Marion, and we saw there that "in the idol, the gaze of man is frozen in its mirror; in the icon, the gaze of man is lost in the invisible gaze that visibly envisages him."[25] For Marion, it is not just that by looking at the icon the gaze plunges into the invisible; the icon is able to turn its gaze back on the beholder. What is it, exactly, about the icon that is able to gaze back at the one beholding? It is something more, much more, than the simple depicted eyes of the Christ or saint.

In his *Art of Seeing: Paradox and Perception in Orthodox Iconography*, Maximos Constas describes the "Sinai Christ," one of the earliest surviving icons, dating from the first part of the sixth century.[26] It is located in St. Catherine's Monastery among the rugged peaks of the Sinai Peninsula, the oldest, continuously inhabited Christian monastery in the world. The location is the reason why this remarkable icon survived. During the period of Eastern iconoclasm (726–843 CE) the place had come under the control and protection of Islam. It is just one of the startling paradoxes associated with this ancient masterpiece.

The size of the panel is relatively quite large (roughly a meter by a half a meter) and Constas gives a detailed description of the painting. The feature that grabs our attention is the distinctive and deliberate asymmetry of the face. The line of the long nose is not in the middle of the depicted face, but only in the middle of the illuminated oval of the face, toward the viewer's left. To the viewer's right an outer shaded edge of the figure's left cheek comprises part of the frontal aspect and so unbalances the two sides of the face. The two sides also differ dramatically in character. The side to the viewer's left is serene, radiating peace and gentleness, its pupil constricted, as if bathed in the light. On the other side, the eye is dilated, as if by fear and stress. The eyebrow on the figure's right is gently curved, smooth and relaxed; the one on the figure's left is arched and knotted as if in shock and pain. The colors on the two sides are also different, green-grey predominating, but with shadings of purple and violet on the figure's left cheek. The most amazing revelation, however, is achieved by transposing the two sides, right to left,

---

25. Marion, *God Without Being*, 19.
26. Constas, *Art of Seeing*, ch. 1. The arresting image of this icon is reproduced on the cover of the present book.

left to right. Constas explains that because of cerebral lateralization—the way the respective sides of our brains serve different functions—our right brains receive information about people's moods and mental states from the left-side facing (right side of the other person). If the two sides of Christ's face are transposed, as Constas does in his book, the effect is quite shocking, with the face appearing distorted and deeply unhinged. As it stands, however, our attention is drawn to the lucid, tranquil right side, while the wounded, violated left recedes from focus. But it obviously remains in peripheral view, and thus an implicit and dynamic contrast and commentary is set up between the two sides. Constas comments,

> Through his large eyes, the Sinai Christ exerts a mesmerizing power over the viewer. Caught within his gaze, our vision is naturally (and thus inexorably) drawn to the right side of his face. There, however, our bliss of repose is disturbed by something stirring in the shadows, a contrary force skirting the edges of our vision, concealed within a realm beyond perception.[27]

The eyes of the icon naturally look at us, but it is the ambiguity and asymmetry of the image which command our attention, forbidding us to look away. The Sinai Christ, or at least its profound aesthetic, has gone on to influence countless other icons, and I believe it is this built-in instability or semiotic slippage which produces Marion's infinite gaze of the icon. It is the very same semiotic slippage which we have read in the "glory" of the Fourth Gospel. The crucified Jesus appeared to his disciples on the evening of the first day of the week and his first words were "Peace be with you" (20:19). Then, "After he said this, he showed them his hands and his side . . . Jesus said to them again, 'Peace be with you . . .'" (20:20–21). The icon (of the painting, of the text) moves from violence to peace, then back to violence, then back to peace again, and so on in an endless regenerative, forgiving circle. The two moments might be called by philosophers a dialectic, but this is not a rational argument. It is an oscillation of signs, from one to the other, plunging us ever deeper into a transformative well of new humanity. Close to the concept of dialectic is the duality of two natures in Christ, and this is also sometimes seen in the twin aspects of the icon; but imposing a dogmatic interpretation is to freeze the iconic movement in metaphysics. What is happening is never so much the difficult concept of two natures, but the circular collapse of violence into peace brought about by and as the revelation of God's relational nonviolence in the earth. But *then*, because this is a revelation of God's "glory" in the earth, we can begin to conceive of how the divine and human natures accompany each other in the portrait. It

---

27. Constas, *Art of Seeing*, 55.

does not happen in a simple binary of two sides of the portrait, or a dialectic of two irreconcilable concepts, but in the semiotic collapse of the human discourse of violence into the divine discourse of grace, occurring in the one person of the Crucified from Nazareth.

Nonviolent Semiosis of Bread and Wine

Iconography might seem a rarefied interest to some Christians. Much closer to home is the practice of the Lord's Supper, an observance embraced in one form or another by every deliberate *ecclesia* in the world. Shortly before he died Jesus enacted a symbolic meal which he encouraged his followers to repeat with *ad libitum* frequency ("as often as you do this . . ."). I have already expressed (of course) a methodological preference for the thought of semiotics rather than symbolism, and the action and elements of the bread and wine can now offer a final demonstration of the enormous richness of this seam in the Gospel of John. It is frequently remarked that the Gospel does not have a narrative of the institution of the Eucharist. In its place the "Bread of Life" discourse serves as a powerful commentary on the semiosis of this meal both in terms of the overall Gospel and in actual first-century Christian practice.[28] Specifically, I believe, it shows how the meal intends a community enactment of semiotic slippage repeated as day-to-day conscious formation of meaning.[29]

Chapter 6 of John's Gospel begins with the miracle of the feeding of the five thousand. The event offers dramatic proof of Jesus's status as Messiah, the Moses-like "prophet who is to come into the world' (6:14); it is followed at once by the attempt of the people to "take him by force to make him king" (6:15). However, this is a drastic misunderstanding from which Jesus must at once extricate himself and escape. The people's reaction is a result of witnessing "the sign that he had done" (6:14), but plainly they completely misread it. Manifestly, the *sēmeia* of Jesus are never simply the external miracles but must be interpreted, and here the Bread of Life discourse serves that urgent purpose.

In which case—to repeat the argument already made—the signs are necessarily implicated with words and the latter must always be taken as part of their being. As Jesus speaks to his interlocutors in the aftermath of the loaves, they prompt an irony, already noted, by asking, "What sign are

---

28. Brown, *Gospel according to John*, 257–91.

29. Thinking on it in this way, at the end point of the present volume, offers the outline of a "sacramental catechesis" for any community seeking the sense of revelation and transformation supplied by the semiotic turn.

you going to give us then, so that we may see it and believe you?" (6:30). The éclat of the multiplication itself needs to be reread, to be radically interpreted. The power of the act could so easily be taken up in a kind of first-century Napoleanic Messiah meaning—the ability to supply an army on the march, in the wilderness. And that is indeed why the people wish to make Jesus king. But the meaning is entirely the inverse. Jesus leads the conversation forward, getting to the point where he identifies *himself* with the bread or manna supplied by God in the wilderness: "I am the bread of life" (6:35). He adds that those who come to him will never be hungry, and those who believe in him will never be thirsty. Thus, the bread just consumed in the desert can only be understood on the basis of relation to the person of Jesus, setting in motion a code of assimilation or ingestion. A connection to the Lord's Supper and Eucharist is impossible to avoid, and it seems clear that the author is using the two traditions—multiplication of loaves and the Eucharist—to comment on each other reciprocally.

It becomes another instance of "iconic doubling," of "glory," of the plunging of human meaning into a free-fall of absolute self-giving and nonviolence. The immense power of feeding a multitude in the wilderness is itself the self-surrender and giving of the cross. At the same time, the "I am" of the "I am the bread of life" statement is also to be understood in these terms. The divine claims of Jesus in the Fourth Gospel can only be read as semiotic collapse of anything and everything that we have previously understood of God as generative violence and the power of violence. The truth of this reading is backed up by the further shocking implications of Jesus's statements.

The language is so graphic it is not surprising that "when many of his disciples heard it, they said, 'This teaching is difficult: who can accept it?'" (6:60). It is indeed disciples who balk at the concept, and it seems very probable that the challenge is directed toward members within the first-century Christian community. The raw signifiers of Jesus-as-food-and-drink suggest something which offends deeply not just general human sensibility, but the explicit central law of biblical Judaism. The problem, therefore, cannot be simply the physicality of the language, requiring a "spiritual" otherworldly interpretation. The very grounds of human meaning are at stake. "Very truly, I tell you, unless you eat the flesh of the Son of Man and drink his blood, you have no life in you. Those who eat my flesh and drink my blood have eternal life, and I will raise them up on the last day; for my flesh is true food and my blood is true drink" (6:53–55). How intolerable is this!

We hear, at Genesis 1:29–30, that at the creation God gave to humans and animals the grains, fruits and plants of the earth to eat. Then, after the flood, God concedes to Noah and his descendants to eat the flesh of animals and fish, on the sole condition that "you shall not eat flesh with its life, that is, its blood" (Gen 9:4). The primally imagined order of creation is without violence, but in the conditions of actually existing humanity meat-eating is permitted, yet with an arrangement which preserves the sacredness of life by excluding the consumption of blood. The prohibition is repeated and reinforced in the priestly legislation at Leviticus 17:10–14: "for the life of every creature is its blood." Leviticus adds the sacrificial connotation that the blood is intended solely for ritual, spilled for "atonement" at the altar (17:11). These exclusions are not just random rules which can be displaced at a whim, but central to the identity and ritual of Judaism and the cosmic order their world represents. The decision of the Council of Jerusalem in Acts 15 shows how cardinal this rule remained in the early church: even if circumcision was unnecessary Gentile converts should "abstain . . . from blood" (v. 20). John's language could not fail, therefore, to offend. Our more contemporary habit of spiritualizing the content does a disservice to its primal shock. What then is the function of these exigent tropes which reverse and explode the legislation of Genesis and Leviticus and the anthropological prohibitions they contain?

The only way these words could have valid relational meaning is if the flesh and blood of Jesus on the cross had emptied the universe of violence, such that the original priestly taboos of the Bible were made redundant. And this had to be a living experience for the author and the Beloved Disciple, the witness behind the words. The primitive semiotic boundaries against eating human flesh and drinking blood could only be undone by a revolution in human and theological meaning, when a particular flesh and blood became an event of absolute nonviolence and peace. The author of John uses signifiers bound up from the dawn of humanity in taboos and prohibitions, and she deliberately thrusts them into the debate in completely transgressive terms. The point is not to create a shock for its own sake but to overturn human meaning established "from the beginning." The most taboo item in the human semiotic register becomes a signal of radical human freedom from violence, and in the process a revolutionary level of intimacy. Or vice versa. Love and the surrender of love bring the letting go of violence. "Eating and drinking Jesus" are signs then of an entirely new semiosis and anthropology, and it is only by meditating continually on the total collapse of the old human way that they are saved from being simply an outrage.

Such new semiosis also necessarily had to involve divine revelation—a God—completely in sympathy. Otherwise this God would quickly require the event be returned to the sacrificial sacred which blood always signified. By and large this is in fact what happened in Western church history, in the Anselmian revisionism of the meaning of Christ's death. But the actual semiotic slippage of gospel meaning has resulted in the Girardian reading of the nonviolent Logos, and now we are obliged to follow through in terms of categorical divine revelation—of an eternal God who is foreign to any kind of violence. Once again, therefore, we are in the slippage of the icon, its revolutionary oscillation, but this time in terms of the woundedness of flesh and blood received as the nonviolent self-giving of bread and wine, and with that the transformation of all human and divine meaning. The coupled sets of signs create together a transforming semiosis opening an entirely new way of being.

Proto-Semiosis of the Gospel

The Beloved Disciple runs to the tomb on Easter Sunday morning, outracing Simon Peter, who arrives behind. They come because alerted by Mary Magdalene, who went to the tomb while it was still dark; finding the stone removed she ran back to inform the disciples. Mary mysteriously disappears from the narrative, only to reappear very quickly afterward in the revelatory encounter with Jesus in "the garden." Once again, the labile identity of the Beloved Disciple disrupts the text, taking a significant precedence—looking in the tomb first, then entering and believing (20:5–8), before quickly evaporating to leave a named disciple in view, this time the woman, Mary Magdalene.

Mary Magdalene is a seminal figure, a crucial conduit or relay to resurrection faith in all the gospel accounts. In the Synoptics she is always the first named individual to enter the tomb and, in Mark and Matthew, the first to experience the appearance of the Risen Christ (Mark 16:1–5, 9; Matt 28:1–9; Luke 24:1–10). In Luke she, and the other women, return to the disciples and then the same sequence as in John occurs, with Peter "running" to the tomb and seeing "the linen cloths by themselves" (Luke 24:12). It is evident in John's Gospel that Mary came back with Peter—there is no break between 20:10 with the "disciples return[ing] to their homes" and then verse 11, "But Mary stood weeping outside the tomb." In any case, it makes complete sense that she would. And yet she cannot be allowed to figure in the whole episode of the Beloved Disciple arriving and looking in the tomb first. This disciple sees "the linen wrappings lying there" (20:5) then defers to Peter, who is the first to enter and, in his turn, see, not just the linen wrappings, but the cloth that had been on Jesus's head "rolled up in a place by itself" (20:7). Mary's role is restricted to alerting the (supposedly) male disciples; and yet the Fourth Gospel goes on to display her loving grief morphing step by step into the proto-recognition of and witness to the Risen One.

Putting these elements together, it seems quite unreasonable to think Mary did not herself look into the tomb when the Beloved Disciple and Peter did—if nothing else her grief would have pushed her to. But, in any case, how could she have carried the message "They have taken the Lord out of the tomb" (20:2) unless she had *first* done exactly this? In other words, it seems very arguable that the Fourth Gospel has subtly shaded out Mary as first witness of the contents of the tomb, substituting the anonymous "Beloved Disciple" and Peter. Why in fact would the Beloved Disciple passively return home instead of doing exactly what Mary did— continue a process of confusion, love and lament that would culminate in vision of the Resurrected One? So it is that the author has elided the Magdalene as the actual beloved disciple and first witness in question, while leaving enough clues to identify her.

The argument attains a sharper importance if we focus on the crucial look of the Beloved Disciple inside the tomb and the highly significant result that "he saw and believed" (20:8). There is a kind of textual one-upmanship over the Lukan tradition which just has the evidence of "linen cloths by themselves." Here there is also the cloth that had been on Jesus's head "rolled up in a place by itself," first seen by Peter then, immediately following, by the Beloved Disciple. This detail forcefully suggests a firsthand eyewitness, someone who recalled extra details no one else did. But what, then, is it about this electric scene-setting which seems to elicit "belief" in the disciple? The belief is immediately qualified by the statement "for as yet they did not understand the scripture, that he must rise from the dead" (20:9). In other words, there is a kind of belief here which is not yet the full Easter faith. The statement seems like a segue into Mary's still-to-come encounter with the Risen Christ, but what then is the nature of the partial belief?

It is not the transcendent miracle of triumph over death which is at stake, but it could very well be the mental environment in which this was recognized and the way its all-important semiosis is already beginning to shape emerging Christian truth. The primary information or "evidence" around the tomb does not display anger and revenge in the aftermath of the cross, the energy of a violent counter-eruption and settling of accounts to come. On the contrary, whatever the resurrection was, it involved a quiet, feminine and domestic "rolling up" of a piece of cloth. It is this quietness or gentleness in the midst of absolute life-giving power which begins to elicit a transformative response, something which is already the "glory" of the sign that prompts belief (John 2:11). It is not a full credal belief, but it is the revolutionary relation of nonviolence that the semiotics of the gospel bring to the world: the first glance around the empty tomb fulfilling entirely the nonviolence of the cross. It begins at once a free-fall slippage into new human meaning. And, in this case, if Mary Magdalene is indeed the "first" Beloved Disciple it means that it was her eyes—the neural semiotics processing and signifying information in her brain—that were already being prepared for the subsequent full encounter with her Risen Lord.

If now, in this light, we go back to the tradition of the bread-and-wine/flesh-and-blood we can see more easily how the primary semiosis of the whole Easter experience floods through and from these signs. The thought of a nonretaliatory God, not counting people's sins against them (2 Cor 5:19), cannot arise spontaneously in a world constructed out of mimetic violence. It needs to be given conditions to grow slowly out of a distinctive people with a unique set of experiences, and there needs to be a particular nexus where these possibilities coalesce into an actual new transcendence, one of nonviolent divinity. The signs of bread and wine in the early Christian community (1 Cor 11:23–27) could not overcome their intrinsic scandal (eating human flesh and blood) without this special nexus, including, crucially, the emptying out of all semiosis of violence. What I have attempted to show in John's Gospel are the core lines of signification, reversals and relational shifts by which this could come about, based in the privileged experience of the Beloved Disciple. All meaning is semiosis and the Gospel of John sees the semiosis of new meaning as edible, precisely because its crucial signs are absolutely without violence—without the built-in rivalry and murder of old meaning. The Fourth Gospel presents the gospel's proto-semiosis experienced by the Beloved Disciple—probably the person of Mary Magdalene. Any signs coming out of this Gospel, including the flesh and blood of the Son of Man as food and drink, are continuous with the signs of the empty tomb, the first dawn and beginning of a world without violence. In essence gospel signs are all proto-semiosis. The labor of this book has been to get to the point where we can recognize them as such, and as the necessary underpinning of Girardian revelatory anthropology.

Bibliography

Antonello, Pierpaolo, and Paul Gifford, eds. *How We Became Human: Mimetic Theory and the Science of Evolutionary Origins*. East Lansing: Michigan State University Press, 2015.
Aquinas, Thomas. *De aeternitate mundi*. Translated by Robert T. Miller. https://sourcebooks.fordham.edu/basis/aquinas-eternity.asp.
Aristotle. *Categories and De Interpretatione*. Translated by J. L. Ackrill. Oxford: Oxford University Press, 1975.
Augustine of Hippo. *Confessions*. Translated by Henry Chadwick. Oxford: Oxford University Press, 2009.
———. *On Genesis: A Refutation of the Manichees*. In *On Genesis*, translated by Edmund Hill, 39–102. The Works of St. Augustine: A Translation for the 21st Century 13. Edited by John E. Rotelle. Brooklyn: New City, 1990–2019.
Barnhart, Bruno. *The Good Wine: Reading John from the Center*. New York: Paulist, 1993.
Bartlett, Anthony W. *Cross Purposes: The Violent Grammar of Christian Atonement*. 2001. Reprint, London: T. & T. Clark, 2018.
———. *Virtually Christian: How Christ Changes Human Meaning and Makes Creation New*. Winchester, UK: O Books, 2011.
Bonhoeffer, Dietrich. *Letters and Papers from Prison*. Edited by Eberhard Bethge. New York: Collier, 1971.
Brent, Joseph. *Charles Sanders Peirce: A Life*. Bloomington: Indiana University Press, 1993.
Brown, Raymond E. *The Community of the Beloved Disciple: The Life, Loves, and Hates of an Individual Church in New Testament Times*. New York: Paulist, 1979.
———. *The Gospel according to John*. 2 vols. Anchor Bible 29, 29A. Garden City, NY: Doubleday, 1966–70.
Bultmann, Rudolf. *The Gospel of John: A Commentary*. Translated by G. R. Beasley-Murray. Philadelphia: Westminster, 1971.
Burch, Robert. "Charles Sanders Peirce." *Stanford Encyclopedia of Philosophy*. Edited by Edward N. Zalta. Fall 2017 ed. https://plato.stanford.edu/archives/fall2017/entries/peirce/.
Campbell, Douglas A. *The Deliverance of God: An Apocalyptic Rereading of Justification in Paul*. Grand Rapids: Eerdmans, 2009.

Caputo, John D. *The Prayers and Tears of Jacques Derrida*. Bloomington: Indiana University Press, 1997.
Charlesworth, James H. *The Beloved Disciple: Whose Witness Validates the Gospel of John?* Valley Forge, PA: Trinity Press International, 1995.
Chiang, Ted. "Story of Your Life." In *Stories of Your Life and Others*, 97–145. New York: Vintage, 2016.
Constas, Maximos. *The Art of Seeing: Paradox and Perception in Orthodox Iconography*. Contemporary Christian Thought Series 25. Alhambra, CA: Sebastian, 2014.
Conway, Erik. "Global Warming Consensus." *Ask NASA Climate* (blog), June 13, 2013. https://climate.nasa.gov/blog/938/.
Deely, John. *Augustine and Poinsot: The Protosemiotic Development*. Postmodernity in Philosophy 1. Scranton: University of Scranton Press, 2009.
———. *Four Ages of Understanding: The First Postmodern Survey of Philosophy from Ancient Times to the Twenty-First Century*. Toronto: University of Toronto Press, 2001.
———. *The Human Use of Signs, or, Elements of Anthroposemiosis*. Lanham, MD: Rowman & Littlefield, 1994.
———. *The Impact on Philosophy of Semiotics: The Quasi-error of the External World, with a Dialogue between a "Semiotist" and a "Realist."* South Bend, IN: St. Augustine's, 2003.
Denzinger, Heinrich. *Enchiridion Symbolorum: Compendium of Creeds, Definitions, and Declarations of the Catholic Church*. 43rd ed. San Francisco: Ignatius, 2012.
Derrida, Jacques. *The Gift of Death*. Translated by David Willis. Chicago: University of Chicago Press, 1995.
———. *Of Grammatology*. Translated by Gayatri Chakravorty Spivak. Baltimore: Johns Hopkins University Press, 1974. Originally published as *De la grammatologie* (Paris: Minuit, 1967).
———. "Plato's Pharmacy." In *Dissemination*, translated by Barbara Johnson, 63–171. Chicago: University of Chicago Press, 1981.
———. "Positions: Interview with Jean-Louis Houdebine and Guy Scarpetta." In *Positions*, translated by Alan Bass, 37–96. Chicago: University of Chicago Press, 1981.
———. "Semiology and Grammatology: Interview with Julia Kristeva." In *Positions*, translated by Alan Bass, 15–36. Chicago: University of Chicago Press, 1981.
———. *Specters of Marx*. Translated by Peggy Kamuf. Abingdon, UK: Routledge, 1994.
———. *Speech and Phenomena*. Translated by David B. Allison. Evanston: Northwestern University Press, 1973.
———. *Writing and Difference*. Translated by Alan Bass. 1978. Reprint, 1990. Originally published as *L'écriture et la différence* (Paris: Seuil, 1967).
Descartes, René. *Discourse on Method; and, Meditations on First Philosophy*. Translated by Donald A. Cress. 4th ed. Indianapolis: Hackett, 1999.
Eco, Umberto. *Semiotics and the Philosophy of Language*. Bloomington: Indiana University Press, 1986.
———. *A Theory of Semiotics*. Advances in Semiotics. Bloomington: Indiana University Press, 1979.
Geninasca, Jacques. *Signs and Parables: Semiotics and Gospel Texts*. Pittsburgh: Pickwick, 1978.
Gilson, Étienne. *God and Philosophy*. 2nd ed. New Haven: Yale University Press, 2002.

Girard, René. *Battling to the End: Conversations with Benoît Chantre*. East Lansing: Michigan State University Press, 2009.

———. *Deceit, Desire and the Novel: Self and Other in Literary Structure*. Translated by Yvonne Freccero. Baltimore: Johns Hopkins University Press, 1976.

———. *The One by Whom Scandal Comes*. Translated by M. B. DeBevoise. East Lansing: Michigan State University, 2014.

———. *Violence and the Sacred*. Translated by Patrick Gregory. Baltimore: Johns Hopkins University Press, 1977.

———. *When These Things Begin: Conversations with Michel Treguer*. Translated by Trevor Cribben Merrill. East Lansing: Michigan State University Press, 2014. Originally published as *Quand ces choses commenceront: Entretiens avec Michel Treguer* (Paris: Arléa, 1996).

Girard, René, et al. *Evolution and Conversion: Dialogues on the Origin of Culture*. New York: T. & T. Clark, 2007.

Girard, René, et al. *Things Hidden since the Foundation of the World*. Translated by Stephen Bann and Michael Metteer. Stanford: Stanford University Press, 1987. Originally published as *Des choses cachées depuis la fondation du monde* (Paris: Grasset, 1978).

Groth, Miles. "What Is Metaphysics?" Translation of Martin Heidegger. https://wagner.edu/psychology/files/2013/01/Heidegger-What-Is-Metaphysics-Translation-GROTH.pdf.

Guagliardo, Vincent. "Being and Anthroposemiotics." In *Semiotics 1993*, edited by Robert Corrington and John Deely, 50–56. Lanham, MD: University Press of America, 1994.

Haven, Cynthia L. *Evolution of Desire: A Life of René Girard*. East Lansing: Michigan State University Press, 2018.

Hegel, G. W. F. *Hegel's Philosophy of Mind*. Translated by William Wallace and A. V. Millar. Oxford: Clarendon, 1971.

Heidegger, Martin. *Basic Writings: From "Being and Time" (1927) to "The Task of Thinking" (1964)*. Edited by David Farrell Krell. Harper Perennial Modern Thought. New York: HarperCollins, 2008.

———. *Being and Time*. Translated by John Macquarrie and Edward Robinson. 1962. Reprint, New York: Harper Perennial Modern Classics, 2008.

———. *Contributions to Philosophy (Of the Event)*. Translated by Richard Rojcewicz and Daniela Vallega-Neu. Bloomington: Indiana University Press, 2012.

———. *Holzwege*. Frankfurt a.M.: V. Klostermann, 1957.

———. *Identity and Difference*. Translated by Joan Stambaugh. Chicago: University of Chicago Press, 1969.

———. *An Introduction to Metaphysics*. Translated by Ralph Manheim. New Haven: Yale University Press, 1959.

———. *Pathmarks*. Edited by William McNeill. Cambridge: Cambridge University Press, 1998. Originally published in German as *Wegmarken* (Frankfurt a.M.: V. Klostermann, 1967).

Heraclitus. *Fragments: The Collected Wisdom of Heraclitus*. Translated by Brooks Haxton. New York: Penguin, 2003.

Houser, R. E. "Avicenna and Aquinas: Essence, Existence, and the *Esse* of Christ." *The Saint Anselm Journal* 9 (2013) 1–21.

Hume, David. *An Enquiry Concerning Human Understanding*. Edited by Peter Millican. Oxford World's Classics. Oxford: Oxford University Press, 2008.
Keller, Helen. *The Story of My Life*. New York: New American Library, 1988.
Kierkegaard, Søren. *Fear and Trembling/Repetition*. Translated and edited by Howard V. Hong and Edna H. Hong. Rev. ed. Princeton: Princeton University Press, 1983.
Kunze, Donald. *Thought and Place: The Architecture of Eternal Places in the Philosophy of Giambattista Vico*. Emory Vico Studies. New York: P. Lang, 1987.
Levinas, Emmanuel. *Totality and Infinity: An Essay on Exteriority*. Translated by Alphonso Lingis. Pittsburgh: Duquesne University Press, 1969. Originally published as *Totalité et infini* (The Hague: Martinus Nijhoff, 1961).
Lévi-Strauss, Claude. *The Elementary Structures of Kinship*. Boston: Beacon, 1969.
———. *Structural Anthropology*. Translated by Claire Jacobson. New York: Basic Books, 1963.
Marion, Jean-Luc. *God Without Being: Hors-Texte*. Translated by Thomas A. Carlson. 2nd ed. Chicago: University of Chicago Press, 2012.
McCabe, Bret. "Structuralism's Samson." *Johns Hopkins Magazine*, Fall 2012. http://hub.jhu.edu/magazine/2012/fall/structuralisms-samson.
McKenna, Andrew J. "Darwin and Girard: Natural and Human Science." Raven Foundation Online, 2015. https://ecommons.luc.edu/cgi/viewcontent.cgi?article=1005&context=modernlang_facpubs.
———. *Violence and Difference: Girard, Derrida, and Deconstruction*. Urbana: University of Illinois Press, 1992.
McKirahan, Richard D. *Philosophy before Socrates: An Introduction with Texts and Commentary*. 2nd ed. Indianapolis: Hackett, 2010.
Neville, Robert Cumming. *The Truth of Broken Symbols*. Albany: State University of New York, 1996.
Origen. *Commentary on John*. In vol. 9 of *The Ante-Nicene Fathers*, edited by Allan Menzies. 1896. Reprint, Pickerington, OH: Beloved Publishing, 2014.
Peirce, Charles Sanders. *The Collected Papers of Charles Sanders Peirce*. Vols. 1–6 edited by Charles Hartshorne and Paul Weiss; vols. 7–8 edited by A. W. Burks. Cambridge: Harvard University Press, 1931–58.
———. *The Essential Peirce: Selected Philosophical Writings*. Vol. 1, *1867–1893*. Edited by Nathan Houser and Christian Kloesel. Bloomington: Indiana University Press, 1992.
———. "Evolutionary Love." *The Monist* 3 (1893) 176–200.
Penn, Arthur, dir. *The Miracle Worker*. 1962; Big Sky Ranch, Simi Valley, CA; Playfilm Productions.
Plato. *Phaedrus*. Translated by Benjamin Jowett. Overland Park, KS: Digireads.com Publishing, 2019.
Poinsot, John. *Tractatus de Signis: The Semiotic of John Poinsot* (from *Artis Logicae Prima et Secunda*, Alacá, Spain, 1631–32). Bilingual arrangement by John Deely. Berkeley: University of California Press, 1985.
Ricoeur, Paul. *Interpretation Theory: Discourse and the Surplus of Meaning*. Fort Worth: Texas Christian University Press, 1976.
Roberts, Alexander, and James Donaldson, eds. *The Ante-Nicene Fathers*. 10 vols. 1885–87. Reprint, New York: Scribner's, 1913.
Robin, Richard S., ed. *Annotated Catalogue of the Papers of Charles S. Peirce*. Amherst: University of Massachusetts Press, 1967.

Rosenblum, Bruce, and Fred Kuttner. *Quantum Enigma: Physics Encounters Consciousness*. 2nd ed. Oxford: Oxford University Press, 2011.
Russell, Bertrand. *Wisdom of the West*. Edited by Paul Foulkes. New York: Crescent, 1959.
Salier, Willis Hedley. *The Rhetorical Impact of the Sēmeia in the Gospel of John*. Wissenschaftliche Untersuchungen zum Neuen Testament 2. Reihe 186. Tübingen: Mohr Siebeck, 2004.
Saussure, Ferdinand de. *Course in General Linguistics*. Translated by Wade Baskin. Edited by Perry Meisel and Haun Saussy. New York: Columbia University Press, 2011.
Schneiders, Sandra M. *Written That You May Believe: Encountering Jesus in the Fourth Gospel*. New York: Crossroad, 2003.
Stalker, D. M. G. "Exodus." In *Peake's Commentary on the Bible*, edited by M. Black and H. H. Rowley, 208–40. London: Nelson, 1962.
Taylor, Charles. *The Language Animal: The Full Shape of the Human Linguistic Capacity*. Cambridge: Belknap Press of Harvard University Press, 2016.
Ticciati, Susannah. *A New Apophaticism: Augustine and the Redemption of Signs*. Leiden: Brill, 2013.
Tillich, Paul. *Dynamics of Faith*. New York: Harper, 1957.
Trabant, Jürgen. *Vico's New Science of Ancient Signs: A Study of Sematology*. Translated by Sean Ward. New York: Routledge, 2004.
Trible, Phyllis. *Rhetorical Criticism: Context, Method, and the Book of Jonah*. Minneapolis: Fortress, 1994.
Verene, Donald Phillip. *Vico's Science of Imagination*. Ithaca: Cornell University Press, 1981.
Vico, Giambattista. *The New Science of Giambattista Vico*. Translation of the 3rd ed. of *Scienza Nuova* (Naples, 1744) by Thomas Goddard Bergin and Max Harold Fish. Ithaca: Cornell University Press, 1968.
Wittgenstein, Ludwig. *Major Works*. New York: HarperCollins, 2009.

Index

Abraham, 29, 73–77, 86, 149n1, 160
agapism, 120, 122
anthroposemiotics, 95–7
Antonello, Pierpaolo, 44
Aquinas
    and Latin age, 107–8
    being-as-first-known (*ens ut primum cognitum*), 93–94, 98
    esse name for God, xx, 83–86, 88, 93
    nothing, creation from, 88
    theology and, 86, 90
    Trinity and, 111n15
Augustine, 80–81, 87–88, 117
Avicenna (*Ibn Sīnā*), 85

being
    as first known, 93–99
    as presence (Derrida), 53, 59, 60
    for Aquinas, 83–86
    for Heidegger, xxvi, 62, 88–91, 94–97, 134–35, 140–42
    hypostasis and, 142, 147
    logos and, 144–45
    love and, xi, 99, 135
    protocol for written term, 83n4
    relation and, xxi–xxii, 99, 109, 116, 136, 138–39
    semiotics and, 61n22, 95–7, 107
    violence and, 90–91, 98, 145n27, 148
    withdrawal and, 142, 146n32 (*see also* ontology)

Beloved Disciple, 150–54, 157, 166, 171–74
Bible
    beginnings in, 16–18, 20
    creation in, 87–88, 91
    Derrida and, 59, 72–78;
    sacred and, ix, 49, 171
    transformative semiotics and, xiv, xx, xxiii, xxvii, 20–21, 23–29, 38, 47–49, 79, 82, 91–92, 99, 121, 129–30, 147, 171
    Vico and, 105–6
    see also revelation
binaries, 37, 39, 40–42
Bonhoeffer, Dietrich, xxiii
Brown, Raymond, 149–50, 151–52, 161n21

Cain, 17–18
Cartesian dualism, 94, 102
categories, 109, 118–19
Chiang, Ted, xxvii–xxix
climate change, 132–33
codes
    analyzed by Eco, 126–29
    code invention, 128–9
    Genesis as, 88, 91
    in brain, 12
    in nature, 8
    in national flag, 9
    John's Gospel and, 154, 157, 165–66
color, and meaning, 7–14, 124

compassion, 20, 24–25, 125, 153, 162
Constas, Maximos, 167–68
Creatio ex nihilo, 87–88
   as *creatio sine violentia*, 91

Dasein
   as *there-being*, 90, 94
   as relation, 140–41
ceconstruction, 59, 61, 65–66, 70, 143
Deely, John
   history of thought from semiotic perspective, x, xxv, 80–84, 89, 93–95, 101–4, 139
   ontological relation and, 108–11
   Peirce as point of arrival, 112–13, 119
   plays down cultural turn to human subject, 107, 124
Derrida, Jacques, x, xxiv–xxv, 50–53, 57–68, 70–79. See also *différance*, the messianic, the other, trace
Descartes, 101–2
dictionary, 3–4
différance, 59–61, 77

Eco, Umberto, 19, 81n3, 125–29
empircist paradox, 102–3
encyclopedia, 4, 4n1
ens ut primum cognitum (being as first known)
   Aquinas and, 93
   Heidegger and, 94–95
   Peirce's firstness and, 119
   signs and, 95–97
   transformed by love, 98–99
eschatology, xi, xxii
esse, God as, 84–86
Eucharist
   Marion and, 143
   as code and semiosis of nonviolence, 169–71
Exodus, and name of God, 85, 135, 159–60

facts, alternative, 131–32
falsehood, 19, 31, 111, 124, 127. *See also* lies

forgiveness, xxii, 20, 24, 99, 125, 144, 147, 162, 168
Four Ages of Understanding, concept of, xxv, 81–83
Fox and rabbit, image of function of sign, 64, 139

Galileo, 102
Genesis, 17, 18, 87–88, 90–92, 170–71
Girard, René
   account of beginnings, 18–20
   as background to present book, ix–x, xiii–xv, xx, xxiv
   bible and, 23–24, 31, 47–49, 165
   and Lévi-Strauss, 32–37, 53
   parallels to Heidegger, 88–89, 90, 96–97
   radical concept of Christian logos, xxvi, 143–46, 172
   relation to Derrida, 50–51, 65, 67, 70
   roots in Saussure, 33, 53
   semiotics, generative, 31–32, 38–44, 46–49, 97, 129, 136, 147
glory
   and slippage, 162–65
   and icon, 166–69
"God," as nonviolent signifier, 92
   violent origins of, 19
gospel
   as nonviolence, xx, xxiii
   semiotic reading of, 92, 98, 121, & throughout final chapter (10)
grace (nonviolence of expelled Logos), 146
Guagliardo, Vincent, 95–97

Hamlet, 71–72
Haven, Cynthia, 51, 65
Hegel, G. W. F., 61, 78n21,
Heidegger, Martin
   account of being, 62, 88–91, 94–97, 134–35, 140–42
   of human existence, 90, 94, 140–41
   of no-thing and dread, 89–90, 96
   break from Descartes, 94

covert Christian character of
thought, 78n21, 94, 141–42,
144–45
metaphysics and, 135
violence and, 90, 91, 96, 141–42,
145n27
separation of Heraclitean and
Johannine logos, 145–46
Heraclitus, logos of, 69–70
Holy Spirit, 164n23
human, emergence of, 19, 35, 39–44
humanism, 21, 26
Hume, David, 102–3
hupostasis (phonetic spelling of Greek
word translated "hypostasis")
as relation, xxi, xxvi, 138–40
as self-giving love, 144, 145

icon
analyzed by Marion, xxvi, 135–38
invisibility of relation, 137–38
see also Sinai Christ, and glory
idol, mirrored gaze, 136–37
interpretant, 114–16, 123

Jesus, 26–29, 92, 137, 156, 159–60
John (Gospel of)
"beginning" in, 161, 165
community behind composition,
149n1
"I am" sayings, 156, 159–60, 165;
irony in, 157, 160–62
man born blind, 156–58
Mary Magdalene, 152–53, 172–74
semiosis in, 154–56, 157–58, 159,
162, 164 166, 168
symbolism, 150n2, 158–59
women in, 153, 154n11
see also Beloved Disciple, glory,
Sinai Christ
Johns Hopkins Symposium, 1966, 50–1
justice (in Derrida), 71–73

Kant, Emmanuel, 103, 113
Keller, Helen, 45
Kierkegaard, Søren, 73

language
emergence of, 39–44
function of difference, 54–58
lattice, of sign relations, 109, 110n14
Levinas, Emmanuel, 72n11
Lévi-Strauss, Claude, 32–37, 51–53, 68
lies
proprium of semiosis, 19, 123–24
with possibility of truth, 125, 127
see also falsehood
Locke, John, 102
Logocentrism, 59, 79
logos
Christian logos characterized by
nonviolence, self-giving relation,
145–46
Heidegger's radical disjunction of
Johannine from Heraclitean,
144–45
Heraclitean, 69–70
love, xi, xxvi, xxix, 20, 24, 26, 99, 125,
135–36, 141,165, 166, 171. See
also agapism

Marion, Jean-Luc, revelatory
phenomenology, 134–38, 140–
43, 146, 167
Matrix, the, movie, 103, 116, 132
meaning
origins of, 12, 15, 18–19, 28, 36–37,
38–44, 45, 67, 95–96
other and, 72, 113–14, 138
revolution in, xx, xxi–xxv, xxvii,
24–25, 28–29, 48–49, 72, 74, 79,
83, 99, 128–30
messianic, the, xi, 59, 75–78
Metaphysics, 19, 41–3, 52, 68–9, 86, 92,
97, 142–43, 166
mimesis (mimetic desire), 32n2

narrative, 28, 133, 147. See also Taylor,
Charles
neurons, 11, and "neural studio," 12–14,
127
nihilation, 89–90, 97
nonviolence
relation of, xxiii, 99, 136, 162, 168

revolution of, xx, 49, 87, 99, 122, 125, 143, 153
solution to human crisis, 24
theology of, 29, 49, 91–2, 144–47, 164n23, 172–74

objectivism, 2–8
ontological difference, 134
ontological relation
  concept of 109–11, 116–17, 123–24
  signs and, 116, 123, 132–33
  transformation and, 136, 139, 143
ontology, xi, 88, 91, 94–5, 98, 140–42, 147. *See also* being
onto-theology, 88, 98, 135, 142, 144
other, the, claim of, 72–75
otherness, at core of semiotics, 95–9

peace, xxii–xxiii, 19, 86, 87, 91, 99, 118, 122, 162, 167–68, 171
Peirce, Charles Sanders
  categories in, 118–19
  key figure for Deely, 89
  semiotics of, xxv, 9–10, 112–16, 122
  truth as communal and evolutionary, 117, 120–22, 124
pharmakon/pharmakos, 66–67
Platonism, xxi, xxiii, 48, 69
Poinsot, John, 82, 108–10, 111n15
postmodernism, xxiii, 22; for Deely, 82–83
poststructuralism, 41, 51
primary scene, 18–20, 39–40
proto-semiosis, of the gospel, 172–74
pyramid, as model of sign and trace, 60–61, 63

reality/realism, xi, xxii, 61n22, 82, 84, 89, 107, 109, 117, 122–24, 133
relation, xxi–xxiii, xxv, 99, 106–11, 115, 119, 125, 129, 132, 133n3, 136. See also *hupostasis*
re-meaning (diagram of), 28–29
representation, via interpretant, 115
revelation, anthropological, xx, 20, 23–4, 48, 91, 146
Ricoeur, Paul, 68n5
ritual, 37, 43–4, 171

rose, "a rose is a rose is a rose," 5

sacred, the, 19, 36, 41–3, 46, 97, 141
sacrifice, ix, 17, 98, 106, 137, 144
Saussure, Ferdinand de, 33, 53–56, 57–58, 122
scapegoat, xiv, 32, 66, 125, 139
Schneiders, Sandra, 150n2, 151–55, 158
science, 8, 36, 46, 103, 123, 133, 133n3, 139
semeion (in John's Gospel), xxvi, 157–58, 161, 165, 169, 173
sememe, 126, 154
semiology, 33n4, 122
semio-ontology, xxvi, 61, 87, 96, 98, 125, 132
semiosis
  as process, xxiii, 23, 26, 75, 95, 118
  feminine, 153, 173
  gospel of John as, 149–74
  love and, 121
  unlimited, 126–27
semiotics
  generative, xxiv, 30, 32, 38–45, 46
  origins in Augustine, 80–81
  science of, xiv, 33, 53–5, 57, 61–2, 81–2, 81n3, 104–5, 106–11, 114–16, 122, 126–29
  theological, xix, xxi–xxiii, xxvi, 48, 86–87, 91–92, 98–100, 138, 144, 170–71, 173
  transformative, xxvii, 28–9, 46–9, 50, 67, 71, 77–9, 83, 98, 99, 118, 121, 129–30, 138–40, 143
  see also Deely, Eco, Girard, Peirce, Poinsot, Saussure
semioverse, 98, 116, 118
sign, the, xx, xxiv
  difference and, 54–56
  first historical concept of, 80–81
  Girardian, 39, 41–4, 46
  interpretant and, 114–16
  linguistic sign arbitrary, 55
  metaphysics and, 52
  sign and relation, 79, 95, 97, 107–8, 110–11, 115–16, 123, 138–39
  (*see also* ontological relation)
sign function 126, 128

signifier and signified, 54
see also *semeion*
Sinai Christ, xxvii, 167–68
slippage, semiotic, xxvii, 162–66, 168–69, 172–73
Socrates, 17, 66, 70n9
spiritual reading, of Bible, 29
stories, xxiv, 48, 77, 124, 133, 140
structuralism, 32, 36, 41
symbol, 9–10, 43–44, 97, 150n2, 158–59

Taylor, Charles, xxiv, 32n2, 129n24
Theuth, Egyptian god, 17
Thirdness (Peirce), 118–19, 122
trace, 61–64; the other and, 70–71, 72n11
transcendence, violent, 18–19, 142; nonviolent, xxvii, 143, 174
transcendental signifier, 41–2, 47
transformation, xi, xxi, 7, 20, 24, 28–9, 91, 95, 118, 129, 172. *See also* transformative semiotics
triadic thought, 113–14, 118
Trible, Phyllis, 156n15

Trinity
relational mode of being, 111n15
triadic sign, 113
truth, possibility of, 117, 124–25, 127
Turing test, 10–11
turn to the subject, 107, 121, 124

verum esse ipsum factum (truth is made), 105
Vico, 104–7
victim
revelation of, ix, 23, 24, 28, 38, 48, 146
as transcendental signifier, 41–2
violence
generative, xxv, 18–19, 36, 65, 92
metaphysics and, 63, 65, 68–69, 70, 86, 142, 144–45
original, ix, xxix, 19, 35, 39, 142
postmodern, 22–23
revelation of, 20, 23–4, 25, 28
see also logos, nonviolence

women, in Gospel of John, 152–53, 154n11
writing, 17, 48, 57–8, 161n20

"In his cutting-edge book, *Theology Beyond Metaphysics*, Anthony Bartlett reveals the radical way in which God has intervened to liberate and reconstitute human consciousness, transforming it from the inside out with language-signs of nonviolence. I am grateful for its hopeful vision: that the new beginning inaugurated by Jesus is in our day coming to full clarity, with an urgency that cannot fail to transform human reality."

—**James Warren**, author of *Compassion Or Apocalypse: A Comprehensible Guide To The Thought Of René Girard*

"For anyone interested in the theological application of the thought of René Girard, Tony Bartlett has long been essential reading. Here he outdoes himself in the clarity with which he makes potentially complicated matters simple. He brings us to the heart of why and how Girard's insight communicates an epochal shift in lived understanding of both the gospel and what it means to be human. Deep grazing, to which I will have to return to learn more."

—**James Alison**, Catholic priest, theologian, and author

"Bartlett has an expansive vision with the sign at its center. Unfolding it evocatively through Girard, Heidegger, Marion, and the lesser known but no less rewarding semiotics of John Deely, he arrives at John's Gospel, in the company of the Beloved Disciple, to discover Christ as the transformative sign that makes all things new."

—**Susannah Ticciati**, Reader in Christian Theology, King's College London

"In this important book, Anthony Bartlett draws on René Girard's biblical anthropology in vital and telling ways. By engaging—and winningly explaining—advances in semiotics, he rewrites intellectual history. His analyses decouple theology from its unwieldy partnership with metaphysics, while mining key insights in philosophical tradition from Aquinas through Peirce, from Heidegger through Derrida, from Vico to Lévi-Strauss."

—**Andrew J. McKenna**, Emeritus Professor of French, Loyola University Chicago

"In this paradigm-shifting work, Anthony Bartlett unfolds poetic language, potent descriptors, and powerful artifacts for dynamically revealing God as nonviolent. Though this is a deeply philosophical work, this book is an astonishing revelation that should be witnessed to around tables, from the pulpit, and even on our interwebs. Bartlett has given us an invaluable resource for telling a better story to the worlds we inhabit."

—**Dan White Jr.**, co-founder of The Praxis Gathering and author of *Love Over Fear*